ADVENTURES IN AMERICA

Readings in Early American History to 1877

SECOND EDITION

Edited by John A. Trickel
Richland College

KENDALL/HUNT PUBLISHING COMPANY
2460 Kerper Boulevard P.O. Box 539 Dubuque, Iowa 52004-0539

Library of Congress Catalog Card Number: 91–61738

ISBN 0–8403–6744–9

Printed in the United States of America
10 9 8 7 6 5 4 3 2 1

Contents

UNIT IV—CAN THE NATION ENDURE

Introduction

In terms of appeal, relevance, and readability, historical works vary greatly; in addition, those who write history differ in interests, training, writing skills, and purposes. Mindful of these variables while choosing readings for this collection, the editor attempted to accomplish several different goals. One goal was to choose articles that are enjoyable and suitable for a general audience. Another goal was to introduce students to a wide variety of historical interests. Thus, selections from traditional political, economic, and diplomatic points of view are included, as well as articles from environmental, minority, and social perspectives of the American past.

The editor quickly discovered that an invaluable source of scholarly but readable historical articles is presented within the pages of the popular history magazines, some scholarly publications, and historical monographs. Drawing from these sources, the following pieces were assembled. The first group of selections deals with topics from early English colonization through the rupture of American and English relations in 1776. In the second unit are articles dealing with topics from the revolution to the rise of popular politics in the 1820s. The third unit offers works from the Jacksonian Age through the Mexican-American War. The final series deals with the Civil War, from its prelude to its aftermath.

The intent of this collection is to stimulate the students' imagination and peak the students' interest in the diversity of the human experiences in the development of the United States. Students should read these articles for major points, rather than for factual detail, after which they should try to formulate a theme statement explaining the central point of the article. Then, after writing down in brief the major factors used by the author to support the argument presented, students can understand better the various types of historical inquiry and the many interpretations that each permits.

History and the Historian

John A. Trickel

Students frequently ask, "how can history change, it is over, isn't it?" Nothing seems more obvious than the assertion that the past does not change; however, an understanding of the factors surrounding those events does change. So in reality history has two meanings: the record of the past, and, from that record, what historians choose to interpret and write about.

History must be more than simply a chronicle of what happened previously. Any writing about the past contains only a portion of the whole record in which facts are selected, interpretations advanced, and descriptions are completed. Imagine what a "jumble" history would be if every speech, newspaper report, and public document were assembled to tell the story of the past! Yet surely with generations of historians investigating aspects of each period, a "true history" will emerge, will it not? The answer is a qualified "Yes," because in many cases the events seem reasonably clear and consistent. However, all conclusions are tentative, subject to later verification or reinterpretation.

What accounts for this tentativeness? In part, the answer lies in the complexity of events that compose history. For instance, all can agree that a war of independence raged between American colonists and British regulars from 1776 to 1783, with certain events and people playing critical roles. But, placing boundaries on the history of that period is exceedingly difficult. Although battles are certainly part of the war, so, too, are the lives of the soldiers and of their loved ones at home. The politics of the Continental Congress and of Parliament are likewise elements of war, as are their foreign policies. The problem is that all that "happened" in that time frame can be related to the Revolutionary War. Even if the historian concentrates on one campaign or battle, the history will only be part of a larger whole.

History is also often revised, sometimes radically, as a consequence of the discovery of new sources. Papers tucked away in musty attics or dark caves sometimes cast new light on important people or events in the past. Such was the case for ancient historians, for instance, when the Dead Sea Scrolls from the first century A.D. *were uncovered in 1947. Discoveries by Archaeologists constantly add to the knowledge historians have of pre-historic and his-*

toric societies. For instance, in recent years, archaeologists have significantly altered the estimated number of Native Americans who lived in Pre-Columbian America. The article, "Indians and New England" chapter 4 in Unit I, illustrates the knowledge gained from the relatively new interest in environmental history.

Even without new sources, old sources are often reevaluated by new methods. Sophisticated statistical procedures now produce better understanding of economic, social, and political patterns, while computers provide the equipment for model building and factor analysis. Today's historians are better trained in methods borrowed from sociology, psychology, and economics, and, armed with those techniques, information about family life, sex roles, and community and political interrelations better round out the understanding of previous societies.

The Conquest of Utopia

Eric R. Wolf

The Aztecs' cruel, short-lived conquest of central Mexico ended decisively with Spanish conquest in 1521. The reasons for the fall of this powerful empire were both internal and external, and the impact on Spain enormous. The complex results are analyzed in this article by Eric R. Wolf. What additional factor do you think William Cronon (article 4) would add to Wolf's study.

In 1492, Christopher Columbus, sailing under the flag of Castile, discovered the islands of the Caribbean and planted upon their shores the standard of his sovereigns and the cross of his Savior. From these islands, the newcomers began to probe the Middle American coast. In Easter week, 1519, a young adventurer, Hernán Cortés—lawyer by professional training and military man through baptism of fire on Santo Domingo—landed in the vicinity of San Juan de Ulua in Veracruz. He brought with him an army of 508 soldiers—32 of whom were crossbowmen and carried harquebuses—16 horses, and 14 pieces of artillery, together with a navy of 11 ships and 100 sailors. In July and August of that year, Cortés beached his ships and embarked on the conquest of Tenochtitlán. Two years later, on August 13, 1521, Tenochtitlán fell into Spanish hands. One cycle of history had come to an end and another cycle began.

How is one to explain this sudden irreversible change in the fate of Middle America? The entire enterprise of the Spanish Conquest seems shrouded in a curious air of unreality. Hernán Cortés conquers an empire embracing millions of people. For lack of holy water, a Fray Pedro de Gante baptizes hundreds of thousands of Indians with his saliva. A Nuñez Cabeza de Vaca sets out to find the golden cities of Cíbola and the Fountain of Youth, to be shipwrecked, reduced to

Reprinted from Eric R. Wolf, *Sons of the Shaking Earth* (Chicago: University of Chicago Press, 1959), pp. 152–175, with permission of the author and the University of Chicago Press.

starvation, nearly eaten by cannibals, only to return to the fray as soon as he is rescued. Actors, acts, and motives seem superhuman: their lust for gold and for salvation, their undivided loyalty to a distant monarch, their courage in the face of a thousand obstacles seem to defy simple psychological explanations. They not only made history; they struck poses against the backdrop of history, conscious of their role as makers and shakers of this earth. The utterances of a Cortés, a Panfilo Narváez, a Garay, are replete with references to Caesar, Pompey, and Hannibal. Cortés plays not only at being himself; he is also the Amadís of Gaul celebrated in the medieval books of chivalry. They were not satisfied with the simple act; they translated each act into a symbolic statement, an evocation of a superhuman purpose. Struck with admiration of their deeds and postures, their chroniclers took them at their word. In the pages of the history books these men parade in the guise of their own evaluation of themselves: half centaurs, pawing the ground with their hoofs and bellowing with voices like cannon, half gods, therefore, and only half men.

But their image of themselves obscures the real greatness of their achievement, for greatness can be measured only on a human scale, not on a divine. Part of their greatness was undoubtedly due to the military tactics employed by a courageous and cunning general. The Spaniards used cavalry to break through the massed formations of an enemy that had never before encountered horses; they thus avoided hand-to-hand combat in which gunpowder and iron arms would have been of little avail in the face of the wicked Indian swords, beset with obsidian chips. To counteract the Indian firepower of spears and arrows, the Spaniards used the crossbow, the instrument that gained them such a decisive victory in the great battle of Pavia against the remnants of French knighthood. When Spanish cavalry, artillery, and infantry proved impotent against Indian canoes manned by archers in the canals and lagoons surrounding Tenochtitlán, Cortés again carried the battle to the enemy, attacking the embattled capital across the water, from the boards of thirteen ships built on the spot.

None of these military successes would have been possible, however, without the Indian allies Cortés won in Middle America. From the first, he enlisted on his side rulers and peoples who had suffered grievously at the hands of their Mexica enemies. In a decisive way, as Ralph Beals has put it, "the conquest of Tenochtitlán was less a conquest than it was a revolt of dominated peoples." Spanish firepower and cavalry would have been impotent against the Mexica armies without the Tlaxcaltec, Texcocans and others who joined the Spanish cause. They furnished the bulk of the infantry and manned the canoes that covered the advance of the brigantines across the lagoon of Tenochtitlán. They provided, transported, and prepared the food supplies needed to sustain an army in the field. They maintained lines of communication between coast and highland, and they policed occupied and pacified areas. They supplied the raw materials and muscular energy for the construction of the ships that decided the siege of the Mexica capital. Spanish military equipment and tactics carried the day, but Indian assistance determined the outcome of the war.

In an ultimate sense, the time was ripe for a redress in the balance of power in Middle America. Even Moctezuma, in his abode at Tenochtitlán, must have felt this, for we can read in his hesitations, in his hearkening to omens of doom, evidence of the doubt and uncertainty which was gnawing at the vitals of Mexica domination. The Spaniards provided the indispensable additional energy required to reverse the dominant political trend. Yet they were not mere agents of the indigenous will, mere leaders of an indigenous revolt. Cortés' genius lay precisely in his ability to play this role, to surround himself with charisma in the eyes of the Indians. Cortés played this role to the hilt, but with calculated duplicity. For the Spaniards had not come to Middle America to restore an indigenous society. They acted from autonomous motives which were not those of their Indian allies. Accepting the command of a people deeply accustomed to obedience through long participation in a hierarchical social order, they began to enact their own purposes, to realize their own ends, which were those of Spanish society and therefore alien and hostile to those of the Indians among whom they had begun to move.

To understand these ends, we must try to understand Spanish society of that time, a task in which we moderns experience a particular difficulty. The reduced and impoverished Spain of today [1959] obscures our understanding of the once wealthy and powerful empire upon which the sun never set. All too often, we tend to interpret the past by reconstructing it in the image of the present. Again, too often, we view Spain through the lens of a powerful political mythology, a mythology forged both consciously and unconsciously in Protestant countries to advance the liberating cause of Protestantism and republican institutions against Catholicism and monarchical absolutism. According to this mythology, a singularly partisan deity ranged himself on the side of human freedom and economic progress against "feudal" Spain. While in northern Europe right-thinking and industrious men put their shoulders to the wheel of the Industrial Revolution, the

Catholic South remained sunk in medieval sloth. But the rise and decline of a society is not explained by recourse to political demonology; the truth is at once simpler and more complex.

Let us not forget that the Mediterranean and not the European North is the homeland of capitalism and of the Industrial Revolution. Italy, southern France, Spain, and southern Germany witnessed the rise of the first factories, the first banks, the first great fairs. At the time of the discovery of America, the Iberian Peninsula harbored thriving cities, humming with expanding wealth and trade. The sources of this prosperity were manifold: the sale of wool to England or to Flanders; the sale of iron wares to the Levant; the seizure and sale of slaves from the African coast; the quick raid on a Saracen stronghold or a pirate's lair. These were enterprises which demanded the utmost in individual stamina and personal valor; they were also exceedingly profitable. And in response the culture which fed upon an extension of these enterprises elaborated its peculiar image of the manly ideal: the overweening personality possessed of skill and courage. This ideal belonged as much to the medieval past as to the commercial future. It was inherently contradictory and revealed in its contradiction the opposing forces at work within the social system that gave it birth. Its heroes act; but the cultural forms of their acts are not only rich in the symbolic pageantry of the medieval knight-crusader but also supreme examples of the exaltation of Renaissance man pioneering on new frontiers of thought and human behavior. Covertly, more than once, the goal of the act is profit, conceived as personal enhancement through the acquisition of gold and riches.

There were in reality two Spains, or two tendencies at work in the Iberian Peninsula. The first tendency was aristocratic, oriented toward warfare and the gain of riches by warfare. It was exemplified most clearly by the armies of Castile, composed of a warlike nobility and a warlike peasantry. These armies had been forged in the fight against the Moors, first in raid and counterraid, later in the systematic reconquest of the Moorish southland. The nobility, partly organized into religious orders of monastic warriors, saw in warfare a ready source of ego enhancement and looted wealth. Its traditional economic interest lay in the extension of grazing range for its herds of cattle and sheep, coupled with a flourishing export trade in wool to northern Europe. The peasantry, on the other hand, consisted of solider-cultivators, recruited into the army by promises and guaranties of freedom from servile encumbrances and charters of local self-rule. These peasants desired land, free land, to divide among their sons. In warfare, both nobility and peasantry gained their divergent ends.

The other Spain, the other Spanish trend, was less involved in warfare; it pointed toward capital accumulation through rising industry and trade in the hands of a town-based bourgeoisie. Such entrepreneurs existed in all Peninsular towns; but only in eastern Spain, centered in Catalonia, had they gained sufficient power to check the expansionist desires of the aristocratic soldiery. In this part of Spain, a bloody peasant war had smashed the remnants of a feudal system of the classic European kind. Traditional relationships in which a lord exercised economic, judicial, and social control of a group of serfs had given way to new social ties. A free peasantry populated the countryside; a prosperous bourgeoisie, long oriented toward maritime trade, controlled the towns. The country was undergoing incipient industrialization, and the cloth, leather, and iron wares so produced were exchanged in the eastern Mediterranean for the drugs, dyestuffs, and luxury goods of the Orient.

By 1492, these two Spains were headed for collision, a conflict which might well have altered the face of Spain but for the discovery of America. The fall of the last Moorish redoubt put an end to the limitless acquisition of land by conquest and to the easy accumulation of wealth by forceful seizure; 1492 marked the closing of the Spanish frontier. As land became scarce, interests which had run parallel up to that time began to conflict; while the solider-peasant wanted unencumbered land, the aristocrat wanted open range for sheep and cattle or land for dependent cultivators. With the distribution of the fruits of conquest among the conquerors, moreover, readily available wealth became unavailable. How was new wealth to be produced? To this problem the merchant-entrepreneur of the towns had an answer: capital investment in industry coupled with the reduction of aristocratic power. At this moment, however, the doors to the New World swung wide open to reveal a new frontier: dream cities of gold, endless expanses of land, huge reservoirs of dependent labor. The merchant-entrepreneur receded into obscurity; the knight-adventurer, the visionary of wealth through seizure at sword's point, gained new impetus.

It was this new frontier which settled the fate of Spain. Paradoxically, Spanish industry was to be swamped in a tide of gold from the Indies, which spelled its ultimate ruin; paradoxically, also, the new frontier destroyed the class which might have carried such industrialization to a successful conclusion. For in this New World, all men—peasant, merchant, impoverished noble, noble merchant-prince—could dream of becoming lords of land, Indians, and gold. Men who in Spain might have allied themselves politically and economically with the entrepreneurs and traders of the towns against the aristocrat could in this new venture identify themselves with the ideal of the mounted noble. Men who in Spain might have spurred the growth of the middle classes were here converted into its opponents. The year 1492 might have marked Spain's awakening to a new reality; instead, it marked the coming of a new dream, a new utopia.

Where men of varied pasts and varied interests engage in a common enterprise, belief in a universal utopia renders possible their common action. Utopia asks no questions of reality; it serves to bind men in the service of a dream. Belief in it postpones the day of reckoning on which the spoils will be divided and men will draw their swords to validate their personal utopia against the counterclaims of their comrades-in-arms. Some came to the New World to find gold; others to find order; still others to save souls. Yet in their common dream they asked no questions of one another. For the time being, their dream was validated by their common experience on board ship, by their common sufferings in the face of the enemy, by their common victory.

In the course of their common adventure in utopia they also achieved a set of common usages and understandings which made "the culture of the Conquest" different from their ancestral culture and from the culture still to be in the New World. Their purposes had a transcendental simplicity: gold, subjects, souls. This simplicity patterned their behavior and their thought, some of it conscious, self-imposed. The colonist-to-be in search of his liberty casts off the traditional forms which he has experienced as shackles and encumbrances. The royal official in search of order abhors the tangle of inherited forms of the Old World. The friar leaves behind him a world which is old and corrupt; in utopia he seeks austerity and clarity. The very process of migration produces a simplified stock of cultural forms.

Men drawn from all walks of life, the conquerors were not a complete sample of their ancestral society. They did not bring with them complete knowledge of the gamut of Spanish culture. Some of this age-old heritage they could not reproduce in the New World because they lacked acquaintance with it. Some of it, however, vanished in the crucible of their common experience, in their need to develop a common cultural denominator to facilitate their common task. Spain, but recently unified under one crown, had remained a cultural plural, a mosaic of many parts. Yet the culture of the conquerors was, by contrast, highly homogeneous. This simplification extended to material goods: only one plow, of the many Spanish plows, was transmitted to the New World; only a few techniques of fishing were selected from the plethora of Spanish fishing techniques and transplanted into the new setting. Simplification extended also to symbolic behavior: speech undergoes a leveling, a planing-down of the formalities of Castilian Spanish into a plain and utilitarian idiom. Left behind are the many Spanish folk fiestas in honor of a multitude of beloved local saints; they yield in the New World to the measured and standardized performance of the formal celebrations of way stations in the life of Christ. The culture of the conquest was, as George Foster has pointed out, *sui generis.* In vain one looks in the culture of these men for the rich varied regional heritage of the mother country.

Some of the conquerors wanted gold—gold, the actual tangible substance, not the intangible "promises to pay" of later capitalism. In this they were children of their times, caught in the contradiction between medieval magic and the modern search for profits. All over Europe men longed for gold, encountered gold in dreams, dug for it under trees and in caves, sold their souls to the devil for it, labored over retorts to obtain it from base metals such as iron or lead. It was a kind of illness, and Cortés stated it that way—half cynically and half realistically—in addressing the first Mexica noble he met: "The Spaniards are troubled with a disease of the heart for which gold is the specific remedy." The illness was greed, but beyond greed the desire for personal liberty, escape of the ego from bondage to other men, "spiritual autarchy," as Eliseo Vivas has said, "which is achieved only when you are able to say to another man, *a mi no me manda nadie*—no one bosses me; I am lord because I have land and gold and Indians, and I need not beg any favors from you or any one else." This is the new self-made man talking, the medieval adventurer on the threshold of capitalism, knight-errant in cultural form but primitive capitalist in disguise. The goal is medieval—never again to bend one's will to that of another—but the instrument is modern: the instrument of wealth.

Utopia thus bears at the outset the mark of a contradiction between past and future, a contradiction never wholly overcome. The contradiction is most startlingly illuminated when the Spanish entrepreneur is compared with this contemporary English rival. "The Englishmen," says Salvador de Madariaga, "though on the surface more self-seeking, were in depth more socially minded; the Spaniards, though in appearance more statesmanlike and creative, more intent on 'ennobling' cities and setting up kingdoms, were more self-centered. The Englishman, with his dividends, socialized his adventures, gain, botty; the Spaniard, with his hospitals, foundations, cathedrals, colleges and marquisates, raised a monument to his own self. . . ." The rise of puritanism in the Anglo-American world, so brilliantly analyzed by Max Weber and Richard Tawney, destroyed the contradiction between individual goals and cultural means. For in accepting the Protestant ethic of work and capital accumulation as virtue, the entrepreneur made himself an instrument of production, harnessed himself to the process of capital formation. In Anglo-America, the very means thus became the ends; in Ibero-America, means and ends remained at war with one another, contradictory, unresolved.

If some came in search of gold and its promise of personal liberty, others came in search of order. Their deity was the absolute monarch; their religion the new religion of the reason of state. At the end of the fifteenth century the Spanish crown had just emerged victorious in its political battles against its rivals. With the help of the rising middle classes and the peasantry, it had successfully defeated the attempts of the aristocrats who wished to reduce the king once again to the passive position of a mere *primus inter pares.* Yet this political success but threatened to put the king into the hands of the penny-wise merchants who wished to trade support for a veto over his military and bureaucratic expenditures. The long period of the reconquest had also brought with it a spate of *fueros* or local charters which exempted one or the other local or professional body from the application of the general law; many a king had traded local autonomy for support against the Moorish enemy.

In the conquest of the New World, the crown saw its opportunity to escape the limitations of internal Spanish politics. Gold from the Indies would enrich not only the eager adventurer; a fifth of all gold and silver mined in the New World would be the king's, to finance a royal army, navy, and officialdom, to build the bases of absolutist power upon institutions wholly independent of nobility, middle classes, or peasant cultivators. Wealth from the Indies would underwrite a state standing above all classes, above the endless quarrels of contending interest groups. This state would speak with a new voice, with a new will. It would no longer be bound by precedent; it would set aside solutions which had become traditional, overgrown with the "cake of custom" and with compromise. The New World would not have to grow, piecemeal, in the shadows of ancient complexities: it would be a planned world, projected into reality by the royal will and its executioners. Thus utopia would become law, and law utopian. If Spanish towns had been small, cramped within their rings of fortifications, crowded around small irregular squares, then the towns of the New World would be large, open, unfortified; built upon the gridiron plan; centered upon a spacious square dominated by church and city-hall as twin symbols of sacred and secular power; an architectural utopia conceived by Italian architect-dreamers and built in the New World by royal mandate.

Was it true that many Indians lived in scattered hamlets instead of stationary, circumscribed, concentrated settlements? Then let there be a law to force them to live in nucleated towns, each with its own church, each surrounded by its own fields—within a measured radius of 560 yards from the church steeple—so that they could learn to order their lives to the tolling of church bells and to the commands of royal officers. Land and people of utopia had both been conquered by the sword; but it would be the dry scratching of the goose-quill pen upon parchment that would turn utopia into reality. Let each Indian keep twelve chickens and six turkeys and sell them for no more than 4 reales per turkey and 1 1/2 reales per chicken; let each Indian working in a textile mill receive a daily ration of eighteen tortillas or fourteen tamales, plus chili, chickpeas, and beans. No problem was too insignificant to demand solution, and all solutions were solutions of law. Utopia was to be born also with this fatal deficiency implicit in the contradiction of law and reality. Reality is too protean to be wholly covered by law; it soon grows through, around, and over law, leaving but a hollow shell of words, a gesture of etiquette to gloss over the gap between wish and existence. The Latin American world still bears this legacy of law as a gesture to initiate action, to create a new order, and—when the energy of the gesture is spent—to use the law as wish, to wipe out a reality grown beyond law and order, beyond utopia.

Utopia contained many houses. If some men longed for gold, to build upon it their untrameled liberty, and if others sought Indian subjects to rule and exercise in the spirit of the new order, so there were men who came to save souls. Upon the ruins of pagan shrines and idols in a new continent filled with souls hungry for salvation, yet uncorrupted by the age-old vices of the Old World, they would erect their own utopia: the prelude on earth of the Kingdom of Heaven. To these prophets of salvation, the conquest of the New World was the call to a great spiritual task: the defeat of Satan in his own redoubt, the redemption of souls languishing in his power, the annunciation of the faith in the one true God. The shock troops of this new faith were the friars, members of the monastic orders, strongly influenced by the reformist religious currents of the times. In some countries, such movements were soon to feed the flames of the Protestant revolution. If this did not happen in Spain, it was not because Spain lacked inflammable intellectual tinder. The economic and political development of the country had given strong impetus to men who began to question long-accepted opinions and to explore new interpretations of Catholicism. Most of these questioners were influenced by Erasmus of Rotterdam (1466–1536), whose teaching de-emphasized the importance of formal ritual and stressed the promptings to piety of an "inner" voice, and by the utopian and reformist thought of Thomas More (1478–1535) and Luis Vives (1492–1540).

The reason that this new religious current did not explode into open rebellion against accepted religious forms is to be found in the character of the Spanish state and the circumstances which surrounded it rather than in the intellectual heterodoxy of the movement. The Spanish state had no need to break with the papacy: it dictated ecclesiastical appointments in its own territory; it possessed the right to read and suppress papal bulls before making them public; it controlled the office of the Inquisition; it even sponsored autonomy in doctrinal matters through its support of the belief in the immaculate conception of the Virgin Mary, long before this belief became official church dogma at the Council of Trent (1545–63). In other European states the hunger for land and capital was one of the chief underlying motives for religious reformation; after the break with Rome, the estates of the church were divided among the members of the Protestant faction. In Spain, the frontiers had not yet closed. Until 1492 land and wealth were still to be had by fighting the Moors in southern Spain in the name of religion, and that year witnessed the opening of the new frontier in the New World, with its promise of gold and glory for all takers.

Under Cardinal Ximénez de Cisneros, the Erasmists received royal approval. The crown saw in their effort to restore the simplicity and austerity of primitive Christianity—in the face of decay and corruption—a spiritual counterpart to its own efforts to centralize Spain and to endow the new empire with a unified sense of mission. Many of the friars who came to the New World had taken part in this religious renewal. The first twelve friars to set foot in New Spain—the so-called Apostolic Twelve—had all worked to spread the gospel of primitive Christendom in southern Spain. Fray Juan de Zumárraga (1461?–1548), the first archbishop of Mexico, was a follower of Erasmus and familiar with the utopian writings of Sir Thomas More. Vasco de Quiroga (1470–1565), the first bishop of Michoacán, actually established a replica of Sir Thomas More's Utopia among the Indian communities of his bishopric. All these soldiers of the faith favored poverty over wealth, communal property over private property. Carefully they labored to purge Catholicism of the accumulation of ritual, selecting from the profusion of religious ritual only the major ceremonials celebrating the way-stations of Christ's life. This desire for purity and simplicity they also expressed in their great single-naved churches, symbolic of the homogeneity of primitive Christian worship, uncluttered by devotion to smaller altars and lateral naves.

The utopia of gold and liberty crumbled in the tension between exaltation of the self, through valiant deeds, and wealth, the instrument selected for their validation. The utopia of order remained arrested in the legal gesture, attempting to stem the tide of real behavior. The utopia of faith, too, was to founder, hoped-for morality all too often impotent in the face of stubborn secular demand. And yet, conversion proved a success. The romanticists have long delighted in discovering the idols behind altars, the Gods of the Cave transformed into Christs hanging upon the Cross, the earth goddesses disguised as Catholic Virgins, the braziers burning copal gum on the steps of the churches, and other evidences of pre-Conquest heritage in the religious beliefs and practices of modern Indians. There is much that is Indian in the Catholicism of Middle America; but more surprising than the numerous survivals of pre-Conquest ideas and rituals is the organizational success of the Catholic utopia in a country of different religions and languages. Wherever you go in Middle America, you encounter the images of the Catholic saints and the churches built by the conquerors. Christ and the Virgin may have been transmuted by the adoration of men who had worshipped the Sun and the Moon and the Earth and the Lords of the Four Directions; but when an Indian speaks of a human being today, he does not say "a man"; he says "a Christian," a believer.

How is this success to be explained? It is easy to dismember men with cannons; it is more difficult to tame their minds. Certainly military defeat played a part, because it provided a visible demonstration of the impotence and decadence of the Mexica gods. The Children of the Sun had died by the sword as they had lived by the sword. The old gods had failed. When the Spaniards had demanded that the Totonac of Cempoala destroy their idols, the people had recoiled in horror; yet when the conquerors hurled the idols to the ground and broke them to pieces, the idols had remained mute and defenseless. They had not smitten the foreigners; they had failed to show the power that was in them. When the priests released the stones from the Pyramid of Cholula which held back the magic water that was in the mountain so that it would drown the strange men in a flood, the channel remained dry, and their magic deserted them. When the Children of the Sun, the Toltec rulers of Tenochtitlán, called down the wrath of their terrible idol Hummingbird-on-the-Left upon their enemies, Hummingbird-on-the-Left remained silent. The mutilated idols of their gods now rested on the bottom of the lake from which they had set out to conquer the universe for the sun; and the rubble of their temples served as fill for the new city of Mexico which was to arise upon these ruins. The old gods were dead, and powerless.

Not that these old gods had been so greatly loved. We know—or we can guess—that the will of these gods and the burden of human sacrifice rested heavily upon the land. Worship of warrior gods and human sacrifice were religious activities consonant with the military character of Mexica expansion. Inevitably, however, peace and political consolidation brought to the fore alternative religious explanations of a less militaristic character. Quetzalcoatl, the Shining Serpent, served as a symbolic form through which these new interpretations and longings could find expression. His latter-day attributes as a harbinger of peaceful productivity and human wisdom bear surprising similarity to the ideological dictates of Christianity. Indeed, the Spanish friars came to believe that Quetzalcoatl had been none other than the apostle Thomas, come to the New World to convert the Indians. The longing for peace and for an end to bloodshed provided a fertile soil for the diffusion of the Christian message.

Both religions, moreover, believed in a structured and ordered supernatural world, in which more powerful, unseen, and unfathomable divinities stood above local supernatural mediators of lesser scope and power that were yet more immediately tangible. The Middle American peasant, like his Spanish counterpart, focused his religious interest on these lowlier supernatural helpers. He was more interested in the powers that affected his crops, his children, his family, and the people with whom he was in immediate and personal contact, than in the ultimate powers and their manifestations, which absorbed the interest of the religious specialist. Among the gods of a multi-headed pantheon, his daily concern was with the gods of the earth, fertility, rain and water, with illness, with the immediate short-range future, with the malevolence of his neighbors. Where the Spanish peasant worshipped wooden saints, the Middle American peasant worshipped clay idols; both had recourse to the magical practices of folk medicine; both had a strong sense of omens; and both believed in the reality of witches who could be ordinary everyday people during the day and malevolent spirits in animal disguise at night.

The priests, the specialists of both religions, on the other hand, were the heirs of rich and complex intellectual traditions, trained in the esoteric interpretation of religious symbols whether these symbols concerned multiple incarnations of Tezcatlipoca or the implications of the Revelation of St. John the Divine. The concern of the priest was not the concern of the peasant, and yet the same religious structure could embrace both. As long as the priests remained in command, as ultimate mediators between gods and men and ultimate interpreters of this relationship, men could adapt the manifold religious patterns to suit their personal and local concerns. What was true of religious concerns also held true of gods. A god could be one or triune, unique or multiple, and interpretation could stress his oneness at one time, his multiplicity at another. The Mexica pantheon had embraced many local gods, and the Mexica priesthood had labored to equate these gods with their own inherited deities or with one another. The Catholic Church had a similar tradition of flexibility. Just as the cloak of the Virgin hid many a local Persephone or Isis along the shores of the European Mediterranean, or as an Odin hanging himself from the tree of life became a Christ, so a Hummingbird-on-the-Left became a Spanish St. James riding down upon the heathens; a Tlaloc, a Christian Señor de Sacromonte; a God of the Cave, the Lord of Chalma; and Our Lady Spirit, the Virgin of Guadalupe.

The Catholic Church drove out the priests of the old gods and manned the pivotal points of the religious hierarchy with men ordained in its own cult. It destroyed the old idols and put an end to human sacrifices, burned the sacred picture books and relegated to oblivion much of the calendric and divinatory knowledge of its predecessors; but it also offered the common man a way in which he could cast his traditional attachments into new forms. The Catholic Church, like the solar religion of the Mexica rigid at the heights of command but flexible on the level of the peasant household, built a bridge from the old order to the new. As Frank Tannenbaum has said, "It gave the Indian an opportunity . . . to save his faith in his own gods."

This transition from the old to the new was eased also by an astonishing similarity in ritual and symbol between the old and the new religion. A Nahua or an Otomí would hardly know what to make of a Spanish friar who, hampered by the language barrier, pointed first to the sky to indicate heaven and then to earth to indicate hell, as a first lesson in Catholic catechism. But rituals can be observed and learned by imitation. Both religious traditions had a rite of baptism. In Catholicism, the child was baptized and named, thus including him among the true believers. The Mexica similarly bathed and named the child in a religious rite, and the Maya celebrated with a ceremony the first time the child was carried astride the hip. Both religious traditions had a kind of confession. The Mexica and the inhabitants of the Gulf coast confessed their sexual transgressions to a priest of the earth goddess Filth-Eater; the Zapotec had annual public confessions; and the Maya confessed themselves either to priests or members of their families in case of illness. Both religious traditions possessed a ritual of communion. The Catholics drank wine and swallowed a wafer to symbolize their contact with the divine blood and body of Christ; the Mexica consumed images of the gods made of amaranth and liberally anointed with sacrificial blood. Both people used incense in their churches; both fasted and did penance; both went on pilgrimages to holy places; both kept houses of celibate virgins. Both believed in the existence of a supernatural mother; and both believed in virgin birth. Where Catholics held that Mary conceived immaculately through the power of the Holy Spirit, the Mexica believed that their goddess Coatlícue had given birth to Hummingbird-on-the-Left, impregnated by an obsidian knife which fell from the sky. Both people made use of the cross. A white St. Andrew's Cross, representing the four directions of the universe, often graced the hat and shield of the Shining Serpent, and the Maya made frequent use of the symbol of the foliated cross. The Spaniards represented their sacred stories in passion plays; the Middle Americans represented the annual changes of vegetation and activities in their sacrifices.

The Catholic missionaries well recognized the danger which lay in the maintenance of similar outward forms of ritual upon conversion. Yet they were themselves unable to decide whether these similarities were merely the work of Satan laboring to duplicate in his hellish church the rituals of the church sanctified by God, or whether they might not indeed represent the precipitate of some previous Christian teaching, brought to the New World perhaps by no less a personage than the apostle Thomas. Whatever their doubts, the formal similarities between the two religious traditions permitted an easy transition for the worshipper and gave him continuity precisely in the realm in which continuity was vital: the realm of religious behavior.

Nor did the psychology of Spanish Catholicism differ greatly from the psychology of the Mesoamerican solar cult. The Spanish ideal of the austere knight, defending his honor and the Virgin against Moors or other unbelievers, was not far removed from the Mexica ideal of the jaguar-eagle knight, whose obsidian sword insured victory and sacrificial victims for the hungry deities of war. In both religions cruelty against others in warfare and exalted pride went hand in hand with sacrificial penance—cruelty against the self, performed by a Spanish conqueror in a hairshirt, by a Mexica noble torturing his flesh with the sharp spikes of the century plant.

True to their hierarchical habits, the Spaniards expended their greatest religious effort in converting the nobles, who became their first converts, partly because of the similarity of motivation, partly because of a desire to achieve a secure place in the new Spanish hierarchy through baptism and Christian vows. At Tlaxcala, the first center of the Spanish missionary effort, the local aristocracy strove mightily to reserve for itself a monopoly of all new religious offices, even those of cook, janitor, and gardener in the new monasteries. Their children were the first beneficiaries of Spanish ecclesiastical schooling. They used their power to set the feet of their own tributaries upon the new road to salvation; these tributaries thus came to church, as Fray Mendieta said, "more for the sake of outer appearance, to follow the orders of the *principales* who wanted to deceive them than to find a remedy for their souls." With the nobles firmly dedicated to the worship of the new religion, the commoners could be converted in mass, often with no more than a token understanding of the new divinities they were to worship. Pedro de Gante, exemplary Franciscan and kinsman of Charles V, baptized Indians in Mexico City at a daily rate of 14,000.

To the task of mass conversion, moreover, the church brought an exemplary table of organization. Like the Middle American religion, it drew a line between religious specialists and lay worshippers. In both traditions, the priests were the final spokesmen of the divine realm, in contact with a world to which ordinary men had no access. In both religions, long training was required to make a man worthy of his special role, and in both religions fasts, penances, self-torture, and sexual abstinence were required of priests to maintain their spiritual worth in the sight of the divine powers. Throughout the exercise of their spiritual role on earth, dress, residence, speech, and comportment marked them off from ordinary men. Such parallelism again eased the transition from the worship of the old gods to the worship of the new, maintaining as it did the hierarchy of channels through which supernatural commands were passed down to the lay believer.

To be sure, the Catholic Church was organized internally to take maximum advantage of the opportunities so offered. Its division into holy orders and secular clergy made for great flexibility in a situation where an advance guard was needed to establish new beachheads of the faith, while a rear-guard took over and consolidated the gains. The friars were the advance guard; the abiding missionary work of the sixteenth century which laid the basis for all later religious efforts was probably carried out by no more than one thousand individuals. Established in fortified churches within the core areas of the newly won land, they spread out in "missions of penetration" into areas where Spanish political control was often still in doubt, sometimes ahead of Spanish armies, sometimes in their wake. Always they linked these outposts with their home bases through "liaison missions," to which they could retreat or where they could seek new strength to carry on their task of penetration. The secular clergy, the ordinary priesthood, carried out the work of consolidation.

Inevitably there were quarrels and conflicts of jurisdiction as the work progressed, as well as conflicts of temperament. The holy orders recruited men whose personalities differed markedly from those characteristic of the regular clergy. The friars favored individuals who were more adventurous and utopian in outlook, as well as less amenable to routine and less adapted to the day-to-day life of a going society. The secular clergy showed more conservatism, less of a tendency to sacrifice reality to otherworldly visions and schemes. Thus the larger church benefited by its possession of both kinds of men, both kinds of organization. When the task of conversion was completed, the work of shepherding the flock through its daily tribulations could be turned over to men capable of preserving the gains.

The eventual adjustment of the religious dream to mundane reality was less than utopia, and yet it left an impress on the Indian population such as no other religious or political current has done to this day. Ultimately the message of salvation spelled hope for the Indian, not only hope in the transcendental realm of a supernatural life after death but hope on earth, where utopia was yielding to the pressure of all too secular interests. Men would labor to deny him his humanity, to defend his use as a resource, a tool to be used and discarded at will; but against such claims of politicians, lawyers, and theologians, Pope Paul III would in 1537 assert, in his bull "Sublimis Deus":

> The sublime God so loved the human race that He not only created man in such wise that he might participate in the good that other creatures enjoy, but also endowed him with capacity to attain to the inaccessible and invisible Supreme Good and behold it face to face[;] . . . all are capable of receiving the doctrines of the faith. . . . We . . . consider . . . that the Indians are truly men. . . .

To the Indian, the rite of baptism thus proved an assertion of his essential humanity, to be a man with human claims upon other men. Of this right no colonist or royal official could rob him. When the Indian re-emerges from beneath the wreckage of utopia, we find that he has rebuilt and cemented his new life with bonds drawn from the new religion, at once his opium, his consolation, and his hope of ultimate justice.

3

The Jamestown Fiasco

Edmund S. Morgan

The tenuous beginnings of the little English settlement on the James River and the factors in its survival are skillfully woven together by Edmund S. Morgan. The initial struggle for survival was followed by a desperate grasp at economic success.

The first wave of Englishmen reached Virginia at Cape Henry, the southern headland at the opening of Chesapeake Bay, on April 26, 1607. The same day their troubles began. The Indians of the Cape Henry region (the Chesapeakes), when they found a party of twenty or thirty strangers walking about on their territory, drove them back to the ships they came on. It was not the last Indian victory, but it was no more effective than later ones. In spite of troubles, the English were there to stay. They spent until May 14 exploring Virginia's broad waters and then chose a site that fitted the formula Hakluyt had prescribed. The place which they named Jamestown, on the James (formerly Powhatan) River, was inland from the capes about sixty miles, ample distance for warning of a Spanish invasion by sea. It was situated on a peninsula, making it easily defensible by land; and the river was navigable by oceangoing ships for another seventy-five miles into the interior, thus giving access to other tribes in case the local Indians should prove as unfriendly as the Chesapeakes.

Captain Christopher Newport had landed the settlers in time to plant something for a harvest that year if they put their minds to it. After a week, in which they built a fort for protection, Newport and twenty-one others took a small boat and headed up the river on a diplomatic and reconnoitering mission, while the settlers behind set about the crucial business of planting corn. Newport paused at various

Indian villages along the way and assured the people, as best he could, of the friendship of the English and of his readiness to assist them against their enemies. Newport gathered correctly from his attempted conversations that one man, Powhatan, ruled the whole area above Jamestown, as far as the falls at the present site of Richmond. His enemies, the Monacans, lived above the falls (where they might be difficult to reach if Powhatan proved unfriendly). Newport also surmised, incorrectly, that the Chesapeake Indians who had attacked him at Cape Henry were not under Powhatan's dominion. He accordingly tried to make an alliance against the Chesapeakes and Monacans with a local chief whom he mistook for Powhatan. At the same time, he planted a cross with the name of King James on it (to establish English dominion) and tried to explain to the somewhat bewildered and justifiably suspicious owners of the country that one arm of the cross was Powhatan, the other himself, and that the fastening of them together signified the league between them.

If the Indians understood, they were apparently unimpressed, for three days later, returning to Jamestown, Newport found that two hundred of Powhatan's warriors had attacked the fort the day before and had only been prevented from destroying it by fire from the ships. The settlers had been engaged in planting and had not yet unpacked their guns from the cases in which they were shipped. That was a mistake they were not likely to repeat. But for the next ten years they seem to have made nearly every possible mistake and some that seem almost impossible. It would take a book longer than this to recount them all, and the story has already been told many times. But if we are to understand the heritage of these ten disastrous years for later Virginia history, we should look at a few of the more puzzling episodes and then try to fathom the forces behind them.

Skip over the first couple of years, when it was easy for Englishmen to make mistakes in the strange new world to which they had come, and look at Jamestown in the winter of 1609–10. It is three planting seasons since the colony began. The settlers have fallen into an uneasy truce with the Indians, punctuated by guerrilla raids on both sides, but they have had plenty of time in which they could have grown crops. They have obtained corn from the Indians and supplies from England. They have firearms. Game abounds in the woods; and Virginia's rivers are filled with sturgeon in the summer and covered with geese and ducks in the winter. There are five hundred people in the colony now. And they are starving. They scour the woods listlessly for nuts, roots, and berries. And they offer the only authentic examples of cannibalism witnessed in Virginia. One provident man chops up his wife and salts down the pieces. Others dig up graves to eat the corpses. By spring only sixty are left alive.

Another scene, a year later, in the spring of 1611. The settlers have been reinforced with more men and supplies from England. The preceding winter has not been as gruesome as the one before, thanks in part to corn obtained from the Indians. But the colony still is not growing its own corn. The governor, Lord De la Warr, weakened by the winter, has returned to England for his health. His replacement, Sir Thomas Dale, reaches Jamestown in May, a time when all hands could have been used in planting. Dale finds nothing planted except "some few seeds put into a private garden or two." And the people he finds at "their daily and usuall workes, bowling in the streetes."

It is evident that the settlers, failing to plant for themselves, depend heavily on the Indians for food. The Indians can finish them off at any time simply by leaving the area. And the Indians know it. One of them tells the English flatly that "we can plant any where . . . and we know that you cannot live if you want [i.e., lack] our harvest, and that reliefe we bring you." If the English drive out the Indians, they will starve.

With that in mind, we look back a year on a scene in the summer following the starving, cannibal winter. It is August, when corn is ripening. The governor has been negotiating with Powhatan about some runaway Englishmen he is thought to be harboring. Powhatan returns "noe other than prowde and disdaynefull Answers," and so the governor sends George Percy "to take Revendge upon the Paspeheans and Chiconamians [Chickahominies]," the tribes closest to Jamestown. Percy, the brother of the Earl of Northumberland and the perennial second in command at Jamestown, takes a group of soldiers up the James a few miles by boat and then marches inland three miles to the principal town of the Paspaheghs. They fall upon the town, kill fifteen or sixteen Indians, and capture the queen of the tribe and her children.

Percy then has his men burn the houses and "cutt downe their Corne groweinge about the Towne." He takes the queen and her children back to his boats and embarks for Jamestown, but his men "begin to murmur becawse the quene and her Children weare spared." Percy therefore obliges them by throwing the children overboard "and shoteinge owtt their Braynes in the water." Meanwhile he sends another party under Captain James Davis to attack another Indian town (presumably a Chickahominy town), where again they cut down the corn and burn the houses. Upon returning to Jamestown, Percy hears that the governor is displeased that the queen of the Paspaheghs has been spared. Davis wants to burn her, but Percy, "haveinge seene so mutche Bloodshedd that day," insists that she merely be put to the sword. So she is led away and stabbed.

Thus the English, unable or unwilling to feed themselves, continually demanding corn from the Indians, take pains to destroy both the Indians and their corn.

One final scene. It is the spring of 1612, and Governor Dale is supervising the building of a fort at Henrico, near the present site of Richmond. He pauses to deal with some of his men, Englishmen, who have committed a serious crime.

It is not easy to make sense out of the behavior displayed in these episodes. How to explain the suicidal impulse that led the hungry English to destroy the corn that might have fed them and to commit atrocities upon the people who grew up? And how to account for the seeming unwillingness or incapacity of the English to feed themselves? Although they had invaded Indian territory and quarreled with the owners, the difficulty of obtaining land was not great. The Indians were no match for English weapons. Moreover, since the Indians could afford to give up the land around Jamestown as well as Henrico without seriously endangering their own economy, they made no concerted effort to drive the English out. Although Indian attacks may have prevented the English from getting a crop into the ground in time for a harvest in the fall of 1607, the occasional Indian raids thereafter cannot explain the English failure to grow food in succeeding years. How, then, can we account for it?

The answer that comes first to mind is the poor organization and direction of the colony. The government prescribed by the charter placed full powers in a council appointed by the king, with a president elected by the other members. The president had virtually no authority of his own; and while the council lasted, the members spent most of their time bickering and intriguing against one another and especially against the one man who had the experience and the assurance to take command. The names of the councillors had been kept secret (even from themselves) in a locked box, until the ships carrying the first settlers arrived in Virginia. By that time a bumptious young man named John Smith had made himself unpopular with Captain Christopher Newport (in command until their arrival) and with most of the other gentlemen of consequence aboard. When they opened the box, they were appalled to find Smith's name on the list of councillors. But during the next two years Smith's confidence in himself and his willingness to act while others talked overcame most of the handicaps imposed by the feeble frame of government. It was Smith who kept the colony going during those years. But in doing so he dealt more decisively with the Indians than with his own quarreling countrymen, and he gave an initial turn to the colony's Indian relations that was not quite what the company had intended.

Smith, the son of a yeoman, was a rare combination of actor and man of action. He had already won his spurs fighting against the Turks in Hungary, where, as he tells it, he won all the battles except the last, in which he was captured, enslaved, and then rescued by a fair princess. With her assistance he made his escape, then trekked across Europe and was back in England to join the Jamestown expedition at the age of twenty-seven. In spite of his youth, he may have had more experience than anyone else at Jamestown in making war, in living off the land, and in communicating with people whose language he did not know. Certainly he showed more aptitude than anyone else in all these matters. And it was probably his ability to deal with the Indians that prevented them from destroying or starving the settlement.

When the supplies ran out in the first autumn, Smith succeeded in trading with the Indians for corn. Then, on an exploring expedition up the Chickahominy River, he was made a prisoner and brought before Powhatan. This was the point at which another fair princess, Pocahontas, stepped in to save his life—or so Smith later told it; and in spite of the skepticism engendered by the larger-than-life view of himself that Smith always affected, there seems to be no good reason to doubt him. In any case, he returned unharmed; and while he remained in Virginia (until the fall of 1609), he conducted most of the colony's relations (both with Powhatan and with the tribes under Powhatan's dominion.)

Smith took a keener interest in the Indians than anyone else in Virginia for a century to come. The astonishingly accurate map he made of the country shows the locations of the different tribes, and his writings give us most of the information we will ever have about them. But his interest in them was neither philanthropic nor philosophic. As he came to know them, he was convinced that they could be incorporated into the English settlement, but he scorned the notion that gentleness was the way to do it. Although Smith looks a little like a latter-day Drake or Hawkins, he did not see the Indians as Drake saw the Cimarrons. His own model seems to have been Hernando Cortez, and he would gladly have made Powhatan his Montezuma. He was disgusted when orders came from the company requiring that the settlers give the old chief a formal coronation, designed to make him a proper king, ally, and in some sense a vassal of King James. Smith witnessed the ceremony with undisguised contempt. Powhatan himself submitted with ill grace to the dignity thus thrust upon him and made it plain that he did not consider himself anybody's vassal and that he needed none of the proffered English assistance against his enemies.

Smith was sure that kindness was wasted on savages, and within weeks he was successfully bullying and browbeating Powhatan out of hundreds of bushels of corn. Years later, as he reflected in England on the frustrations that continued to beset Virginia, he was sure he had been right, that the Spanish had shown the way to deal with Indians. The English should have learned the lesson of how the Spanish "forced the treacherous and rebellious Infidels to doe all manner of drudgery worke and slavery for them, themselves living like Souldiers upon the fruits of their labours." John Smith's idea of the proper role of the Virginia Indians in English Virginia was something close to slavery. Given the superiority of English arms, he had no doubt of his ability to conquer the lot of them with a handful of men, just as Cortez had conquered the much more populous and formidable Aztecs. Once conquered, they could forthwith be put to work for their conquerors.

Smith was not afraid of work himself; and in the absence of Indian slaves he bent his efforts as much toward getting work out of Englishmen as he did toward supplying their deficiencies from Indian larders. In these first years many Englishmen perceived that the Indians had a satisfactory way of living without much work, and they slipped away "to live Idle among the Savages." Those who remained were so averse to any kind of labor, Smith reported, "that had they not beene forced nolens volens perforce to gather and prepare their victuall they would all have starved, and have eaten one another." While the governing council ruled, under the presidency of men of greater social prestige than Smith, he could make little headway against the jealousies and intrigues that greeted all his efforts to organize the people either for planting or for gathering food. But month by month other members of the council died or returned to England; and by the end of 1608 Smith was left in complete control. He divided the remaining settlers into work gangs and made them a little speech, in which he told them they could either work or starve: "Howsoever you have bin heretofore tolerated by the authoritie of the

Councell from that I have often commanded you, yet seeing nowe the authoritie resteth wholly in my selfe; you must obay this for a law, that he that will not worke, shall not eate (except by sicknesse he be disabled).'' He did not except himself from the rule and assured them that ''every one that gathereth not every day as much as I doe, the next daie shall be set beyond the river, and for ever bee banished from the fort, and live there or starve.'' And lest this only produce a general exodus to the Indians, Smith used his influence with the neighboring tribes to apply the same discipline to any settler who dared choose that course. As a result, in the winter of 1608–9 he lost only seven or eight men.

Had Smith been left in charge, it is not impossible that he would have achieved a society which, in one way or another, would have included the Indians. They might have had a role not much better than the Spanish assigned them, and they might have died as rapidly as the Arawaks from disease and overwork. But it is unlikely that the grisly scenes already described would have taken place (they all occurred after his departure). In spite of his eagerness to subdue the Indians, Smith was in continual contact and communication with them. He bullied and threatened and browbeat them, but we do not read of any atrocities committed upon them under his direction, nor did he feel obliged to hang, break, or burn any Englishman who went off to live with them.

But the Virginia Company in 1609 was not yet ready to abandon its goal of making its own way in Virginia and sharing the country with the Indians on more favorable terms than Smith would have allowed them. The members of the council who returned to England complained of Smith's overbearing ways, with Englishmen as well as Indians. So the company decided not to leave the colony in the hands of so pushy a young man. At the same time, however, they recognized that the conciliar form of government was ineffective, and that a firmer authority was necessary to put their lazy colonists to work. They accordingly asked, and were given, a new charter, in which the king relinquished his government of the colony. Henceforth the company would have full control and would rule through a governor who would exercise absolute powers in the colony. He would be assisted by a council, but their advice would not be binding on him. In fact, he would be as much a military commander as a governor, and the whole enterprise would take on a more military character.

For the next eight or nine years whatever evils befell the colony were not the result of any diffusion of authority except when the appointed governor was absent—as happened when the first governor, Lord De la Warr, delayed his departure from England and his deputy, Sir Thomas Gates, was shipwrecked en route at Bermuda. The starving winter of 1609–10 occurred during this interval; but Gates arrived in May, 1610, followed by De la Warr himself in June. Thereafter Virginia was firmly governed under a clear set of laws, drafted by Gates and by De la Warr's subsequent deputy, Sir Thomas Dale. The so-called *Lawes Divine, Morall and Martiall* were mostly martial, and they set the colonists to work with military discipline and no pretense of gentle government. They prescribed that the settlers be divided into work gangs, much as Smith had divided them, each of which would proceed to its assigned tasks at regular hours. At the beating of a drum, the master of each gang would set them to work and "not suffer any of his company to be negligent, and idle, or depart from his worke" until another beat of the drums allowed it.

The *Laws* prescribed death for a variety of crimes, including rape, adultery, theft, lying, sacrilege, blasphemy, or doing or saying anything that might "tend to the derision" of the Bible. On a more practical level, in order to increase the livestock which had by this time been brought over, the *Laws* made it death to kill any domestic animal, even a chicken. It was also death, in weeding a garden, to take an ear of corn or a bunch of grapes from it, death too to trade privately with anyone on the ships that came to the colony. And the punishments were inflicted with an arbitrary rigor that became a scandal. For stealing two or three pints of oatmeal a man had a needle thrust through his tongue and was then chained to a tree until he starved.

The *Laws* did not even contemplate that the Indians would become a part of the English settlement. Though the company had frowned on Smith's swashbuckling way with Indians, it was disenchanted with Powhatan and convinced that he and those under his dominion did need to be dealt with more sternly. Sir Thomas Gates was instructed to get some Indian children to bring up in the English manner, free of their parents' evil influence. And he was also told to subjugate the neighboring tribes, to make them pay tribute, and to seize the chiefs of any that refused. If he wanted to make friends with any Indians, they must be "those that are farthest from you and enemis unto those amonge whom you dwell." The company's new attitude was incorporated in several provisions of the *Laws*. When Indians came to Jamestown to trade or visit, they were to be placed under guard to prevent them from stealing anything; no inhabitant was to speak to them without the governor's permission; and the settlers were forbidden on pain of death to "runne away from the Colonie, to Powhatan, or any savage Werowance else whatsoever." The company's desire to bring the Indians into the community had given way to an effort to keep settlers and Indians apart.

In their relations to the Indians, as in their rule of the settlers, the new governing officers of the colony were ruthless. The guerrilla raids that the two races conducted against each other became increasingly hideous, especially on the part of the English. Indians coming to Jamestown with food were treated as spies. Gates had them seized and killed "for a Terrour to the Reste to cawse them to desiste from their subtell practyses." Gates showed his own subtle practices by enticing the Indians at Kecoughtan (Point Comfort) to watch a display of dancing and drumming by one of his men and then "espyeinge a fitteinge oportunety fell in upon them putt fyve to the sworde wownded many others some of them beinge after fownde in the woods with Sutche extreorindary Lardge and mortall wownds that itt seemed strange they Cold flye so far." It is possible that the rank and file of settlers aggravated the bad relations with the Indians by unauthorized attacks, but unauthorized fraternization seems to have bothered the governors more. The atrocities committed against the queen of the Paspaheghs, though apparently demanded by the men, were the work of the governing officers, as were the atrocities committed against the Englishmen who fled to live with the Indians.

John Smith had not had his way in wishing to reduce the Indians to slavery, or something like it, on the Spanish model. But the policy of his successors, though perhaps not with company approval, made Virginia look far more like the Hispaniola of Las Casas than it did when Smith was in charge. And the company and the colony had few benefits to show for all the rigor. At the end of ten years, in spite of the military discipline of work gangs, the colonists were still not growing enough to feed themselves and were still begging, bullying, and buying corn from the Indians whose lands they scorched so deliberately. We cannot, it seems, blame the colony's failures on lax discipline and diffusion of authority. Failures continued and atrocities multiplied after authority was made absolute and concentrated in one man.

Another explanation, often advanced, for Virginia's early troubles, and especially for its failure to feed itself, is the collective organization of labor in the colony. All the settlers were expected to work together in a single community effort, to produce both their food and the exports that would make the company rich. Those who held shares would ultimately get part of the profits, but meanwhile the incentives of private enterprise were lacking. The work a man did bore no direct relation to his reward. The laggard would receive as large a share in the end as the man who worked hard.

The communal production of food seems to have been somewhat modified after the reorganization of 1609 by the assignment of small amounts of land to individuals for private gardens. It is not clear who received such allotments, perhaps only those who came at their own expense. Men who came at company expense may have been expected to continue working exclusively for the common stock until their seven-year terms expired. At any rate, in 1614, the year when the first shipment of company men concluded their service, Governor Dale apparently assigned private allotments to them and to other independent "farmers." Each man got three acres, or twelve acres if he had a family. He was responsible for growing his own food plus two and a half barrels of corn annually for the company as a supply for newcomers to tide them over the first year. And henceforth each "farmer" would work for the company only one month a year.

By this time Gates and Dale had succeeded in planting settlements at several points along the James as high up as Henrico, just below the falls. The many close-spaced tributary rivers and creeks made it possible to throw up a palisade between two of them to make a small fortified peninsula. Within the space thus enclosed by water on three sides and palisaded on the fourth, the settlers could build their houses, dig their gardens, and pasture their cattle. It was within these enclaves that Dale parceled out private allotments. They were affirmations of an expectation that would linger for a century, that Virginia was about to become the site of thriving cities and towns. In point of fact, the new "cities" scarcely matched in size the tiny villages from which Powhatan's people threatened them. And the "farmers" who huddled together on the allotments assigned to them proved incapable of supporting themselves or the colony with adequate supplies of food.

According to John Rolfe, a settler who had married John Smith's fair Pocahontas, the switch to private enterprise transformed the colony's food deficit instantly to a surplus: instead of the settlers seeking corn from the Indians, the Indians sought it from them. If so, the situation did not last long. Governor Samuel Argall, who took charge at the end of May, 1617, bought 600 bushels from the Indians that fall, "which did greatly relieve the whole Colonie." And when Governor George Yeardley relieved Argall in April, 1619, he found the colony "in a great scarcity for want of corn" and made immediate preparations to seek it from the Indians. If, then, the colony's failure to grow food arose from its communal organization of production, the failure was not overcome by the switch to private enterprise.

Still another explanation for the improvidence of Virginia's pioneers is one that John Smith often emphasized, namely, the character of the immigrants. They were certainly an odd assortment, for the most conspicuous group among them was an extraordinary number of gentlemen. Virginia, as a patriotic enterprise, had excited the imagination of England's nobility and gentry. The shareholders included 32 present or future earls, 4 countesses, and 3 viscounts (all members of the nobility) as well as hundreds of lesser gentlemen, some of them perhaps retainers of the larger men. Not all were content to risk only their money. Of the 105 settlers who started the colony, 36 could be classified as gentlemen. In the first "supply" of 120 additional settlers, 28 were gentlemen, and in the second supply of 70, again 28 were gentlemen. These numbers gave Virginia's population about six times as large a proportion of gentlemen as England had.

Gentlemen, by definition, had no manual skill, nor could they be expected to work at ordinary labor. They were supposed to be useful for "the force of knowledge, the exercise of counsell"; but to have ninety-odd wise men offering advice while a couple of hundred did the work was inauspicious, especially when the wise men included "many unruly gallants packed thether by their friends to escape il destinies" at home.

What was worse, the gentlemen were apparently accompanied by the personal attendants that gentlemen thought necessary to make life bearable even in England. The colony's laborers "were for most part footmen, and such as they that were Adventurers brought to attend them, or such as they could perswade to goe with them, that never did know what a dayes worke was." Smith complained that he could never get any real work from more than thirty out of two hundred, and he later argued that of all the people sent to Virginia, a hundred good laborers "would have done more than a thousand of those that went."

The company may actually have had little choice in allowing gentlemen and their servants to make so large a number of their settlers. The gentlemen were paying their own way, and the company perhaps could not afford to deny them. But even if unencumbered by these volunteers, the colony might have foundered on the kind of settlers that the company itself did want to send. What the company wanted for Virginia was a variety of craftsmen. Richard Hakluyt had made up a list for Walter Raleigh that suggests the degree of specialization contemplated in an infant settlement: Hakluyt wanted both carpenters and joiners, tallow chandlers and wax chandlers, bowstave preparers and bowyers, fletchers and arrowhead makers, men to rough-hew pikestaffs and other men to finish them. In 1610 and again in 1611 the Virginia Company published lists of the kind of workers it wanted. Some were for building, making tools, and other jobs needed to keep the settlers alive, but the purpose of staying alive would be to see just what Virginia was good for and then start sending the goods back to England. Everybody hoped for gold and silver and jewels, so the colony needed refiners and mineral men. But they might have to settle for iron, so send men with all the skills needed to smelt it. The silk grass that Hariot described might produce something like silk, and there were native mulberry trees for growing worms, so send silk dressers. Sturgeon swam in the rivers, so send men who knew how to make caviar. And so on. Since not all the needed skills for Virginia's potential products were to be found in England, the company sought them abroad: glassmakers from Italy, millwrights from Holland, pitch boilers from Poland, vine dressers and saltmakers from France. The settlers of Virginia were expected to create a more complex, more varied economy than England itself possessed. As an extension of England, the colony would impart its variety and health to the mother country.

If the company had succeeded in filling the early ships for Virginia with as great a variety of specialized craftsmen as it wanted, the results might conceivably have been worse than they were. We have already noticed the effect of specialization in England itself, where the division of labor had become a source not of efficiency but of idleness. In Virginia the effect was magnified. Among the skilled men who started the settlement in 1607 were four carpenters, two bricklayers, one mason (apparently a higher skill than bricklaying), a blacksmith, a tailor, and a barber. The first "supply" in 1608 had six tailors, two goldsmiths, two refiners, two apothecaries, a blacksmith, a gunner (i.e., gunsmith?), a cooper, a tobacco pipe maker, a jeweler, and a perfumer. There were doubtless others, and being skilled they expected to be paid and fed for doing the kind of work for which they had been hired. Some were obviously useful. But others may have found themselves without means to use their special talents. If they were conscientious, the jeweler may have spent some time looking for jewels, the goldsmiths for gold, the perfumer for something to make perfume with. But when the search proved futile, it did not follow that they should or would exercise their skilled hands at any other tasks. It was not suitable for a perfumer or a jeweler or a goldsmith to put his hand to the hoe. Rather, they could join the gentlemen in genteel loafing while a handful of ordinary laborers worked at the ordinary labor of growing and gathering food.

The laborers could be required to work at whatever they were told to; but they were, by all accounts, too few and too feeble. The company may have rounded them up as it did in 1609 when it appealed to the mayor of London to rid the city of its "swarme of unnecessary inmates" by sending to Virginia any who were destitute and lying in the streets.

The company, then, partly by choice, partly by necessity, sent to the colony an oversupply of men who were not prepared to tackle the work essential to settling in a wilderness. In choosing prospective Virginians, the company did not look for men who would be particularly qualified to keep themselves alive in a new land. The company never considered the problem of staying alive in Virginia to be a serious one. And why should they have? England's swarming population had had ample experience in moving to new areas and staying alive. The people who drifted north and west into the pasture-farming areas got along, and the lands there were marginal, far poorer than those that awaited the settlers of tidewater Virginia. Though there may have been some farmers among the early settlers, no one for whom an occupation is given was listed as a husbandman or yeoman. And though thirty husbandmen were included in the 1611 list of men wanted, few came. As late as 1620 the colony reported "a great scarcity, or none at all" of "husbandmen truely bred," by which was meant farmers from the arable regions. In spite of the experience at Roanoke and in spite of the repeated starving times at Jamestown, the company simply did not envisage the provision of food as a serious problem. They sent some food supplies with every ship but never enough to last more than a few months. After that people should be able to do for themselves.

The colonists were apparently expected to live from the land like England's woodland and pasture people, who gave only small amounts of time to their small garden plots, cattle, and sheep and spent the rest in spinning, weaving, mining, handicrafts, and loafing. Virginians would spend their time on the more varied commodities of the New World. To enable them to live in this manner, the company sent cattle, swine, and sheep: and when Dale assigned them private plots of land, the plots were small, in keeping with the expectation that they would not spend much time at farming. The company never intended the colony to supply England with grain and did not even expect that agricultural products might be its principal exports. They did want to give sugar, silk, and wine a try, but most of the skills they sought showed an expectation of setting up extractive industries such as iron mining, smelting, saltmaking, pitch making, and glass-making. The major part of the colonists' work time was supposed to be devoted to processing the promised riches of the land for export; and with the establishment of martial law the company had the means of seeing that they put their shoulders to the task.

Unfortunately, the persons charged with directing the motley work force had a problem, quite apart from the overload of gentlemen and specialized craftsmen they had to contend with. During the early years of the colony they could find no riches to extract. They sent back some cedar wood, but lumber was too bulky a product to bear the cost of such long transportation to market. Sassafras was available in such quantities that the market for it quickly collapsed. The refiners found no gold or silver or even enough iron to be worth mining. Silk grass and silk proved to be a will-o'-the-wisp.

The result was a situation that taxed the patience both of the leaders and of the men they supervised. They had all come to Virginia with high expectations. Those who came as servants of the company had seven years in which to make their employers rich. After that they would be free to make themselves rich. But with no prospect of riches in sight for anybody, it was difficult to keep them even at the simple tasks required for staying alive or to find anything else for them to do.

The predicament of those in charge is reflected in the hours of work they prescribed for the colonists, which contrast sharply with those specified in the English Statute of Artificers. There was no point in demanding dawn-to-dusk toil unless there was work worth doing. When John Smith demanded that men work or starve, how much work did he demand? By his own account, "4 hours each day was spent in worke, the rest in pastimes and merry exercise." The governors who took charge after the reorganization of 1609 were equally modest in their demands.

To have grown enough corn to feed the colony would have required only a fraction of the brief working time specified, yet it was not grown. Even in their free time men shunned the simple planting tasks that sufficed for the Indians. And the very fact that the Indians did grow corn may be one more reason why the colonists did not. For the Indians presented a challenge that Englishmen were not prepared to meet, a challenge to their image of themselves, to their self-esteem, to their conviction of their own superiority over foreigners, and especially over barbarous foreigners like the Irish and the Indians.

If you were a colonist, you knew that your technology was superior to the Indians'. You knew that you were civilized, and they were savages. It was evident in your firearms, your clothing, your housing, your government, your religion. The Indians were supposed to be overcome with admiration and to join you in extracting riches from the country. But your superior technology had proved insufficient to extract anything. The Indians, keeping to themselves, laughed at your superior methods and lived from the land more abundantly and with less labor than you did. They even furnished you with the food that you somehow did not get around to growing enough of yourselves. To be thus condescended to by heathen savages was intolerable. And when your own people started deserting in order to live with them, it was too much. If it came to that, the whole enterprise of Virginia would be over. So you killed the Indians, tortured them, burned their villages, burned their cornfields. It proved your superiority in spite of your failures. And you gave similar treatment to any of your own people who succumbed to the savage way of life. But you still did not grow much corn. That was not what you had come to Virginia for.

By the time the colony was ten years old and an almost total loss to the men who had invested their lives and fortunes in it, only one ray of hope had appeared. It had been known, from the Roanoke experience, that the Indians grew and smoked a kind of tobacco; and tobacco grown in the Spanish West Indies was already being imported into England, where it sold at eighteen shillings a pound. Virginia tobacco had proved, like everything else, a disappointment; but one of the settlers, John Rolfe, tried some seeds of the West Indian variety, and the result was much better. The colonists stopped bowling in the streets and planted tobacco in them—and everywhere else that they could find open land. In 1617, ten years after the first landing at Jamestown, they shipped their first cargo to England. It was not up to Spanish tobacco, but it sold at three shillings a pound.

To the members of the company it was proof that they had been right in their estimate of the colony's potential. But the proof was bitter. Tobacco had at first been accepted as a medicine, good for a great variety of ailments. But what gave it its high price was the fact that people had started smoking it for fun. Used this way it was considered harmful and faintly immoral. People smoked it in taverns and brothels. Was Virginia to supplement England's economy and redeem her rogues by pandering to a new vice? The answer, of course, was yes. But the men who ran the Virginia Company, still aiming at ends of a higher nature, were not yet ready to take yes for an answer.

4

Indians and New Englanders

William Cronon

The effect of European diseases, demands and attitudes all had significant impact on natives. William Cronon points out the impacts of trade demands of Europeans on the Native's society. He also chronicles the effects of early contacts with European fishermen.

The tension between Indian and European property systems did not become instantly apparent the moment the first European visited New England. Indeed, for well over a century before English settlement began in Massachusetts, Europeans and Indians engaged in a largely unrecorded trade which suggested more possibilities for cooperation than for conflict between their respective economies. Hunters and sailors encountering one another on the coasts of Maine, Nova Scotia, and the St. Lawrence discovered very early that they had valuable things to trade: metal goods, weaponry, articles of clothing, and ornamental objects on the part of the Europeans; furs and skins on the part of the Indians. For the Europeans, such trade began as a casual adjunct to the cod fisheries, but in the second half of the sixteenth century, with the rising popularity of felt hats and the decline in European fur production, North American furs became a principal object of trade in their own right. For the Indians, that trade marked a new involvement in an alien commercial economy, as well as the onset of complicated shifts in their ecological circumstances.

It is important to underscore how little we know of this early fur trade and its effects: the various Indian peoples of New England undoubtedly started interacting with European visitors neither at the same time nor in the same way. As early as 1524, Verrazzano found Indians along the Maine coast who were only too familiar with the ways of European sailors. Although they actively sought to trade furs for knives, hooks, and other metal goods, they were nevertheless careful to direct Verrazzano's men to meet them at the rockiest and most dangerous part of the shore, where landing was impossible. There, as Verrazzano reported, "they sent us what they wanted to give on a rope, continually shouting to us not to approach the land," and communicating great hostility. This was in marked contrast to the inhabitants of Narragansett Bay, who apparently had had rather less experience with Europeans. They not only welcomed Verrazzano wholeheartedly but seemed indifferent to his offers of trade. "They did not appreciate cloth of silk and gold," Verrazzano wrote, "nor even of any other kind, nor did they care to have them; the same was true for metals like steel and iron, for many times when we showed them some of our arms, they did not admire them, nor ask for them, but merely examined their workmanship." Northern Indians, who lived closer to the fishing banks, learned of European trade goods and military methods before their southern counterparts; likewise, inhabitants of the coast began European contacts before those of interior villages.

Nevertheless, by the beginning of the seventeenth century, every recorded European exploration found Indians in villages all along the New England coast eager for trade. On the island of Cuttyhunk in 1602, Bartholomew Gosnold obtained the skins of beavers, otters, martens, foxes, rabbits, seals, and deer in exchange for knives and what he called "trifles." In 1605, Champlain was greeted on the Penobscot River by thirty Indians led by a sachem named Bashaba, who assured him that "no greater good could come to them than to have our friendship." Champlain was told that "they desired to live in peace with their enemies, and that we should dwell in their land, in order that they might in future more than ever before engage in hunting beavers, and give us a part of them in return for our providing them with things which they wanted." Already in 1605, Bashaba's speech displayed the extent to which Indians were orienting their economic activity to enable them to trade with Europeans. Bashaba made clear that he understood the demand for beaver on European markets, that he and his followers were prepared to increase their production to meet that demand, and that he saw friendship with Europeans as a way both of obtaining trade goods and of shifting military balances among Indian villages.

These were important lessons, to which we must soon return. For the moment, however, the most significant thing about them was that they were learned primarily not from men like Champlain and Gosnold but from dozens of unknown visitors who left no record of their trips. We know next to nothing about most of the Europeans who journeyed to New England in the sixteenth and early seventeenth centuries, and we can make only the crudest of inferences about how Indians responded to them. Yet there can be no doubt that contacts between the two groups were extensive. Explorers who were greeted by Indians speaking French, English, or Basque could have few illusions about being the first European visitors to an area. When the Pilgrims first landed on Cape Cod in 1620, they discovered "a place like a grave" covered with wooden boards. Digging it up, they found layer upon layer of household goods, the personal possessions that Indians ordinarily buried with their dead: mats, bowls, trays, dishes, a bow, and two bundles. In the smaller of the two bundles was a quantity of sweet-smelling red powder in which were the bones of a young child, wrapped in beads and accompanied by an undersized bow. Still, what troubled the grave-robbers were not these Indian things, many of which they took, but the contents of the larger bundle. There, in the same red powder, were the remnants of a man: some of the flesh remained on the bones, and they realized with a shock that "the skull had fine yellow haire still on it." With the bones, "bound up in a saylers canvas Casacke, and a payre of cloth breeches," were a knife, a needle, and "two or three old iron things," evidently the dead man's most personal belongings. A blond European sailor, shipwrecked or abandoned on the Massachusetts coast, had lived as an Indian, had perhaps fathered an Indian child, and had been buried in an Indian grave. His circumstances may or may not have been unusual—even this we cannot know—but they betokened an already long and continuing exchange between peoples on opposite sides of the Atlantic.

It was anonymous Europeans like the dead sailor in the Cape Cod grave who helped bring about the single most dramatic ecological change in Indian lives, one whose full significance historians have only recently come to understand. Of all the many organisms Europeans carried to America, none of them were more devastating to the Indians than the Old World diseases, what W. H. McNeill has called the microparasites. The ancestors of New England Indians had reached North America perhaps twenty or thirty thousand years before the Europeans, arriving via a land bridge at the Bering Straits during the most recent of the glacial epochs. In the course of their migrations, they failed to bring with them many of the illnesses that were common elsewhere in the world. Their low population densities and their having lived for extended periods under semiarctic conditions served to filter out microorganisms which required large host populations and more temperate climates to survive. Their lack of domesticated animals, especially the grazing ungulates, such as swine, cattle, and horses, which share many diseases with humans, also helped to reduce the number of pathogens they brought with them from Eurasia. As a result, the American Indians were blessed by the absence not only of diseases that Europeans ordinarily experienced in childhood, such as chicken pox and measles, but also of more lethal organisms that were epidemic in the Old World: smallpox, influenza, plague, malaria, yellow fever, tuberculosis, and several others. As William Wood said, the New England Indians were a people of "lusty and healthful bodies, not experimentally knowing the catalogue of those health-wasting diseases which are incident to other countries."

It was, of course, a blessing that proved all too quickly to be a curse. For hundreds of generations, Indian babies had grown to adulthood with no experience of these illnesses, so that Indian mothers transferred to their infants none of the antibodies which might have provided some measure of immunity against them. What the Indians lacked was not so much *genetic* protection from Eurasian disease—though this may have been a partial factor—as the historical experience as a population to maintain *acquired* immunities from generation to generation: each new generation that failed to encounter a disease was left with less protection against it. As a result, European diseases struck Indian villages with horrible ferocity. Mortality rates in initial onslaughts were rarely less than 80 or 90 percent, and it was not unheard of for an entire village to be wiped out. From the moment of their first contact with an Old World pathogen, Indian populations experienced wave upon wave of epidemics as new diseases made their appearance or as new nonimmune generations came to age. A long process of depopulation set in, accompanied by massive social and economic disorganization.

How early this began in New England is impossible to know. The long sea voyage across the Atlantic acted as a disease filter in its own right, since epidemic diseases had usually run their course on board ship before sailors reached North America. Many visits probably occurred with no disease organisms at all being passed on to Indians, and the earliest transfers may well have been of endemic illnesses—diarrheas, dysentery, venereal diseases, respiratory viruses, tuberculosis—which had remained nonvirulent in the shipboard population. Those Indians who saw the most of European visitors were obviously most at risk to acquire any disease that survived the sea journey, and so the inhabitants of northern fur-trading areas probably began to suffer from the new diseases first. By 1616, Pierre Biard could write of disease as being a regular visitor to the Indians of Maine and Nova Scotia. "They are astonished," he said,

> and often complain that, since the French mingle with and carry on trade with them, they are dying fast, and the population is thinning out. For they assert that, before this association and intercourse, all their countries were very populous, and they tell how one by one the different coasts, according as they have begun to traffic with us, have been more reduced by disease.

Biard's description suggests a significant increase in mortality rates among the northern Indians, but does not convey the catastrophic scale of epidemics that occurred elsewhere. The low population densities of the northern hunters probably protected them somewhat from certain diseases (cholera, for instance) that needed a minimum host population in order to reproduce themselves, and may also have limited the diseases that did occur to sporadic outbreaks. Nevertheless, northern death sentences were postponed rather than annulled, and the effects of disease were simply spread over a long period of slow attrition.

Although the corn-growing Indians of southern New England were less involved in the fur trade, their much greater population densities meant that when disease was finally introduced to them, its effects were explosive. The first recorded epidemic in the south began in 1616 and raged for three years on the coast between Cape Cod and Penobscot Bay, reaching villages perhaps twenty or thirty miles inland but sparing both the deeper interior and the coast west of Narragansett Bay. Although contemporary observers describe it as "the plague," New England lacked the rats and human population densities necessary to sustain that disease. Chicken pox seems a more likely cause, since its virus requires only a small host population in order to remain in circulation; it could have traveled in latent form across the Atlantic in the body of a European sailor who might then have developed shingles from which Indians could easily have become infected. Whichever disease the Indians caught, its effects are well documented. Thomas Morton told of villages in which only a single inhabitant was left alive. So many died that no one remained to bury the corpses, and crows and wolves feasted on them where they lay. When colonists arrived a few years after the epidemic had spent itself, they found such quantities of bleached bones and skulls that, as Morton said, "it seemed . . . a new found Golgotha."

Southern New England Indians continued to experience serious outbreaks of disease during the 1620s, and in 1633 they were visited by smallpox, one of the most lethal of European killers. The 1633 epidemic saw mortalities in many villages reach 95 percent. This time villages in the interior and along the coast west of Narragansett Bay fell victim to the viral fury as much as those elsewhere, perhaps an indication of the extent to which their trade connections had been expanded since 1616. William Bradford, Governor of the Plymouth Colony, has left the fullest description of the horrors brought by the disease. "For want of bedding and linen and other helps," he wrote,

> they fall into a lamentable condition as they lie on their hard mats, the pox breaking and mattering and running one into another, their skin cleaving by reason thereof to the mats they lie on. When they turn them, a whole side will flay off at once as it were, and they will be all of a gore blood, most fearful to behold. And then being very sore, what with cold and other distempers, they die like rotten sheep.

There was little Indians could do to protect themselves from the epidemics. Whereas they had previously dealt with their sick companions by gathering at their bedside to sit through the illness with them, they quickly learned that the new diseases could be escaped only by casting aside family and community ties and fleeing. "So terrible is their apprehension of an infectious disease," wrote Roger Williams in the 1640s, "that not only persons, but the Houses and the whole Towne takes flight." With only the sick left to help the sick, even those who might otherwise have survived an epidemic were doomed. Bradford said that

> they were in the end not able to help one another, no not to make a fire nor to fetch a little water to drink, nor any to bury the dead. But would strive as long as they could, and when they could procure no other means to make fire, they would burn the wooden trays and dishes they ate their meat in, and their very bows and arrows. And some would crawl out on all fours to get a little water, and sometimes die by the way and not be able to get in again.

Social disorganization compounded the biological effects of disease. Once villages were attacked by a new pathogen, they often missed key phases in their annual subsistence cycles—the corn planting, say, or the fall hunt—and so were weakened when the next infection arrived. Worse, hungry times that had always been normal in precolonial Indian society—for instance, the late winter among northern hunters—became lethal when accompanied by the new diseases. Chronic illnesses gained their foothold in this way, and broke out whenever Indian populations became particularly susceptible to them. Tuberculosis had become common by the end of the seventeenth century, and influenza in combination with pneumonia recurred regularly in epidemic proportions. Measles, typhus, dysentery, and syphilis all became endemic and contributed to the general decline in Indian populations. As a result, in the first seventy-five years of the seventeenth century, the total number of Indians in New England fell precipitously from well over 70,000 to fewer than 12,000. In some areas, the decline was even more dramatic: New Hampshire and Vermont were virtually depopulated as the western Abenaki declined from perhaps 10,000 to fewer than 500.

The epidemics disrupted most of the networks of kinship and authority that had previously organized Indian lives. When Bradford described a village in which "the chief sachem himself now died and almost all his friends and kindred," he was depicting a phenomenon that took place in many Indian communities. Villages which had lost their sachems and whose populations had declined twentyfold were often no longer viable entities; surviving Indians were forced to move to new villages and create new political alignments. Depopulation and alliances with Europeans gave ambitious individuals who had lacked high rank before an epidemic opportunities to assume new leadership roles. Squanto, for instance, later to become the Pilgrims' interpreter, was the only survivor from his village at the end of the 1616–19 epidemic. A man without a community, "whose ends," as Edward Winslow said, "were only to make himself great in the eyes of his countrymen, by means of his nearness and favor with us," he consciously sought to undermine the authority of the neighboring sachem Massasoit. One of his devices for doing that was to convince other Indians that the colonists "had the plague buried in our storehouse; which, at our pleasure, we could send forth to what place or people we would, and destroy them therewith, though we stirred not from home." This was a particularly blatant attempt to use disease to amass political power; the Indians' willingness to believe it testifies to both their fear and their well-grounded suspicion that the new illnesses were of European origin. But the mere fact of depopulation promoted conditions of turmoil which enabled new leaders to emerge in the ensuing political vacuum.

The social disruption brought by the epidemics was not limited to political leaders. Indian doctors, or powwows, found their ordinary healing practices useless against so potent a biological assault. Indeed, as the Puritan historian Edward Johnson said, the "powwows themselves were oft smitten with deaths stroke." European pathogens thus served to undermine the spiritual and religious practices of Indian communities. John Winthrop, in speaking of victims of smallpox in 1633, said that "divers of them, in their sickness, confessed that the Englishmen's God was a good God; and that, if they recovered, they would serve him." Conversions of this sort were often a kind of hedging of bets with little lasting consequence, but they suggest some of the spiritual trauma brought by the enormous mortalities. As Robert Cushman said of the Indians around Plymouth, "Those that are left, have their courage much abated, and their countenance is dejected, and they seem as a people affrighted."

Indian depopulation as a result of European diseases ironically made it easier for Europeans to justify taking Indian lands. If the English believed that cornfields were the only property Indians had improved sufficiently to own, the wiping out of a village—and the subsequent abandonment of its planting fields—eliminated even this modest right. Over and over again, New England towns made their first settlements on the sites of destroyed Indian villages. Plymouth, for instance, was located "where there is a great deal of Land cleared, and hath beene planted with Corne three or foure years agoe"—planted, in fact, just before the 1616 epidemic broke out. More than fifty of the earliest settlements had similar locations, thus saving their inhabitants much initial work in clearing trees. To Puritans, the epidemics were manifestly a sign of God's providence, "in sweeping away great multitudes of the natives . . . that he might make room for us there." John Winthrop saw this "making room" as a direct conveyance of property right: "God," he said, "hath hereby cleared out title to this place."

As Indian villages vanished, the land on which they had lived began to change. Freed from the annual burnings and soon to be subject to an entirely different agricultural regime, and land's transformations were often so gradual as to be imperceptible. But a few changes were directly attributable to the depopulation caused by the epidemics. Fields which had still stood in grass when the Pilgrims arrived in 1620 were rapidly being reclaimed by forest by the time of the 1630 Puritan migrations to Massachusetts. William Wood spoke of places "where the Indians died of the plague some fourteen years ago" that were covered with "much underwood . . . because it hath not been burned." Between Wessaguscus and Plymouth, the regrowth of forest had already made one extensive area "unuseful and troublesome to travel through, insomuch that it is called ragged plain because it tears and rents the clothes of them that pass." Some Indian fields were rapidly overgrown by the strawberries and raspberries in whose abundance colonists took so much delight, but these were an old-field phenomenon that would not reproduce themselves for long without the growing conditions Indians had created for them. When the Puritan migrations began, the animals that had relied on the Indians to maintain their edge habitats were still abundant beyond English belief, but in many areas the edges were beginning to return to forest. Declining animal populations would not be noticed for many years, but habitat conditions were already shifting to produce that effect.

Because Old World pathogens had such profound effects on Indian lives, any analysis of the fur trade must bear those effects constantly in mind. Changes in the ways Indians organized subsistence, made political alliances, and interacted with the environment stemmed directly from the new market in furs and trade goods, but the larger context was that of a society facing biological havoc. One historian, Calvin Martin, has gone so far as to assert that Indians became involved in the fur trade because they believed that game animals, rather than Europeans, had brought the epidemics upon them. In Martin's view, Indian demand for European trade goods was decidedly secondary to the Indians' belief that they were conducting a holy war against animals that were persecuting them with disease. Elegant as his thesis may be, it is supported by very little evidence, and none of it from New England. Martin is right to note the apparent paradox of Indian participation in the fur trade: by so willingly overhunting the beaver and other game animals, Indians across North America were responsible for attacking one of the major bases of their own subsistence. But to appeal to a spiritual holy war to explain this phenomenon trivializes the social and economic circumstances that led Indians to engage in trade in the first place. The connection between the epidemics and the fur trade was real, but neither so direct nor so purely spiritual as Martin would have us believe.

The fur trade could not have existed without Indians: in order for the English to exploit beavers and other furbearers, it was essential that they have the willing cooperation of Indian partners. This fact sprang from the very hunting skills which English observers regarded as "laziness" in Indian males. Writing of the beaver, William Wood admitted that "these beasts are too cunning for the English, who seldom or never catch any of them; therefore we leave them to those skillful hunters [Indian males] whose time is not so precious." In fact, the Indians' time was not less precious: they simply hunted much more efficiently than the English—even with their supposedly "inferior" technology—and stopped when they were satisfied with what they had caught. (Perhaps their leisure time seemed to them *more* precious than the English thought their own.) No amount of English labor could have yielded so great a return on invested capital as did the Indians' labor in hunting and processing beaver. But to obtain that return, English colonists needed to offer goods that the Indians found as desirable as the Europeans found furs.

Trade was nothing new to the New England Indians. "Amongst themselves," said Roger Williams, "they trade their Corne, skins, Coates, Venison, Fish, etc." Within villages, it was difficult to distinguish such trade from the gift giving that was so important in maintaining political and economic alliance networks. But trade also took place between villages, especially of goods that some possessed in greater quantities by reason of ecological circumstances. An interior village in the upland forest, for instance, which had an abundance of chestnuts, might regularly exchange them with a coastal village that had an abundance of chestnuts, might regularly exchange them with a coastal village that had an abundance of shellfish. Northern New England Indians could obtain a much greater variety and quantity of furs than those in the south, and these could be traded for corn and beans with southern Indians who had agricultural surpluses. But even exchange between villages had important political overtones, since it served as a token of their diplomatic relations. Champlain in 1606 observed a transaction in which one sachem felt he had not received value for value: he "went away very ill-disposed towards them for not properly recognizing his presents, and with the intention of making war upon them in a short time." Most exchanges, whether internal or external to a village, were articulated in the language of gift giving.

In addition to the implicit gift relationship, what distinguished this trade from that of European merchants was its preponderantly local nature. Trade took place largely between adjacent villages; no entrepreneurial class existed whose chief role was to move commodities over long distances. Goods of high value might still travel hundreds of miles, but generally only by being traded from village to village. As John Smith said, villages "have each trade with other so farre as they have society on each others frontiers, for they make no such voyages as from *Pennobscot* to *Cape Cod,* seldome to *Massachset.*" Trade was either between individuals for goods each would personally use, or between sachems for goods that could be redistributed to followers. The European fur trade could come into existence only by being assimilated into this earlier context.

The objects Europeans could offer in trade had certain qualities that were completely new to Indian material culture. Brass and copper pots allowed women to cook over a fire without the risk of shattering their earthen vessels, and were much more easily transported. Woven fabrics were lighter and more colorful than animal skins and nearly as warm. Iron could be sharpened and would hold an edge better than stone, so that European hatchets and knives had advantages over Indian ones. Indians had no firearms, and were unfamiliar with alcohol. But in spite of the newness of these things, it is wrong to see the acquisition of European technology as in itself necessitating a revolution in Indian social life. European tools did not instantly increase Indian productivity in any drastic way. Most were readily incorporated into subsistence practices and trade patterns that had existed in precolonial times. They were in fact often reconverted into less utilitarian but more highly valued Indian objects: the many early explorers who came across Indians wearing brass and copper jewelry, for instance, were probably seeing what Indians believed to be—along with arrowheads—the proper use of European brass and copper kettles.

Indians had first to learn the uses of European fabrics and metals before they would trade for them; as Verrazzano discovered at Narragansett Bay, this did not always happen automatically. What Indians valued was often less the inherent technical qualities of a material object than its ascriptive qualities as an object of status. (In this, they were not fundamentally different from Europeans who sought to obtain animal skins so as to display personal wealth.) A kettle or a metal arrowhead might have virtues that saved labor and were desirable in their own right, but these did not become compelling until other Indians owned them and an individual's importance began to be measured by their possession. Indians eventually sought many of the things Europeans offered in trade, not for what *Europeans* thought valuable about them, but for what those things conveyed in *Indian* schemes of value. In effect, they became different objects. Being rare and exotic, European goods could function as emblems of rank in Indian society and as gifts in the exchanges that created and maintained alliance networks. Indian individuals seeking to increase their political power, especially in the wake of the epidemics, often tried to accumulate trade goods that could be used to gain more allies. Transactions of this kind involved exchanges of values that were functionally more symbolic than utilitarian; as with the property systems we have already examined, Indians and Europeans understood their acquisitions differently, for the simple reason that those acquisitions were embedded in different social and ecological contexts.

Some of the most highly desired goods offered by Europeans in fact had little to do with European technologies at all. After using up their tiny initial store of trade goods, the Plymouth colonists had, as Bradford said, "little or nothing else" to offer Indians "but this corn which themselves had raised out of the earth." Agricultural produce had been the major substance offered by southern Indians in trade with northern ones, and Plymouth at first behaved little differently from an Indian village in trading its maize for furs. What stimulated the trade was not so much new European technologies—nothing other than the sailing ship was necessary to pursue it—as a new European economic need: the need to find commodities that would repay debts to European merchants. In this sense, Europeans took hold of the traditional maize-fur trade network and transformed it from a system of binary village exchange to a link in the new Atlantic economy. Colonial governments reserved the fur trade as a sovereign right for themselves and the merchants who served as their agents, and began to amass corn both by trading with southern Indians and by taxing the colonists themselves. For a short while, it seemed as if corn raising would prove a most profitable enterprise: when Francis Higginson said that it was "almost incredible what great gaine some of our English Planters have had by our Indian Corne," he was excited not about the grain itself but about its easy convertibility into furs. Transported in English ships from southern New England to the Maine coast, corn remained one element of the fur trade throughout the seventeenth century, but its importance nevertheless declined. Its disadvantages limited its desirability as a staple commodity: it was bulky, relatively difficult to transport, and its value fluctuated considerably relative to both the size of the annual corn crop and the northern Indians' success in hunting for food.

It was another commodity—like maize, more Indian than European—that revolutionized the New England fur trade: wampumpeag, the strings of white and purple beads we know today as wampum. Made by grinding and drilling the shells of whelks and quahogs until they were hollow cylinders a quarter of an inch long and an eighth of an inch in diameter, its manufacture was ecologically limited to the Long Island Sound area where these shellfish flourished. Never made in great quantities during precolonial times, wampum was a highly valued token of personal power and wealth. It was initially rare outside the coastal villages in which it was made, so that elsewhere, as Bradford noted, only "the sachems and some special persons . . . wore a little of it for ornament." Lesser individuals dared not accumulate too much of it unless they were willing to challenge those with higher prestige. It was exchanged mainly at well-circumscribed ritual moments: in the payment of tribute between sachems, as recompense for murder or other serious crimes, in the transfer of bridewealth when proposing marriage, as payment for a powwow's magical services, or in gift exchanges to betoken friendship and alliance. It was, in other words, a medium of gift giving whose value was widely accepted among the Indians of southern New England.

To Europeans, wampum was ideally suited to become the medium for a wider, more commercial exchange—to become what John Locke called "money." The Indians' adoption of European metal drills increased their production of wampum, making it more widely available for trade. But, as with corn, the chief European innovation was to introduce a new functional role into Indian economies, that of the merchant who transported goods between communities which, for cultural and ecological reasons, valued those goods differently. The Dutch first discovered wampum's value in 1622, and were astonished at how much it facilitated their trade. Fearing that the Pilgrims would become rivals in the Connecticut fur trade if they found out about wampum independently, the Dutch West India Company's agent, Isaack de Rasieres, decided to introduce them to it himself. He accordingly sold them £50 worth of it in 1627 and encouraged them to try trading it on the Maine coast (rather than on the Connecticut, where the Dutch trading houses were located). Although Maine Indians were initially reluctant to acquire wampum, within two years it had become the single most important commodity Plymouth had to offer. Presumably because of the high prestige that Indians associated with its possession, Plymouth traders "could scarce ever get enough for them, for many years together," and were able to cut off other traders who lacked wampum and had only European goods to sell.

Control of wampum rapidly became crucial to both Indians and Europeans. The political crisis created by the epidemics made wampum a necessary acquisition for any sachem trying to expand—or even retain—his or her power. As greater and greater quantities became available to more and more individuals, even to those who had once been of low rank, an inflationary cycle in the price of prestige objects fueled trade all the more. Possession of wampum became increasingly common, with widening effects on status systems. Here again, wampum was part of the reorganization of Indian economic and political life which followed in the wake of the epidemics: competition for its acquisition established new leaders, promoted dependence on European traders, and helped shift the tribute obligations which had previously existed among Indian villages. "Strange it was," said Bradford, "to see the greater alteration it made in a few years among the Indians themselves."

On the European side, the importance of wampum to the fur trade made it imperative that colonies have a guaranteed supply of it. That meant controlling trade with the Indians of Long Island Sound—Pequots, Mohegans, Narragansetts, and villages on Long Island—who could procure the necessary whelks and quahogs. At first their wampum was obtained by flooding them with high-status European goods such as kettles and firearms; in response, they expanded their production of it and, as Bradford said, "became rich and potent by it." The number of Europeans trying to trade with the wampum makers encouraged the Indians to become shrewd bargainers who played one trader off against another. According to Roger Williams, they "beate all markets and try all places, and runne twenty thirty, yea forty mile, and more, and lodge in the Woods, to save six pence." In part because of the guns which these markets gave the Indians of the south coast, many colonists increasingly feared the Indians' power and sought a less dangerous way of acquiring their wampum. Governor Bradford went so far as to write a poem about the problem:

> But now they know their advantage so well,
> And will not stick, to some, the same to tell,
> That now they can, when they please or will,
> The English drive away, or else them kill.

The colonists' economic problem of obtaining a sure supply of wampum and the military problem of dealing with independent Indian arms were finally solved simultaneously by means of armed force: the slaughter of the Pequots in 1637 and the assassination of the Narragansett sachem Miantonomo in 1643. Exacting a regular military tribute in wampum proved a safer and more reliable source of supply than trading guns for it.

The fur trade was thus far more complicated than a simple exchange of European metal goods for Indian beaver skins. It revolutionized Indian economies less by its new technology than by its new commercialism, at once utilizing and subverting Indian trade patterns to extend European mercantile ones. European merchants created an expanded regional economy in New England by shuttling between several different trading partners: wampum producers along Long Island Sound, corn growers—both Indians and colonists—in the south generally, European manufacturers, and the Indians—located primarily in the north—who hunted furs. Trade linked these groups with an abstract set of equivalent values measured in pelts, bushels of corn, fathoms of wampum, and price movements in sterling on London markets. The essential lesson for the Indians was that certain things began to have *prices* that had not had them before. In particular, one could buy personal prestige by killing animals and exchanging their skins for wampum or high-status European goods.

Formerly, there had been little incentive for Indians to kill more than a fixed number of animals. As Nicolas Denys observed of the northern Indians, "they killed animals only in proportion as they had need of them. They never made an accumulation of skins of Moose, Beaver, Otter, or others, but only so far as they needed them for personal use." The one occasion for which furs *were* accumulated in precolonial times—when they were exchanged with southern villages for corn and other goods—was in fact an exception to prove the rule. Aside from limitations on the amount of grain Indians could move overland or by canoe, such precolonial trade was kept to modest levels by two factors. Need—as measured by use and by the success of harvest or hunt—still determined the volume of trade: there was little reason for the inhabitants of a village to trade for more food than they could eat, or more clothes than they could wear. Taking place mainly between villages, the trade was conducted by sachems and other high-prestige individuals, and so was held in check by the status relationships within a village and the diplomatic relations between villages. It had few of the expansionist tendencies of European commerce.

Precolonial trade enforced an unintentional conservation of animal populations, a conservation which was less the result of an enlightened ecological sensibility than of the Indians' limited social definition of "need." One Indian at the end of the eighteenth century remembered that in earlier times his people had not killed "more than necessary." He said this was because "there was none to barter with them that would have tempted them to waste their animals, as they did after the Chuckopek or white people came on this island, consequently game was never diminished." As we have seen, European trade changed all of this. It introduced Indians to a new set of prestige goods which could only be obtained by trade; moreover, the disruption of earlier status systems by the epidemics eliminated many of the social sanctions which had formerly restricted individual accumulation. Indian economies thus became attached to international markets, not for technological, but for social and political reasons. For them, it was a market of much more limited circulation than it was for Europeans: Indian notions of status were measured by a handful of goods, whereas Europeans could accumulate wealth with virtually any material possession. Nevertheless, even a limited market in prestige was enough to turn Indians into the leading assailants of New England's fur-bearing mammals. Certain animal populations began to decline in consequence, even though the epidemics meant that fewer Indians were hunting them. The commercialization of the Indian's earlier material culture thus brought with it a disintegration of their earlier ecological practices.

Chief among the animals which suffered from the fur trade was of course the beaver, whose low reproductive rates and sedentary habits made it easily threatened by concentrated hunting. Never abundant in southern New England, it was disappearing from Massachusetts coastal regions by 1640 and had ceased to be of much economic significance in the Narragansett country by 1660. The southern trade lasted longest on major rivers that drained extensive regions to the north, where Indian hunters continued to find beavers to kill. On the Connecticut River, European traders established in turn the towns of Wethersfield, Hartford, Windsor, and Springfield as fur posts. Each successive one captured Indian trade from those below it, and the arrival of agricultural settlers eventually brought the fur trade of each to an end. Springfield, established by William Pynchon in 1636, maintained its hold longer than most. Although its trade had declined by 1650 to the point that Edward Johnson could describe it as of "little worth," Pynchon's son John managed between 1652 and 1658 to procure from Indians nearly 9000 beaver pelts, in addition to hundreds of moose, otter, muskrat, fox, raccoon, mink, marten, and lynx skins. Output gradually declined, experienced a sharp drop in the 1670s during the conflicts surrounding King Philip's War, and from then on continued only at much reduced levels. By the end of the century, the fur trade had lost its economic importance to the area. The same fate overtook the string of trading posts—Concord, Chelmsford, and Lancaster—which were established on the Merrimac River.

Other southern animals were also at risk. As Pynchon's records showed, virtually any furbearer could be sold for its pelt. But in the vicinity of denser English settlements, especially Boston, there was also a market for meat, one in which both Indians and colonists participated. In the early 1630s, a male turkey weighing forty pounds brought four shillings in eastern Massachusetts, while other birds—heathcocks, ducks, geese, and so on—cost from four- to sixpence. In Springfield, Pynchon bought venison from the Indians by paying wampum for it. To increase colonial meat supplies, the Massachusetts General Court gave exclusive hunting privileges to designated colonists who improved a pond by setting decoys on it, or who used nets to hunt birds on certain islands. Other colonists used Indian servants to hunt food for them. For their part, Indians found colonial guns particularly helpful in hunting birds and large mammals. They sold enough of what they killed for Governor Bradford to object that

> The gain hereof to make they know so well,
> The fowl to kill, and us the feathers sell.
> For us to seek for deer it doth not boot,
> Since now with guns themselves at them can shoot.
> That garbage, of which we no use did make,
> They have been glad to gather up and take;
> But now they can themselves fully supply,
> And the English of them are glad to buy.

Bradford's main anxiety was that Indians owned guns at all, but he was also irritated by their killing and selling things which English colonists might otherwise have obtained for nothing.

Overhunting combined with reductions in edge habitats led some of the meat species to decline in numbers even by the end of the seventeenth century. Already in 1672, John Josselyn said of the turkey that English and Indian hunters had "now destroyed the breed, so that 'tis very rare to meet with a wild turkie in the woods." Only domesticated ones could be seen in eastern Massachusetts. A century later, the bird which William Wood had seen in flocks of a hundred had become so rare throughout New England that a popular farmer's manual could define the word "turkey" as "a large domestick fowl, brought from Turkey, and is called by the name of its country." The fact that the domesticated bird of Europe had originally been brought from America by Spanish colonists in the sixteenth century had apparently been forgotten. Other birds would eventually be eliminated as well—the passenger pigeon, which had existed in so many "millions of millions," began to disappear toward the end of the eighteenth century—but the fate of these other species was not finally sealed until the rise of metropolitan markets for fowl in the nineteenth century.

More important to southern Indians was the gradual disappearance of the white-tailed deer and other large herbivores. Deer were threatened by changes in their habitat, augmented numbers of hunters, and competition from domestic livestock. They were so reduced by the end of the seventeenth century that Massachusetts enforced its first closed season on their hunting in 1694, and in 1718 all hunting of them was forbidden for a closed term of three years. By the 1740s, a series of "deer reeves"—early game wardens—were regulating the deer hunt, but to little avail. At the end of the eighteenth century, Timothy Dwight noted that deer were "scarcely known below the forty-fourth degree of north latitude," having vanished from all but the northern stretches of Vermont, New Hampshire, and Maine. With them, save for in the far north, had gone the elk, bear, and lynx. "Hunting with us," said Dwight, "exists chiefly in the tales of other times."

By the time this happened, of course, the colonists no longer relied on hunting for any significant portion of their subsistence. The real losers were the Indians, whose earlier way of life was encountering increasing ecological constraints. Indian settlement patterns began to change in the 1630s. On the south coast, Indians took to occupying coastal sites year-round in order to stockpile shellfish so that they could make wampum on an expanded scale. This new sedentarism was reinforced, and promoted elsewhere in New England, by military conflicts—themselves a consequence of the political turmoil which followed the epidemics and expanding European trade—that led villages to prefer permanently fortified sites inhabited by relatively dense populations. Attacks by colonists and intertribal warfare concentrated Indians with particularly dramatic consequences: Gookin described how it forced "many of them to get together in forts; by which means they were brought to such straits and poverty, that had it not been for relief they had from the English, in compensation for labour, doubtless many of them had suffered famine." But even when the threat of violence was not so immediate, Indians were living in fixed locations on a more permanent basis. Earlier subsistence practices which had depended on seasonal dispersal were gradually being abandoned, with important social and ecological effects. Denser settlement patterns encouraged the spread of infectious diseases and increased pressure on adjacent hunting and planting areas. As a result, Indians found themselves relying on a narrowing range of foodstuffs.

As Indians increasingly sold the skins they hunted, they had to have an alternative for their own clothing. Despite some initial reluctance, they found it in European fabric, which, next to wampum, was by mid-century the single most important commodity they bought with fur. At Pynchon's trading post in the 1650s, Indian transactions for textiles outnumbered transactions for metal goods more than fivefold. Elsewhere, the price in beaver skins for a blanket was identical to that for a gun. European clothing was not only high in prestige value but cheaper than fur to own: a large beaver pelt cost nearly twice as much in wampum as a finished cloth coat. Raw cloth, which Indians preferred, was even cheaper. By the 1670s, Daniel Gookin could write:

> The Indians' clothing in former times was of the same matter as Adam's was, viz. skins of beasts, as deer, moose, beaver, otters, raccoons, foxes, and other wild creatures. . . . But, for the most part, they sell the skins and furs to the English, Dutch, and French, and buy of them for clothing a kind of cloth, called duffils, or trucking cloth, about a yard and a half wide.

From duffils they learned to fashion their clothing, and eventually they had no choice but to do so. The decline in deer populations made their reliance on European fabrics inescapable.

By the 1660s, southern New England Indians had for several decades been relying on wampum and furs to trade for textiles, arrowheads, knives, guns, and kettles. Gookin reported that "they generally disuse their former weapons." During the seventeenth century, earlier forms of these implements lost prestige value and young Indians growing up gained less and less experience in making them. Villages thus became vulnerable to changes in their trade base in a way they had not been before. Wampum, which in the 1640s had circulated as legal tender among colonists as well as Indians, lost much of its value in the 1660s when European demand for beaver declined and new supplies of silver coin from the West Indies reduced the scarcity of colonial specie. As a result, although wampum continued to circulate in the Indian trade, the colonists no longer defined it legally as money. "It is but a commodity," declared the Providence Court, and "it is unreasonable that it should be forced upon any man." Demand for wampum fell, and Indians on the south coast suddenly found themselves isolated from markets on which they had come to rely. Indians for whom pelts had been their main access to trade had comparable experiences when their fur supplies gave out. These changes contributed to the conflicts leading up to King Philip's War in 1675–76, but their longer-term effect was to force Indians who depended on trade goods to turn to the only major commodity they had left: their land.

The second half of the seventeenth century saw Indians in southern New England lose most of their land. The colonists accomplished this dispossession in ways which have been recounted at length elsewhere and need not be repeated here. Whether seized as the spoils of war, stolen by colonial subterfuge, or simply sold by Indians to obtain trade goods, the net effect was the same: decreasing quantities of land remained free for the Indians' use. The denser settlement patterns they had adopted earlier became less and less a matter of choice as they found themselves more and more surrounded by colonists. Subsistence practices which had never before had deleterious ecological consequences began gradually to have them. Planting fields could no longer be so easily abandoned when their fertility declined, and agricultural yields fell, making crops a less reliable source of food. Hunting too became more difficult. Adjacent colonial settlements eventually tried to restrict Indian hunting on English land, and such key food sources as deer became harder to obtain. Toward the end of the seventeenth century, many Indians were actually beginning to keep European livestock. If the evidence from one archaeological site in Connecticut can be generalized, by 1700 some Indian villages were relying on domesticated animals for over half their mammalian meat supply. The keeping of cattle on Indian land further decreased the forage available for wild deer herds and so continued the erosion of hunting resources. From an ecological point of view, Indian subsistence practices were in many ways more and more like those of European peasants. As European trade had done earlier, European agriculture reorganized Indian relationships within both the New England regional economy and the New England ecosystem.

Many of the changes I have been describing apply primarily to southern New England. In the north, where Indian populations were much smaller in relation to their land base and fewer colonists came to settle, pressure on animal populations resulted almost wholly from trade rather than competition over land. Low Indian densities meant fewer hunters and for that reason larger concentrations of the very animals Europeans most desired, so that the fur trade was far more active in Maine and eastern Canada than it was farther south. In response, Indians extended their hunting of furbearers to seasons when those animals had not traditionally been taken, and winter subsistence activities which had earlier relied on a wide range of species turned increasingly to the handful that had become tradeable commodities. When Indians returned to the coast in summer to sell their catch, they sought not only wampum and the preferred European tools, but food as well, including corn, bread, peas, prunes, and alcohol. Because of their larger and more concentrated involvement with the fur trade, their eventual dependence on it was even greater than that of southern New England Indians. Nicolas Denys, writing in 1672, said that they had "abandoned all their own utensils." In effect, furbearers were being asked to supply not only clothing and winter food but many other aspects of subsistence as well.

As in the case of southern New England Indians, certain forms of European technology became integrated into northern subsistence practices, with important effects. Once Indians stopped cutting up brass and copper kettles for jewelry, they were liberated from the large and cumbersome wooden kettles, made from tree stumps, which they had once used for cooking. Denys said that the earlier "immovable kettles were the chief regulators of their lives, since they were able to live only in places where these were." European kettles enabled villages to follow animal populations more readily and without the necessity of resorting to base camps; to Indians, they seemed "the most valuable article they can obtain from us." Likewise, the musket, although rarely used for hunting beaver or the smaller furbearers because of its inaccuracy, made the killing of large herbivores a simpler task. Shooting a moose provided far more food with much less labor than killing many birds or small game animals. A solitary beast which had once been hunted only when deep snows slowed its movements, the moose suddenly became an easier prey. As a result, it was gone from parts of eastern Canada by the mid-seventeenth century, and the same pattern repeated itself in northern New England. At the end of the eighteenth century, the colonial historian James Sullivan said of Maine that "the moose, a monstrous large animal, has been plenty there in former days, but it is rare to see one at the present time."

What encouraged the destruction of the beaver, on the other hand, was less new technologies than new market relations. Because supplies of the animal lasted much longer in the north than in the south, northern Indians developed a new set of institutions for controlling the hunt. Reduction in beaver populations, as well as conflict over who should be permitted to trap where, led to major shifts in Indian notions of property. Northern villages had formerly divided their hunting territories on a shifting and ad hoc basis; now, as families tried to hang on to their share of a declining beaver hunt, such territories became more and more fixed. By the eighteenth century, Maine Indians had allocated their lands into family hunting territories whose possession was inherited from generation to generation. In 1764, the fur trader Joseph Chadwick wrote that "their hunting ground and streams were all parcelled out to certain families, time out of mind." By turning uncaught beavers into private property, Indian families sought to guarantee their conservation: "it was their rule," said Chadwick, "to hunt every third year and kill two-thirds of the beaver, leaving the other third part to breed." Indians had once conserved their game animals, probably without fully realizing it, by their seasonal rotation from habitat to habitat, moving wherever food could be had with least effort. Now their dependence on trade forced them to control the beaver hunt much more self-consciously in order to assure that there would be animals to bring to market. The beaver, in other words, had ceased to be an object of use, conserved because the need for it was slight; instead, it had become a commodity of exchange, conserved because the need for it was great.

In part because of the family hunting territories, the beaver survived in Maine, albeit in much reduced numbers. The Maine fur trade continued throughout the eighteenth century, but the effects of colonial warfare, overhunting by English trappers, and competition from Canadian furs combined to make it less and less profitable. At the end of the French and Indian Wars, Maine Indians were complaining that "since the late war English hunters kill all the Beaver they find on said streams, which had not only empoverished many Indian families, but destroyed the breed of Beavers." Elsewhere in New England, the beaver barely survived into the nineteenth century; the southern fur trade was no longer very profitable by 1700, and the animal itself remained only in isolated areas. By 1797, Benjamin Trumbull could write of Connecticut's beavers—as well as its otters, foxes, martens, raccoons, minks and muskrats—using the past tense. Samuel Williams, in his *History of Vermont,* said that "the beaver has deserted all the southern parts of Vermont, and is now found only in the most northern, and uncultivated parts of the state." Even there, the animal would be gone before long.

The elimination of the beaver had ecological consequences beyond the loss of the animals themselves. Their passing left New England with a wealth of place names which no longer made much sense: scattered across the map of the region one still finds Beaver Brooks,

Beaver Stations, Beaver Creeks, and Beaver Ponds. More importantly, they left behind a series of artifacts that would await European settlers when they came to clear the land. When colonists cut a road through freshly opened countryside, they often went out of their way to cross streams on abandoned beaver dams rather than to build bridges. The sites of old dams were often chosen as preferred mill sites. Some beaver ponds became spawning grounds for shad and salmon, thus providing sites where fish for food and fertilizer could be had with a minimum of labor. But it was when the old dams collapsed for want of maintenance that they conferred their greatest benefit on colonial settlers. Behind them was many years' accumulation of leaves, bark, rotten wood, and rain-washed silt; in addition, their ponds had killed acres of trees which had once stood on the banks of pre-beaver streams. When the pond disappeared with the breaching of its dam, the rich black soil was suddenly exposed to the sun and rapidly became covered with grass that grew "as high as a man's shoulders." Not only did this provide forage for moose and deer—as long as those animals remained to browse there—but it became ideal mowing ground when settlers arrived with their cattle. As the English traveler Henry Wansy remarked, "It is a fortunate circumstance to have purchased lands where these industrious animals have made a settlement. At some of them, there have been four ton of hay cut on an acre." The old pond bottoms, which could be as much as two hundred acres in extent, provided excellent agricultural land as well. As one colonial writer put it, "Without these natural meadows, many settlements could not possibly have been made, at the time they were made." The death of the beaver in fact paved the way for the non-Indian communities that would soon arrive.

By 1800, the joint efforts of Indians and colonists had decimated many of the animals whose abundance had most astonished early European visitors to New England. Timothy Dwight in the early nineteenth century said of Connecticut that "we have hardly any wild animals remaining besides a few small species of no consequence except for their fur." Such animals had fallen victim especially to the new Indian dependence on a market in prestige goods. The Indians, not realizing the full ramifications of what that market meant, and finally having little choice but to participate in it, fell victims too: to disease, demographic collapse, economic dependency, and the loss of a world of ecological relationships they could never find again. No one understood this better than the Indians themselves. In 1789, the Mohegans petitioned the state of Connecticut for assistance, explaining:

> The times are Exceedingly Alter'd, Yea the times have turn'd everything upside down, or rather we have Chang'd the good Times, Chiefly by the help of the White People, for in times past, our Fore-Fathers lived in Peace, Love, and great harmony, and had everything in Great plenty. . . . But alas, it is not so now, all our Fishing, Hunting and Fowling is entirely gone.

Even if they exaggerated the peace, love, and harmony of precolonial Indian life, they did not mistake its plenty. Indian economies had maintained and relied on that plenty, and could not exist without the ecological relationships it implied. But although selling the animals had been the Indians' major contribution to their new circumstances, it was by no means the only reason their world had turned upside down. Ecological changes wrought by the colonists themselves were far more extensive, and needed no Indian partners for their accomplishment.

5

Common Sense

Bernard Bailyn

Common Sense *is a powerful Revolutionary document. In it, Thomas Paine successfully attached many myths concerning American reliance on British support. He assaulted the utility of the empire, he claimed the monarchy was corrupt and archaic, and he pleaded that the very voice of nature cried out for independence. Bernard Bailyn astutely analyzes the nature and role of this powerful pamphlet.*

Common Sense is the most brilliant pamphlet written during the American Revolution, and one of the most brilliant pamphlets ever written in the English language. How it could have been produced by the bankrupt Quaker corsetmaker, and the sometime teacher, preacher, and grocer, and twice-dismissed excise officer who happened to catch Benjamin Franklin's attention in England and who arrived in America only 14 months before *Common Sense* was published is nothing one can explain without explaining genius itself. For it is a work of genius—slapdash as it is, rambling as it is, crude as it is. It "burst from the press," Benjamin Rush wrote, "with an effect which has rarely been produced by types and papers in any age or country." Its effect, Franklin said, was "prodigious." It touched some extraordinarily sensitive nerve in American political awareness in the confusing period in which it appeared.

It was written by an Englishman, not an American. Paine had only the barest acquaintance with American affairs when, with Rush's encouragement, he turned an invitation by Franklin to write a history of the Anglo-American controversy into the occasion for composing a passionate tract for American independence. Yet not only does *Common Sense* voice some of the deepest aspirations of the American

This article is an excerpt from Bernard Bailyn, "Common Sense," in *Fundamental Testaments of the American Revolution* (The Library of Congress, 1973), reprinted by permission of Bernard Bailyn.

people of the eve of the Revolution but it also evokes, with superb vigor and with perfect intonation, longings and aspirations that have remained part of American culture to this day.

What is one to make of this extraordinary document after 200 years? What questions, in the context of the current understanding of the causes and meaning of the Revolution, should one ask of it?

Not, I think, the traditional one of whether *Common Sense* precipitated the movement for independence. To accomplish that was of course its ostensible purpose, and so powerful a blast, so piercing a cry so widely heard throughout the colonies—everyone who could read must have seen it in one form or another—could scarcely have failed to move some people some of the way. It undoubtedly caused some of the hesitant and vaguely conservative who had reached no decision to think once more about the future that might be opening up in America.

For it appeared at what was perhaps the perfect moment to have a maximum effect. It was published on January 10, 1776. Nine months before, the first skirmishes of the Revolutionary War had been fought, and seven months before, a bloody battle had taken place on Breed's Hill, across the bay from Boston, which was the headquarters of the British army in America, long since surrounded by provincial troops. Three months after that, in September 1775, a makeshift American army had invaded Canada and taken Montreal. In December its two divisions had joined to attack Quebec, and though that attack, on December 30–31, had failed miserably, the remnants of the American armies still surrounded the city when Paine wrote *Common Sense,* and Montreal was still in American hands.

That a war of some sort was in progress was obvious, but it was not obvious what the objective of the fighting was. There was disagreement in the Continental Congress as to what a military victory, if it came, should be used to achieve. A group of influential and articulate leaders, especially those from Massachusetts, were convinced that only independence from England could properly serve American needs, and Benjamin Franklin, recently returned from London, had reached the same conclusion and had found like-minded people in Philadelphia. But that was *not* the common opinion of the Congress, and it certainly was not the general view of the population at large. Not a single colony had instructed its delegates to work for independence, and not a single step had been taken by the Congress that was incompatible with the idea—which was still the prevailing view—that America's purpose was to force Parliament to acknowledge the liberties it claimed and to redress the grievances that had for so long and in so many different ways been explained to the world. All the most powerful unspoken assumptions of the time—indeed, common sense—ran counter to the notion of independence.

If it is an exaggeration, it is not much of an exaggeration to say that one had to be a fool or a fanatic in early January 1776 to advocate American independence. Militia troops may have been able to defend themselves at certain points and had achieved some limited goals, but the first extended military campaign was ending in a squalid defeat below the walls of Quebec. There was no evidence of an area of agreement among the 13 separate governments and among the hundreds of conflicting American interests that was broad enough and firm enough to support an effective common government. Everyone knew that England was the most powerful nation on earth, and if its navy had fallen into disrepair, it could be swiftly rebuilt. Anyone whose common sense outweighed his enthusiasm and imagination knew that a string of prosperous but weak communities along the Atlantic coast left uncontrolled and unprotected by England would quickly be pounced on by rival European powers whose ruling political notions and whose institutions of government were the opposite of what Americans had been struggling to preserve. The most obvious presumption of all was that the liberties Americans sought were British in their nature: they had been achieved by Britain over the centuries and had been embedded in a constitution whose wonderfully contrived balance between the needs of the state and the rights of the individual was thought throughout the western world to be one of the finest human achievements. It was obvious too, of course, that something had gone wrong recently. It was generally agreed in the colonies that the famous balance of the constitution, in Britain and America, had been thrown off by a vicious gang of ministers greedy for power, and that their attention had been drawn to the colonies by the misrepresentations of certain colonial officeholders who hoped to find an open route to influence and fortune in the enlargement of Crown power in the colonies. But the British constitution had been under attack before, and although at certain junctures in the past drastic action had been necessary to reestablish the balance, no one of any importance had ever concluded that the constitution itself was at fault; no one had ever cast doubt on the principle that liberty, as the colonists knew it, rested on—had in fact been created by—the stable balancing of the three essential socio-constitutional orders, the monarchy, the nobility, and the people at large, each with its appropriate organ of government: the Crown, the House of Lords, and the House of Commons. If the balance had momentarily been thrown off, let Americans, like Britishers in former ages, fight to restore it: force the evildoers out, and recover the protection of the only system ever known to guarantee both liberty and order. America had flourished under that benign system, and it was simply common sense to try to restore its balance. Why should one want to destroy the most successful political structure in the world, which had been constructed by generations of constitutional architects, each building on and refining the wisdom of his predecessors, simply because its present managers where vicious or criminal? And was it reasonable to think that these ill-coordinated, weak communities along the Atlantic coast could defeat England in war and then construct a system of government free of the defects that had been revealed in the almost-perfect English system?

Since we know how it came out, these seem rather artificial and rhetorical questions. But in early January 1776 they were vital and urgent, and *Common Sense* was written to answer them. There was open warfare between England and America, but though confidence in the English government had been severely eroded, the weight of opinion still favored restoration of the situation as it had been before 1764, a position arrived at not by argument so much as by recognition of the obvious sense of the matter, which was rooted in the deepest presuppositions of the time.

In the weeks when *Common Sense* was being written the future—even the very immediate future—was entirely obscure; the situation was malleable in the extreme. No one then could confidently say which course history would later declare to have been the right course to have followed. No one then could know who would later be seen to have been heroes and who weaklings or villains. No one then could know who would be the winners and who the losers.

But Paine was certain that he knew that answers to all these questions, and the immediate impact that *Common Sense* had was in large part simply the result of the pamphlet's ringing assertiveness, its shrill unwavering declaration that all the right was on the side of independence and all the wrong on the side of loyalty to Britain. History favored Paine, and so the pamphlet became prophetic. But in the strict context of the historical moment of its appearance, its assertiveness seemed to many to be more outrageous than prophetic, and rather ridiculous if not slightly insane.

All of this is part of the remarkable history of the pamphlet, part of the extraordinary impact it had upon contemporaries' awareness.

Yet I do not think that, at this distance in time and in the context of what we now know about the causes of the Revolution, the question of its influence on the developing movement toward independence is the most useful question that can be asked. We know both too much and too little to determine the degree to which *Common Sense* precipitated the conclusion that Congress reached in early July. We can now depict in detail the stages by which Congress was led to vote for independence—who played what role and how the fundamental, difficult, and divisive problem was resolved. And the closer we look at the details of what happened in Congress in early 1776 the less important *Common Sense* appears to have been. It played a role in the background, no doubt; and many people, in Congress and out, had the memory of reading it as they accepted the final determination to move to independence. But, as John Adams noted, at least as many people were offended by the pamphlet as were persuaded by it—he himself later called it "a poor, ignorant, malicious, short-sighted, crapulous mass"—and we shall never know the proportions on either side with any precision.

What strikes one more forcefully now, at this distance in time, is something quite different from the question of the pamphlet's unmeasurable contribution to the movement toward independence. There is something extraordinary in this pamphlet—something bizarre, outsized, unique—quite aside from its strident appeal for independence, and that quality, which was recognized if not defined by contemporaries and which sets if off from the rest of the pamphlet literature of the Revolution, helps us understand, I believe, something essential in the Revolution as a whole. A more useful effort, it seems to me, than attempting to measure its influence on independence is to seek to isolate this special quality.

Certainly the language is remarkable. For its prose alone, *Common Sense* would be a notable document—unique among the pamphlets of the American Revolution. Its phraseology is deeply involving—at times clever, at times outrageous, frequently startling in imagery and penetration—and becomes more vivid as the pamphlet progresses.

In the first substantive part of the pamphlet, ostensibly an essay on the principles of government in general and of the English constitution in particular, the ideas are relatively abstract but the imagery is concrete: "Government, like dress, is the badge of last innocence; the palaces of kings are built upon the ruins of the bowers of paradise." As for the "so much boasted constitution of England," it was "noble for the dark and slavish times in which it was erected''; but that was not really so remarkable, Paine said, for ''when the world was overrun with tyranny, the least remove therefrom was a glorious rescue.'' In fact, Paine wrote, the English constitution is ''imperfect, subject to convulsions, and incapable of producing what it seems to promise,'' all of which could be ''easily demonstrated'' to anyone who could shake himself loose from the fetters of prejudice. For ''as a man who is attached to a prostitute is unfitted to choose or judge of a wife, so any prepossession in favor of a rotten constitution of government will disable us from discerning a good one.''

The imagery becomes arresting in Part 2, on monarchy and hereditary succession, institutions which together, Paine wrote, formed ''the most prosperous invention the Devil ever set on foot for the promotion of idolatry.'' The heathens, who invented monarchy, at least had the good sense to grant divinity only to their *dead* kings; ''the Christian world has improved on the plan by doing the same to their living ones. How impious is the title of sacred majesty applied to a worm, who in the midst of his splendor is crumbling into dust!'' Hereditary right is ridiculed by nature herself, which so frequently gives ''mankind an *ass for a lion.*''

What of the true origins of the present-day monarchs, so exalted by myth and supposedly sanctified by antiquity? In all probability, Paine wrote, the founder of any of the modern royal lines was ''nothing better than the principal ruffian of some restless gang, whose savage manners or preeminence of subtility obtained him the title of chief among the plunderers; and who, by increasing in power and extending his depredations, overawed the quiet and defenseless to purchase their safety by frequent contributions.'' The English monarchs? ''No man in his senses can say that their claim under William the Conqueror is a very honorable one. A French bastard, landing with an armed banditti and establishing himself king of England against the consent of the natives is in plain terms a very paltry rascally original.'' Why should one even bother to explain the folly of hereditary right? It is said to provide continuity and hence to preserve a nation from civil wars. That, Paine said, is ''the most barefaced falsity ever imposed upon mankind.'' English history alone disproves it. There had been, Paine confidently declared, ''no less than eight civil wars and nineteen rebellions'' since the Conquest. The fact is that everywhere hereditary monarchy has ''laid . . . the world in blood and ashes.'' ''In England a king hath little more to do than to make war and give away places; which in plain terms is to impoverish the nation and set it together by the ears. A pretty business indeed for a man to be allowed eight hundred thousand sterling a year for, and worshipped into the bargain!'' People who are fools enough to believe the claptrap about monarchy, Paine wrote, should be allowed to do so without interference: ''let them promiscuously worship the Ass and the Lion, and welcome.''

But it is in the third section, ''Thoughts on the Present State of American Affairs,'' that Paine's language becomes most effective and vivid. The emotional level is extremely high throughout these pages and the lyric passages even then must have seemed prophetic:

> The sun never shined on a cause of greater worth. . . . 'Tis not the concern of a day, a year, or an age; posterity are virtually involved in the contest, and will be more or less affected even to the end of time by the proceedings now. Now is the seedtime of continental union, faith, and honor. The least fracture now will be like a name engraved with the point of a pin on the tender rind of a young oak; the wound will enlarge with the tree, and posterity read it in full grown characters.

The arguments in this section, proving the necessity for American independence and the colonies' capacity to achieve it, are elaborately worked out, and they respond to all the objections to independence that Paine had heard. But through all of these pages of argumentation, the prophetic, lyric note of the opening paragraphs continues to be heard, and a sense or urgency keeps the tension high. ''Everything that is right or reasonable,'' Paine writes, ''pleads for separation. The blood of the slain, the weeping voice of nature cries, 'TIS TIME TO PART.'' *Now* is the time to act, he insists: ''The present winter is worth an age if rightly employed, but if lost or neglected the whole continent will partake of the misfortune.'' The possibility of a peaceful conclusion to the controversy had vanished, ''wherefore, since nothing but blows will do, for God's sake let us come to a final separation, and not leave the next generation to be cutting throats under the violated unmeaning names of parent and child.'' Not to act now would not eliminate the need for action, he wrote, but only postpone it to the next generation, which would clearly see that ''a little more, a little farther, would have rendered this continent the glory of the earth.'' To talk of reconciliation, ''with those in whom our reason forbids us to have faith, and our affections, wounded through a thousand pores, instruct us to detest, is madness and folly.'' The earlier harmony was irrecoverable: ''Can ye give to prostitution its former innocence? Neither can ye reconcile Britain and America. . . . As well can the lover forgive the ravisher of his mistress as the continent forgive the murders of Britain.'' And the section ends with Paine's greatest peroration:

> O ye that love mankind! Ye that dare to oppose not only the tyranny but the tyrant, stand forth! Every spot of the old world is overrun with oppression. Freedom hath been hunted round the globe. Asia and Africa had long expelled her. Europe regards her like a stranger, and England hath given her warning to depart. O! receive the fugitive, and prepare in time an asylum for mankind.

In the pamphlet literature of the American Revolution there is nothing comparable to this passage for sheer emotional intensity and lyric appeal. Its vividness must have leapt out of the pages to readers used to greyer, more solid prose.

But language does not explain itself. It is a reflection of deeper elements—qualities of mind, styles of thought, a writer's personal culture. There is something unique in the intellectual idiom of the pamphlet.

Common Sense, it must be said, is lacking in close rigor of argumentation. Again and again Paine's logic can be seen to be grossly deficient. His impatience with following through with his arguments at certain points becomes almost amusing. In the fourth and final section, for example, which is on America's ability to achieve and maintain independence. Paine argues that one of America's great advantages is that, unlike the corrupt European powers, it is free of public debt, a burden that was wellknown to carry with it all sorts of disabling social and political miseries. But then Paine recognizes that mounting a full-scale war and maintaining independence would inevitably force America to create a national debt. He thereupon proceeds to argue, in order, the following: 1) that *such* a debt would be ''a glorious memento of our virtue''; 2) that even if it *were* a misery, it would be a cheap price to pay for independence and a new, free constitution—though not, for reasons that are not made entirely clear, a cheap price to pay for simply getting rid of the ministry responsible for all the trouble and returning the situation to what it was in 1764: ''such a thought is unworthy a man of honor, and is the true characteristic of a narrow heart and a peddling politician.'' Having reached that point, he goes the whole way around to make the third point, which is that ''no nation ought to be without a debt,'' though he had started with the idea that the absence of one was an advantage. But this new notion attracts him, and he begins to grasp the idea, which the later federalists would clearly see, that ''a national debt is a national bond''; but then, having vaguely approached that idea, he skitters off to the curious thought that a national debt could not be a grievance so long as no interest had to be paid on it; and that in turn leads him into claiming that America could produce a navy twice the size of England's for 1/20th of the English national debt.

As I say, close logic, in these specific arguments, contributes nothing to the force of *Common Sense*. But the intellectual style of the pamphlet is extraordinarily impressive nevertheless, because of a more fundamental characteristic than consistency or cogency. The great intellectual force of *Common Sense* lay not in its close argumentation on specific points but in its reversal of the presumptions that underlay the arguments, a reversal that forced thoughtful readers to consider, not so much a point here and a conclusion there, but a wholly new way of looking at the entire range of problems involved. For beneath all of the explicit arguments and conclusions against independence, there were underlying, unspoken, even unconceptualized presuppositions, attitudes, and habits of thought that made it extremely difficult for the colonists to break with England and find in the prospect of an independent future the security and freedom they sought. The special intellectual quality of *Common Sense,* which goes a long way toward explaining its impact on contemporary readers, derives from its reversal of these underlying presumptions and its shifting of the established perspectives to the point where the whole received paradigm within which the Anglo-American controversy had until then proceeded came into question.

No one set of ideas was more deeply embedded in the British and the British-American mind than the notion, whose genealogy could be traced back to Polybius, that liberty could survive in a world of innately ambitious and selfish if not brutal men only where a balance of the contending forces was so institutionalized that no one contestant could monopolize the power of the state and rule without effective opposition. In its application to the Anglo-American world this general belief further presumed that the three main socioconstitutional contestants for power—the monarchy, the nobility, and the people—had an equal right to share in the struggle for power: these were the constituent elements of the political world. And most fundamental of all in this basic set of constitutional notions was the unspoken belief, upon which everything else rested, that complexity in government was good in itself since it made all the rest of the system possible, and that, conversely, simplicity and uncomplicated efficiency in the structure of government were evil in that they led to a monopolization of power, which could only result in brutal state autocracy.

Paine challenged this whole basic constitutional paradigm, and although his conclusions were rejected in America—the American state and national governments are of course built on precisely the ideas he opposed—the bland, automatic assumption that all of this made sense could no longer, after the appearance of *Common Sense,* be said to exist, and respect for certain points was permanently destroyed.

The entire set of received ideas on government, Paine wrote, was false. Complexity was not a virtue in government, he said—all that complexity accomplished was not to make it impossible to tell where the faults lay when a system fell into disarray. The opposite, he said, was in fact true: "the more simple anything is, the less liable it is to be disordered and the easier repaired when disordered." Simplicity was embedded in nature itself, and if the British constitution had reserved the natural order of things, it had done so only to serve the unnatural purposes of the nobility and the monarchy, neither of which had a right to share in the power of the state. The nobility was scarcely even worth considering; it was nothing but the dead remains of an ancient "aristocractical tyranny" that had managed to survive under the cover of encrusting mythologies. The monarchical branch was a more serious matter, and Paine devoted pages of the pamphlet to attacking its claim to a share in the constitution.

As the inheritor of some thuggish ancestor's victory in battle, the "royal brute of Great Britain," as he called George III, was no less a ridiculous constitutional figure than his continental equivalents. For though by his constitutional position he was required to know the affairs of his realm thoroughly and to participate in them actively, by virtue of his exalted social position, entirely removed from everyday life—"distinguished like some new species"—he was forever barred from doing just that. In fact the modern kings of England did nothing at all, Paine wrote, but wage war and hand out gifts to their followers, all the rest of the world's work being handled by the Commons. Yet by virtue of the gifts the king had at his disposal, he corrupted the entire constitution, such as it was. The king's only competitor for power was the Commons, and this body he was able to buy off with the rewards of office and the intimidation of authority. The whole idea of balance in the British constitution was therefore a fraud, for "the *will* of the king is as much the *law* of the land in Britain as in France, with this difference, that instead of proceeding directly from his mouth, it is handed to the people under the formidable shape of an act of Parliament." Yet, was it not true that individuals were safer in England than in France? Yes, Paine said, they are, but not because of the supposed balance of the constitution: "the plain truth is that *it is wholly owing to the constitution of the people and not to the constitution of the government* that the crown is not as oppressive in England as in Turkey."

This was a very potent proposition, no matter how poorly the individual subarguments were presented, for it was well known that even in the best of times formal constitutional theory in England bore only a vague relation to the informal, ordinary operation of the government, and although penetrating minds like David Hume had attempted to reconceive the relationship so as to bring the two into somewhat closer accord, no one had tried to settle the matter by declaring that the whole notion of checks and balances in the English constitution was "farcical" and that two of the three components of the supposed balance had no rightful place in the constitutional forms at all. And no one—at least no one writing in America—had made so straightforward and unqualified a case for the virtues of republican government.

This was Paine's most important challenge to the received wisdom of the day, but it was only the first of a series. In passage after passage in *Common Sense* Paine laid bare one after another of the presuppositions of the day which had disposed the colonists, consciously or unconsciously, to resist independence, and by exposing these inner biases and holding them up to scorn he forced people to think the unthinkable, to ponder the supposedly self-evident, and thus to take the first step in bringing about a radical change.

So the question of independence has always been thought of in filial terms: the colonies had once been children, dependent for their lives on the parent state, but now they had matured, and the question was whether or not they were strong enough to survive and prosper alone in a world of warring states. This whole notion was wrong, Paine declared. On this, as on so many other points, Americans had been misled by "ancient prejudices and . . . superstition." England's supposedly protective nurturance of the colonies had only been a form of selfish economic aggrandizement; she would have nurtured Turkey from exactly the same motivations. The fact is, Paine declared, that the colonies had never needed England's protection; they had indeed suffered from it. They would have flourished far more if England had ignored them, for their prosperity had always been based on a commerce in the necessities of life, and that commerce would have flourished, and would continue to flourish, so long as "eating is the custom of Europe." What in fact England's maternal nurture had given America was a burdensome share of the quarrels of European states with whom America, independent of England, could have lived in harmony. War was endemic in Europe because of the stupidities of monarchical rivalries, and England's involvements had meant that America too was dragged into quarrels in which it had no stake whatever. It was a ridiculous situation even in military terms, for neutrality, Paine wrote, is "a safer convoy than a man of war." The whole concept of England's maternal role was rubbish, he wrote, and rubbish, moreover, that had tragically limited America's capacity to see the wider world as it was and to understand the important role America had in fact played in it and could play even more in the future.

> . . . the phrase *parent* or *mother country* hath been jesuitically adopted by the king and his parasites with a low papistical design of gaining an unfair bias on the credulous weakness of our minds. Europe, and not England, is the parent country of America. This new world hath been the asylum for the persecuted lovers of civil and religious liberty from *every part* of Europe . . . we claim brotherhood with every European Christian, and triumph in the generosity of the sentiment. . . . Not one third of the inhabitants even of this province [Pennsylvania] are of English descent. Wherefore I reprobate the phrase of parent or mother country applied to England only, as being false, selfish, narrow, and ungenerous.

The question, then, of whether America had developed sufficiently under England's maternal nurture to be able to live independent of the parent state was mistaken in its premise and needed no answer. What was needed was freedom from the confining imagery of parent and child which had crippled the colonists' ability to see themselves and the world as they truly were.

So too Paine attacked the fears of independence not defensively, by putting down the doubts that had been voiced, but aggressively, by reshaping the premises on which those doubts had rested. It had been said that if left to themselves the colonies would destroy themselves in civil strife. The opposite was true, Paine replied. The civil strife that America had known had flowed from the connection with England and was a necessary and inescapable part of the colonial relationship. Similarly, it had been pointed out that there was no common government in America, and doubts had been expressed that there ever could be one; so Paine sketched one, based on the existing Continental Congress, which he claimed was so fairly representative of the 13 colonies that anyone who stirred up trouble "would have joined Lucifer in his revolt." In his projected state, people would worship not some "hardened, sullen-tempered Pharaoh" like George III, but law itself and the national constitution, "for as in absolute governments the king is law, so in free countries the law *ought* to be KING." The question was not whether America could create a workable free constitution but how, in view of what had happened, it could afford not to.

So too it had been claimed that America was weak and could not survive in a war with a European power. Paine commented that only in America had nature created a perfect combination of limitless resources for naval construction and a vast coastal extension, with the result that America was not simply capable of self-defense at sea but was potentially the greatest naval power in the world—if it began to build its naval strength immediately, for in time the resources would diminish. So it was argued that America's population was too small to support an army: a grotesquely mistaken idea, Paine said. History proved that the larger the population the *smaller* and *weaker* the armies, for large populations bred prosperity and an excessive involvement in business affairs, both of which had destroyed the military power of nations in the past. The City of London, where England's commerce was centered, was the most cowardly community in the realm: "the rich are in general slaves to fear, and submit to courtly power with the trembling duplicity of a spaniel." In fact, he concluded, a nation's bravest deeds are always done in its youth. Not only was America now capable of sustaining a great military effort, but now was the *only* time it would *ever* be able to do so, for its commerce was sure to rise, its wealth to increase, and its anxiety for the safety of its property to become all-engrossing:

> The vast variety of interests, occasioned by an increase of trade and population, would create confusion. Colony would be against colony. Each being able, would scorn each other's assistance: and while the proud and foolish gloried in their little distinctions, the wise would lament that the union had not been formed before.

So on the major questions Paine performed a task more basic than arguing points in favor of independence (though he did that too); he shifted the premises of the questions and forced thoughtful readers to come at them from different angles of vision and hence to open for scrutiny what had previously been considered to be the firm premises of the controversy.

Written in arresting prose—at times wild and fierce prose, at times lyrical and inspirational, but never flat and merely argumentative, and often deeply moving—and directed as a polemic not so much at the conclusions that opponents of independence had reached but at their premises, at their unspoken presumptions, and at their sense of what was obvious and what was not, *Common Sense* is a unique pamphlet in the literature of the Revolution. But none of this reaches its most important inner quality. There is something in the pamphlet that goes beyond both of these quite distinguishing characteristics, and while it is less susceptible to proof than the attributes I have already discussed, it is perhaps the most important element of all. It relates to the social aspects of the Revolution.

Much ink has been spilled over the question of the degree to which the American Revolution was a social revolution, and it seems to me that certain points have now been well established. The American Revolution was not the result of intolerable social or economic conditions. The colonies were prosperous communities whose economic condition, recovering from the dislocations of the Seven Years' War, improved during the years when the controversy with England rose in intensity. Nor was the Revolution deliberately undertaken to recast the social order, to destroy the last remnants of the *ancien régime,* such as they were in America. And there were no "dysfunctions" building up that shaped a peculiarly revolutionary frame of mind in the colonies. The Anglo-American political community could have continued to function "dysfunctionally" for ages untold if certain problems had not arisen which were handled clumsily by an insensitive ministry supported by a political population frozen in glacial complacency, and if those problems had not stirred up the intense ideological sensibilities of the American people. Yet in an indirect way there was a social component in the Revolutionary movement, but it is subtle and latent, would in, at times quite obscurely, among other elements, and difficult to grasp in itself. It finds it most forceful expression in the dilated prose of Paine's *Common Sense.*

The dominant tone of *Common Sense* is that of rage. It was written by an enraged man—not someone who had reasoned doubts about the English constitution and the related establishment in America, but someone who hated them both and who wished to strike back at them in a savage response. The verbal surface of the pamphlet is heated, and it burned into the consciousness of contemporaries because below it was the flaming conviction, not simply that England was corrupt and that America should declare its independence, but that the whole of organized society and government was stupid and cruel and that it survived only because the atrocities it systematically imposed on humanity had been papered over with a veneer of mythology and superstition that numbed the mind and kept people from rising against the evils that oppressed them.

The aim of almost every other notable pamphlet of the Revolution—pamphlets written by substantial lawyers, ministers, merchants, and planters—was to probe difficult, urgent, and controversial questions and make appropriate recommendations. The aim of *Common Sense* was to tear the world apart—the world as it was known and as it was constituted. *Common Sense* has nothing of the close logic, scholarship, and rational tone of the best of the American pamphlets. Paine was an ignoramus, both in ideas and in the practice of politics, next to Adams, Wilson, Jefferson, or Madison. He could not discipline his thoughts; they were sucked off continuously from the sketchy outline he apparently had in mind when he began the pamphlet into the boiling vortex of his emotions. And he had none of the hard, quizzical, grainy quality of mind that led Madison to probe the deepest questions of republicanism not as an ideal contrast to monarchical corruption but as an operating, practical, everyday process of government capable of containing within it the explosive forces of society. Paine's writing was not meant to probe unknown realities of a future way of life, or to convince, or to explain; it was meant to overwhelm and destroy. In this respect, *Common Sense* bears comparison not with the writings of the other American pamphleteers but with those of Jonathan Swift. For Swift too had been a verbal killer in an age when pamphleteering was important to politics. But Swift's chief weapon had been a rapier as sharp as a razor and so pointed that if first entered its victim unfelt. Paine's writing has none of Swift's marvelously ironic subtlety, just as it has none of the American pamphleteers' learning and logic. Paine's language is violent, slashing, angry, indignant.

This inner voice of anger and indignation had been heard before in Georgian England, in quite special and peculiar forms. It is found in certain of the writings of the extreme leftwing libertarians; and it can be found too in the boiling denunciations of English corruption that flowed from the pens of such would-be prophets as Dr. John Brown, whose sulfuric *Estimate of the Manners and Principles of the Times* created such a sensation in 1757. But its most vivid expression is not verbal but graphic: the paintings and engravings of William Hogarth, whose awareness of the world had taken shape in the same squalor of London's and the provinces' demimonde in which Paine had lived and in which he had struggled so unsuccessfully. In Paine's pamphlet all of these strains and sets of attitudes combine: the extreme left-wing political views that had developed during the English Civil War period as revolutionary republicanism and radical democracy and that had survived, though only underground, through the Glorious Revolution and Walpole's complacent regime; the prohetic sectarian moralism that flowed from 17th-century Puritan roots and that had been kept alive not in the semiestablished nonconformism of Presbyterians and Independents but in the militancy of the radical Baptists and the uncompromising Quakers whom Paine had known so well; and finally, and most important, the indignation and rage of the semi-dispossessed, living at the margins of respectable society and hanging precariously over the abyss of debtors prison, threatened at every turn with an irrecoverable descent into the hell that Hogarth painted so brilliantly and so compulsively in his savage morality tales—those dramatic "progresses" that depict with fiendish, almost insane intensity the passages people in Paine's circumstances took from marginal prosperity, hope, and decency, through scenes of seduction, cruelty, passion, and greed, into madness, disease, and a squalor that became cosmic and apocalyptic in Hogarth's superb late engraving entitled *The Bathos*.

These were English strains and English attitudes—just as *Common Sense* was an English pamphlet written on an American theme—and they were closer in spirit to the viciousness of the Parisian demimonde depicted in the salacious reportage of Restif de La Bretonne than to the Boston of the Adamses and the Philadelphia of Franklin. Yet for all the differences—which help explain why so many American radicals found *Common Sense* so outrageous and unacceptable there are similarities too. In subdued form something of the same indignation and anger lurks around the edges and under the surface of the American Revolutionary movement. It is not the essential core of the Revolution, but it is an important part of it, and one of the most difficult aspects to depict. One catches a sense of it in John Adams' intense hatred of the Hutchinson-Oliver establishment in Boston, a hatred that any reader of Adams' diary can follow in innumerable blistering passages of that wonderful book, and that led to some of the main triggering events of the Revolution. It can be found too in the denunciations of English corruption that sprang so easily to the lips of the New England preachers, especially those most sunk in provincial remoteness and closest to the original fires of Puritanism which had once burned with equal intensity on both sides of the Atlantic. And it can be found in the resentment of otherwise secure and substantial Americans faced with the brutal arrogance and irrational authority of Crown officials appointed through the tortuous workings of a patronage system utterly remote from America and in no way reflective of the realities of American society.

Common Sense expresses all of this in a magnified form—a form that in its intensity no American could have devised. The pamphlet sparked into flame resentments that had smoldered within the American opposition to England for years, and brought into a single focus the lack of confidence in the whole European world that Americans had vaguely felt and the aspirations for a newer, freer, more open world, independent of England, which had not, until then, been freely expressed. *Common Sense* did not touch off the movement for a formal declaration of independence, and it did not create the Revolutionary leaders' determination to build a better world, more open to human aspirations, than had ever been known before. But it stimulated both; and it exposes in unnaturally vivid dilation the anger—born of resentment, frustration, hurt, and fear—that is an impelling force in every transforming revolution.

6

A Most Undisciplined, Profligate Crew

James Kirby Martin

The problems of maintaining discipline in an all voluntary military force is always difficult. The changing nature of the United States troops caused even greater traumas. Problems magnified due to the fact that the soldiers had true grievances against their level of support by their fellow Americans. The nature of the protests, and the differences between enlisted men's and officers' concerns are described by James Kirby Martin in the following article.

A sequence of events inconceivable to Americans raised on patriotic myths about the Revolution occurred in New Jersey during the spring of 1779. For months the officers of the Jersey brigade had been complaining loudly about everything from lack of decent food and clothing to pay arrears and late payments in rapidly depreciating currency. They had petitioned their assembly earlier, but nothing had happened. They petitioned again. Using "the most plain and unambiguous terms," they stressed that "unless a speedy and ample remedy be provided, the total dissolution of your troops is inevitable." The Jersey assembly forwarded the petition to the Continental Congress without comment. After all, the officers, although from New Jersey, were a part of the Continental military establishment.

The assembly's behavior only further angered the officers, and some of them decided to demonstrate their resolve. On May 6 the brigade received orders to join John Sullivan's expedition against the Six Nations. That same day, officers in the First Regiment sent forth yet another petition. They again admonished the assembly about pay and supply issues. While they stated that they would prepare the regiment for the upcoming campaign, they themselves would resign as a group unless the legislators addressed their demands. Complaints had now

"A Most Undisciplined, Profligate Crew" by James Kirby Martin is reprinted from *Arms and Independence,* by R. Hoffman and P. J. Albert, editors, (Charlottesville, Virginia: University of Virginia Press, 1984).

turned into something more than gentlemanly protest. Protest was on the verge of becoming nothing less than open defiance of civil authority.

When George Washington learned about the situation, he was appalled. "Nothing, which has happened in the course of the war, . . . has given me so much pain." It upset him that the officers seemingly had lost sight of the "principles" that governed the cause. What would happen, he asked rhetorically, "if their example should be followed and become general?" The result would be the "ruin" and "disgrace" of the rebel cause, all because these officers had "*reasoned wrong about the means of obtaining a good end.*"

So developed a little known but highly revealing confrontation. Washington told Congress that "the causes of discontent are too great and too general and the ties that bind the officers to the service too feeble" to force the issue. What he did promise was that he would not countenance any aid that came "in [such] a manner extorted. On the other hand, the officers had been asking the assembly for relief since January 1778, but to no avail. They, too, were not about to be moved.

The New Jersey legislature was the political institution with the ability to break the deadlock. Some of the legislators preferred disbanding the brigade. The majority argued that other officers and common soldiers might follow the First Regiment's lead and warned that the war effort could hardly succeed without a Continental military establishment. The moment was now ripe for compromise. The assemblymen agreed to provide the officers with whatever immediate relief could be mustered in return for the latter calling back their petitions. That way civil authorities would not be succumbing to intimidation by representatives of the military establishment, and the principle of subordination of military to civil authority would remain inviolate. The assembly thus provided an immediate payment of £200 to each officer and $40 to each soldier. Accepting the compromise settlement as better than nothing, the brigade moved out of its Jersey encampment on May 11 and marched toward Sullivan's bivouac at Easton, Pennsylvania. Seemingly, all now had returned to normal.

The confrontation between the New Jersey officers and the state assembly serves to illuminate some key points about protest and defiance in the Continental ranks during the years 1776–83. Most important here, it underscores the mounting anger felt by Washington's regulars as a result of their perceived (and no doubt very real) lack of material and psychological support from the society that had spawned the Continental army. It is common knowledge that Washington's regulars suffered from serious supply and pay shortages throughout the war. Increasingly, historians are coming to realize that officers and common soldiers alike received very little moral support from the general populace. As yet, however, scholars have not taken a systematic look at one product of this paradigm of neglect, specifically, protest and defiance. The purpose of this essay is to present preliminary findings that will facilitate that task.

A second purpose of this essay is to outline those basic patterns of protest and to indicate why protest and defiance did not result in serious internal upheaval between army and society.

During the past twenty years, historians have learned that there were at least two Continental armies. The army of 1775–76 might be characterized as a republican constabulary, consisting of citizens who had respectable amounts of property and who were defending hearth and home. They came out for what they believed would be a rather short contest in which their assumed virtue and moral commitment would easily carry the day over seasoned British regulars not necessarily wedded to anything of greater concern than filling their own pocketbooks as mercenaries.

The first army had a militialike appearance. There was not much discipline or rigorous training. These early soldiers had responded to appeals from leaders who warned about "our wives and children, with everything that is dear to us, [being] subjected to the merciless range of uncontrolled despotism." They were convinced that they were "engaged . . . in the cause of virtue, of liberty, of *God.*" Unfortunately, the crushing blows endured in the massive British offensive of 1776 against New York undercut such high-sounding phrases about self-sacrifice. The message at the end of 1775 had been "Persevere, ye guardians of liberty." They did not.

The second Continental establishment took form out of the remains of the first. Even before Washington executed his magnificent turnabout at Trenton and Princeton, he had called for a "respectable army," one built on long-term enlistments, thorough training, and high standards of discipline. The army's command, as well as many delegates in Congress, now wanted soldiers who could stand up against the enemy with more than notions of exalted virtue and moral superiority to upgird them. They called for able-bodied men who could and would endure for the long-term fight in a contest that all leaders now knew could not be sustained by feelings of moral superiority and righteousness alone.

To assist in overcoming manpower shortages, Congress and the states enhanced financial promises made to potential enlistees. Besides guarantees about decent food and clothing, recruiters handed out bounty moneys and promises of free land at war's end (normally only for long-term service). Despite these financial incentives, there was no great rush to the Continental banner. For the remainder of the war, the army's command, Congress, and the states struggled to maintain minimal numbers of Continental soldiers in the ranks.

In fact, all began to search diligently for new recruits. Instead of relying on propertied freeholders and tradesmen of the ideal citizen-soldier type, they broadened the definition of what constituted an "able-bodied and effective" recruit. For example, New Jersey in early 1777 started granting exemptions to all those who hired substitutes for long-term Continental service—and to master who would enroll indentured servants and slaves. The following year Maryland permitted the virtual impressment of vagrants for nine months of regular service. Massachusetts set another kind of precedent in 1777 by declaring blacks (both slave and free) eligible for the state draft. Shortly thereafter, Rhode Islanders set about the business of raising two black battalions.

The vast majority of Continentals who fought with Washington after 1776 were representative of the very poorest and most repressed persons in Revolutionary society. A number of recent studies have verified that a large proportion of the continentals in the second establishment represented ne'er-do-wells, drifters, unemployed laborers, captured British soldiers and Hessians, indentured servants, and slaves. Some of these new regulars were in such desperate economic straits that states had to pass laws prohibiting creditors from pulling them from the ranks and having them thrown in jail for petty debts. (Obviously, this was not a problem with the unfree.)

The most important point to be derived from this dramatic shift in the social composition of the Continental army is that few of these new common soldiers had enjoyed anything close to economic prosperity or full political (or legal) liberty before the war. As a group, they had something to gain from service. If they could survive the rigors of camp life, the killing diseases that so often ravaged the armies of their times, and the carnage of skirmishes and full-scale battles, they could look forward to a better life for themselves at the end of the war. Not only were they to have decent food and clothing and regular pay until the British had been irrevocably beaten, they had also been promised free land (and personal freedom in the cases of indentured servants, black slaves, and criminals). Recruiters thus conveyed a message of personal upward mobility through service. In exchange for personal sacrifice in the short run, there was the prospect of something far better in the long run, paralleling and epitomizing the collective rebel quest for a freer political life in the New World.

To debate whether these new Continentals were motivated to enlist because of crass materialism or benevolent patriotism is to sidetrack the issue. A combination of factors was no doubt at work in the mind of each recruit or conscript. Far more important, especially if we are to comprehend the ramifications of protest and defiance among soldiers and officers, we must understand that respectably established citizens after 1775 and 1776 preferred to let others perform the dirty work of regular, long-term service on their behalf, essentially on a contractual basis. Their legislators gave bounties and *promised* many other incentives. Increasingly, as the war lengthened, the civilian population and its leaders did a less effective job in keeping their part of the agreement. One significant outcome of this obvious civilian ingratitude was protest and defiance coming from Washington's beleaguered soldiers and officers.

That relations between Washington's post- 1776 army and Revolutionary society deteriorated dramatically hardly comes as a surprise to those historians who have investigated surviving records. Widespread anger among the rank and file became most demonstrable in 1779 and 1780, at the very nadir of the war effort. Gen. John Paterson, who spoke out in March 1780, summarized feelings among many officers when he said, "it really gives me great pain to think of our public affairs; where is the public spirit of the year 1775? Where are those flaming *patriots* who were ready to sacrifice their lives, their fortunes, their all, for the public?" These statements indicate that the army had come to believe that Revolutionary civilians had taken advantage of them—and had broken their part of the contract for military services.

There were real dangers hidden behind these words. With each passing month beginning in 1777, Washington's regulars, especially that small cadre that was signing on for the long-term fight, became more professional in military demeanor. Among other things, the immediate thoughts of individual soldiers, whether recruited, dragooned, or pressed into service, became attached to their respective primary units in the army, such as the particular companies or regiments in which they served. The phenomenon was nothing more than a developing comradeship in arms. Any threat or insult thus became an assault on the group. The bonding effect of unit cohesion suggests that collective protest and defiance would become more of a danger to a generally unsupportive society with each passing month, unless civilians who had made grand promises started to meet their contractual obligations more effectively.

Indeed, the most readily observable pattern in Continental army protest and defiance was that it took on more and more of a collective (and menacing) character through time. At the outset, especially beginning in 1776, most protest had an individual character. Frequently it was the raw recruit, quite often anxious for martial glory but quickly disillusioned with the realities of military service once in camp, who struck back against undesirable circumstances. Protest could come through such diverse expressions as swearing, excessive drinking, assaulting officers, deserting, or bounty jumping. One source of such behavior was the dehumanizing, even brutal nature of camp life. Another had to do with broken promises about pay, food, and clothing. A third was a dawning sense that too many civilians held the soldiery in disregard, if not utter contempt.

It must be remembered that middle- and upper-class civilians considered Washington's new regulars to be representative of the "vulgar herd" in a society that still clung to deferential values. The assumption was that the most fit in terms of wealth and community social standing were to lead while the least fit were to follow, even when that meant becoming little more than human cannon fodder. Perhaps James Warren of Massachusetts summarized the social perceptions of "respectable" citizens as well as any of the "better sort" when he described Washington's troops in 1776 as "the most undisciplined, profligate Crew that were ever collected" to fight a war.

While civilians often ridiculed the new regulars as riffraff, troublemakers, or mere hirelings (while conveniently ignoring the precept that military service was an assumed obligation of all citizens in a liberty-loving commonwealth), individual soldiers did not hold back in protesting their circumstances. In many cases, they had already acknowledged the personal reality of down-trodden status before entering the ranks. Acceptance of these circumstances and the conditions of camp life did not mean, however, that these new soldiers would be passive. Thus it may be an error to dismiss heavy swearing around civilians or repeated drunkenness in camp as nothing more than manifestations of "time-honored military vices," to borrow the words of one recent student of the war period.

Only over time did individual acts of protest take on a more collective character. That transition may be better comprehended by considering the phenomenon of desertion. While it is true that a great many soldiers did not think of desertion as a specific form of protest, they fled the ranks with greater frequency when food and clothing were in very short supply or nonexistent, as at Valley Forge. However, primary unit cohesion worked to militate against unusually high desertion levels. Sustained involvement with a company or regiment reduced the likelihood of desertion. Hence as soldiers came to know, trust, and depend upon one another, and as they gained confidence in comrades and felt personally vital to the long-term welfare of their primary group, they were much less likely to lodge a statement of individual protest through such individualized forms as desertion.

The first few days and weeks in the ranks were those in which these poor and desperate new regulars asked themselves whether vague promises of a better lot in life for everyone, including themselves, in a postwar republican polity was worth the sacrifice now being demanded. Many enlistees and conscripts concluded that it was not, and they fled. Since they had little proof that they could trust the civilian population and its leaders, they chose to express their defiance through desertion. Unit cohesion, in turn, helped sustain those who read the equation differently, and it eased the pain of enduring a long war in return for the remote prospect of greater personal freedom, opportunity, and prosperity.

Then there were those individuals who neither deserted nor became hardcore regulars. By and large, this group defied civil and military authority through the practice of bounty jumping. The procedure, which Washington once referred to as "a kind of business" involved enlisting, getting a bounty, and deserting, then repeating the same process with another recruiting agent in another location. Some of the most resourceful bounty jumpers got away with this maneuver seven, eight, or even nine times, if not more.

Bounty jumping was invariably the act of protesting individuals; looting and plundering (like desertion) combined individual with collective protest. Certainly there were numerous occasions when hungry soldiers looted by themselves. Just as often, groups of starving men "borrowed" goods from civilians. Even before the second establishment took form, looting had become a serious problem. One sergeant, for example, described how he and his comrades, searching desperately for food, "liberated" some geese belonging to a local farmer in 1776 and devoured them "Hearty in the Cause of Liberty of taking what Came to their Hand."

Above all else, two patterns stand out with respect to common soldier protest. First, as the war effort lengthened, defiance became more of a collective phenomenon. Second, such protest had a controlled quality. While there was unremitting resentment toward civilians who were invariably perceived as insensitive and unsupportive, protest rarely metamorphosed into wanton violence and mindless destruction. Soldiers looted and pillaged, but they rarely maimed, raped, or murdered civilians. Pvt. Joseph Plumb Martin attempted to explain why. Even though "the monster Hunger, . . . attended us," he wrote, and the new regulars "had borne as along as human nature could endure, and to bear longer we considered folly," he insisted that his comrades had become, in the end, "truly patriotic." They were persons who "loved their country, and they had already suffered everything short of death in its cause." The question by 1779 and 1780 was whether these hardened, cohesive veterans would be willing to endure even more privation.

In reflecting positively on the loyalty of his comrades, Martin was commenting on a near mutiny of the Connecticut Line in 1780. Indeed, the specter of collective defiance in the form of line mutinies had come close to reality with the near insubordination of the New Jersey officers in 1779. They had not demonstrated in the field, but they had made it clear that conditions in the army were all but intolerable—and that civil society, when desperate to maintain a regular force in arms, could be persuaded to concede on basic demands. Washington had used the phrase "extorted"; he had also pointed out that, "notwithstanding the expedient adopted for a saving appearances," this confrontation "cannot fail to operate as a bad precedent."

Among long-term veterans, anger was beginning to overwhelm discipline. There had been small-scale mutinies before, such as the rising of newly recruited Continentals at Halifax, North Carolina, in February 1776. In 1779 Rhode Island and Connecticut regiments threatened mutinies, but nothing came of these incidents. Then in 1780 another near uprising of the Connecticut Line occurred. Invariably, the issues had the same familiar ring: lack of adequate civilian support as demonstrated by rotten food, inadequate clothing, and worthless pay (when pay was available). On occasion, too, the heavy hand of company- and field-grade officers played its part. The near mutiny of the Connecticut Line in 1780 had been avoided by a fortuitous shipment of cattle and by promises from trusted officers of better treatment. In the end, the Connecticut Line calmed itself down, according to Martin, because the soldiery was "unwilling to desert the cause of our country, when in distress." Nevertheless, he explained that "we knew her cause involved our own, but what signified our perishing in the act of saving her, when that very act would inevitably destroy us, and she must finally perish with us."

By the end of 1780, there were some veterans who would have disputed Martin's reasoning. They had all but given up, let come what might for the glorious cause. On January 1, 1781, the Pennsylvania Line proved that point. Suffering through yet another harsh winter near Morristown, New Jersey, the Pennsylvanians mutinied. Some one thousand determined comrades in arms (about 15 percent of the manpower available to Washington) ostensibly wanted nothing more to do with fighting the war. On a prearranged signal, the Pennsylvanians paraded under arms, seized their artillery, and marched south toward Princeton, their ultimate target being Philadelphia. These veterans had had their fill of broken promises, of the unfulfilled contract. They maintained that they had signed on for three years, not for the duration. If they were to stay in the ranks, then they wanted the same benefits (additional bounty payments, more free land, and some pay in specie) that newer enlistees had obtained.

Formal military discipline collapsed as the officers trying to contain the mutineers were brushed aside. The soldiers killed one and wounded two other officers, yet their popular commander, Anthony Wayne, trailed along, attempting to appeal to their sense of patriotism. Speaking through a committee of sergeants, the soldiers assured Wayne and the other officers that they were still loyal to the cause, and they proved it by handing over two spies that Sir Henry Clinton had sent out from New York to monitor the situation. Moreover, the mutineers, despite their anger and bitterness, behaved themselves along their route and did not unnecessarily intimidate civilians who got in their way.

Later checking demonstrated that many of the mutineers were duration enlistees, yet that was a moot point. When the soldiers reached Trenton, representatives of Congress and the Pennsylvania government negotiated with them and agreed to discharge any veteran claiming three years in rank. Also, they offered back pay and new clothing along with immunity from prosecution for having defied their officers in leaving their posts. Once formally discharged, the bulk of the mutineers reenlisted for a new bounty. By late January 1781 the Pennsylvania Line was once more a functioning part of the Continental army.

These mutineers won because Washington was in desperate need of manpower and because they had resorted to collective defiance, not because their society wanted to address what had been grievances based on the contract for service. Unlike their officers, who had just won a major victory in driving for half-pay pensions, they were not in a position to lobby before Congress. Hence they employed one of the most threatening weapons in their arsenal, collective protest against civil authority, but only after less extreme measures had failed to satisfy their claims for financial justice. They were certainly not planning to overthrow any government or to foment an internal social revolution against better-placed members of their society. They had staked their hopes on a better life in the postwar period and had already risked their lives many times for the proposed republican polity. All told, the extreme nature of this mutiny demonstrated, paradoxically, both that Washington's long-term Continentals were the most loyal and dedicated republican citizens in the new nation, and that they were dangerously close to repudiating a dream that far too often had been a personal nightmare because of the realities of societal support and of service in the Continental army.

More worrisome in January 1781 than the matter of appropriate appreciation of the soldiers' actions was whether this mutiny, and its stillborn predecessors, would trigger further turbulence in the ranks. Also camped near Morristown during the winter of 1780–81 were veteran soldiers of the New Jersey Line. Their officers were aware that the Jersey regulars sympathized with the Pennsylvanians and had been in constant communication with them. Then, on January 20, 1781, the New Jersey Line, having witnessed the success of its comrades, also mutinied. The soldiers had each recently received $5 in specie as a token toward long overdue pay, but they were bothered by the better bounties and terms of enlistment offered newer recruits. Their leaders urged them on by shouting: "Let us go to Congress who have money and rum enough but won't give it to us!"

Within a few days, the Jersey Line had won acceptable concessions and was back under control. Washington, however, had decided that enough was enough. "Unless this dangerous spirit can be suppressed by force," he wrote to Congress, "there is an end to all subordination in the Army, and indeed to the Army itself." To back up his strong words, the commander ordered Gen. Robert Howe and about five hundred New England troops near West Point to march to the Jersey camp at Pompton to make sure that the mutineers were back in line and summarily to execute the most notorious leaders. Howe did as instructed. He reached Pompton on January 27, three days after grievances had been redressed. Deploying his men around the campsite just before dawn, Howe caught the Jersey soldiers off guard. He ordered them to fall in without arms, then singled out three ringleaders and ordered their summary execution, to be shot to death by nine of their comrades. A Jersey officer intervened in one case, but the other two were put to death by firing squad.

It was a brutal ending for men who had dreamed of a better future despite all of society's violations of the contract. Perhaps because of the calculated coldheartedness of Washington's orders, or perhaps because the war picture began to brighten in 1781, there were no major uprisings among Washington's regulars after the mutiny of the New Jersey Line. Then again, the soldiery may have been too worn down physically and mentally to continue their protest and defiance in the name of financial justice, humane treatment, and psychological support.

An important question that must be raised in conclusion has to do with political perceptions and fears: given real concerns in Revolutionary society that a regular army could obtain too much power, could corrupt the political system, and could threaten the civilian sector with some form of tyranny, such as a military dictatorship, why did officers and soldiers never unite effectively and put maximum pressure on the frail Revolutionary political structure by protesting in unison? They could have easily played on fears of a coup. But about the closest such union was the Jersey officers' defiance of 1779. Thus, while common soldiers got drunk, deserted, looted, or mutinied, officers pursued their own (and largely separate) avenues of protest. This is curious, especially since the officers too worried about the personal financial cost of service; they too came to resent civilian indifference, ineptitude, and greed; and they too were dismayed over society's inability to treat them with respect. They feared that their virtuous behavior and self-sacrifice would go unappreciated if not completely unrecognized and unrewarded. Having so much in common with their brethren in the rank and file, then, it is worth considering why the officers almost never aligned with them. For if they had, the alliance might have been powerful enough to have fomented something truly menacing to the vitals of Revolutionary society.

The officer corps developed its own forms of protest, and the pattern paralleled that of the common soldiers. The movement was from a dominant expression of individual defiance (resignations in 1776 and 1777) to collective protest (the drive for half-pay pensions which began in earnest during the fall of 1777 and climaxed with the Newburgh Conspiracy of 1782–83). Like common soldiers, the officers had collectivized their protest. In that sense, unit cohesion among comrades had come into play, but such cohesion never broke through the vertical hierarchy of military rank.

Part of the reason lay in the social gulf separating the two groups. As befit the deferential nature of their times as well as their concern for maintaining sharp distinctions in rank as a key to a disciplined fighting force, officers, many of whom were drawn from the "better sort" in society, expected nothing less than steady, if not blind obedience to their will from the rank and file. In their commitment to pursuing the goals of the Revolution, the officers were anything but social levelers. Indeed, many of them feared that the Revolution might get out of hand and lead to actual internal social upheaval, particularly if the "vulgar herd" gained too much influence and authority, whether in or out of the army. They hesitated to turn their troops against society because these same soldiers could always turn against them as well and, through brute force, undermine all assumed claims to economic and social preeminence in Revolutionary America.

Washington's veteran officers, even though they complained and protested with vehemence, also willingly accepted their responsibilities as the army's leadership cadre. The officers administered harsh discipline to deserters, looters, bounty jumpers, and mutineers whenever it seemed necessary—and sometimes when it was not. They generally supported Washington's desire to set the legal limit for lashes at 500 strokes, and many of them often sanctioned whippings of more than 100 lashes, despite the Articles of War of 1776. For example, officers took with relish to Washington's general orders at Morristown in 1780 to inflict 100 to 500 lashes on duly tried plunderers and to administer up to 500 lashes on the spot, even before formal hearings, when soldiers were caught breaking military laws.

Many officers thus used their authority with impunity and rarely expressed sympathy for the plight of common soldiers in the ranks. They were much more concerned with societal stability and the protection of property, as well as with military decorum and hierarchy, all of which precluded the officer corps from working in harmony with the soldiery when protesting common grievances against the civilian sector.

Washington's officers, in reality, were caught between the rank and file, for which they had little sympathy, and the larger society, which had little sympathy for them. They pursued their half-pay pension demands, resorting to such defiant acts as threatening to resign en masse during the late summer of 1780. Later they became even more extreme as some toyed with the idea of a full mutiny, if not the possibility of a coup, during the Newburgh crisis. In the end, they failed in their short-term quest for pensions or commutation, as the soldiery fell short in its drive for minimal levels of respectable support. Perhaps those quests would have been more successful had officers and regulars been able to unite.

7

Creation of the Constitution

Esmond Wright

The Constitution was the product of brilliant political compromise and perceived needs of a revolutionary society. Esmond Wright clearly examines the various factors in the creation of this enduring plan of government, and how the many compromises that made it possible were passed.

The Federal Convention of May 1787 had a somewhat accidental origin. The Mount Vernon Conference of 1785, called to discuss the navigation of the Potomac, had adjourned its meetings to a second conference at Annapolis in 1786, attended by representatives of five states. Two of these representatives, Alexander Hamilton and James Madison, persuaded their colleagues that bound up with commerce were many other questions; the time had come for the creation of a "Constitution of the Federal Government adequate to the exigencies of the Union." A conference was needed of a more fundamental sort. Technically the task of such a conference was to draft amendments to the Articles, but all interested had hopes of devising a completely new document. The body that met in the Philadelphia State House was thus not strictly legal, nor was it very punctual. Rhode Island was not represented. The New Hampshire delegation arrived too late. But in the end fifty-five delegates attended, and thirty-nine of them signed the final draft.

Even allowing for retrospective piety, Jefferson was justified in speaking of them as "an assembly of demi gods." Thirty-two of them were to become front-rank figures, with among them two Presidents, two Chief Justices, and six future state governors. A number of them had served in the Army; nearly three fourths in Congress and in state governments; thirty were college graduates; they were relatively young (average age forty-two) and traveled—a considerable number had lived abroad or at least in a state other than that they represented; the majority were men of means, and some of great wealth, and from the seaboard; over half were lawyers and all but four nationalists. The Philadelphia Convention, in a rare piece of elective good fortune, contained many of those who were the accepted leaders of their states, and many who sought a stronger regime. Their achievement is familiar enough, and well chronicled. Yet it was chronicled only with difficulty. The official secretary, William Jackson, was far from efficient. His notes were not published until 1818, and when they appeared, James Madison of Virginia proceeded, in accordance with them, to alter his own notes, which had been much more fully kept. These were themselves not issued until 1840, four years after his death, by which time fiction about the Founders bulked as large as fact. And Madison's notes, now transformed, were far from reliable. Not until Max Farrand's *The Records of the Federal Convention* appeared in 1911 was it possible to see clearly just what had occurred in Philadelphia.

Among the records not the least vivid are the comments of one delegate on another, and particularly those of William Pierce of Georgia on all the rest.

The Virginia delegation was punctual and very strong. Its most prominent figure was Washington, who had already expressed the view that the confederation was "shadow without substance," "a rope of sand." With a canniness more appropriate to a Yankee than a Virginian, he hesitated about going lest the Convention fail. He went, in the end, and since he was in the chair could keep his own counsel. The delegation included George Mason, who had drafted the Virginia Declaration of Rights, ambitious young Governor Edmund Randolph, and lawyer George Wythe, "remarked," said Pierce, "for his exemplary life." Its directing intelligence, however, was James Madison, "the best informed Man of any point in debate . . . a Gentleman of great modesty—with a remarkable sweet temper."

From New York came Yates, Lansing, and Hamilton—"of small stature and lean. His manners are tinctured with stiffness, and sometimes with a degree of vanity that is highly disagreeable." From Massachusetts came Rufus King and Elbridge Gerry—"A hesitating and laborious speaker . . . goes extensively into all subjects that he speaks on, without respect to elegance or flower of diction." From Connecticut came shoemaker-politician Roger Sherman—"extremely artful in accomplishing any particular object"—and Oliver Ellsworth.

There was William Paterson from New Jersey ("a Classic, a Lawyer and an Orator"), and from Delaware John Dickinson, the Sicyès-turned-conservative among constitution-makers, to whom Pierce was antipathetic—"With an affected air of Wisdom he labors to produce a trifle,—his language is irregular and incorrect,—his flourishes (for he sometimes attempts them), are like expiring flames, they just shew themselves and go out." Luther Martin and James McHenry were there from Maryland; orator John Rutledge, proud Pierce Butler and the cousins Pinckney from South Carolina; and, not least, the Pennsylvania delegation, in talent matching Virginia's. It included the "financier of the Revolution," Robert Morris—"he never once spoke on any point"—who ended in a debtors' prison; and the Scots-educated jurist James Wilson—"no great Orator"—who did likewise. There was Gouveneur Morris, who "charms, captivates and leads away the senses of all who hear him. . . . But with all these powers he is fickle and inconstant—never pursuing one train of thinking—nor ever regular." A crippled arm and lack of a leg did not prevent Morris from seeing himself as the *beau sabreur* of the American, as he was to seek to be of the French, Revolution; in his zest and wit a d'Artagnan, Percy Blakeney, and Münchausen rolled into one. Accompanied wherever he went by two French valets, he was rightly called "exotic" by Hamilton. And there was his only rival as Münchausen, Dr. Franklin, to Pierce "the greatest phylosopher of the present age . . . the very heavens obey him, and the Clouds yield up their lightning to be imprisoned in his rod. But what claim he was to the politician posterity must determine."

Posterity was to be kinder to all of them—Blount from North Carolina apart—even than was William Pierce. The majority of them certainly represented the Federalist viewpoint. Those most obviously identified with a radical point of view were absent. Jefferson and Paine were in Europe, as was John Adams. Patrick Henry, though elected, refused to attend. Samuel Adams was not elected. There was more than a decade of political difference between 1776 and 1787.

A group, then, of unusually talented men, able to debate in secret and keep secret what they said; a basic agreement on what needed to be done to strengthen the government; and small concern, in contrast with the men of 1774–76, with the "why" of political action. The lawyers, Madison and Hamilton preeminently, were now concerned with the mechanics of state-building. To Madison, as a student of constitutions, and to Hamilton, with his taste for executive energy in government, this was a congenial task. The American Constitution was, of course, in Professor Farrand's phrase, "a bundle of compromises"; in the fact that controversy could be resolved by compromise lay its political strength. Again and again recourse was had to statements that sought to reconcile opposing viewpoints, or to a deliberately evasive form of words; thus, the two-year term for congressmen was a compromise between one year and three. Yet in essence there was only one compromise. The Great, the Connecticut, or the Sherman Compromise—since it was largely his doing— was fundamental; it determined the shape of the central government: the decision on Federalism.

Arriving early, the Virginians had prepared, or had listened to Madison's elaboration of, a plan whereby there was to be a legislature of two houses, the lower to be elected by the people and the upper to be elected by the lower. Both houses—one directly, the other indirectly—would thus reflect population rather than statehood; this Virginia Plan was, therefore, acceptable to the larger states. There were also to be a single executive and judiciary, both chosen by the legislature. There was bitter feeling on this point, for the disparity of the states in size was striking. Delaware had 60,000 people; Rhode Island 68,000; Virginia, excluding Kentucky, had 750,000, of whom 300,000 were slaves; and Massachusetts, excluding Maine, 380,000, very few of whom were slaves.

New Jersey countered Virginia's Plan with its own, one much closer to the Articles, presented by William Paterson: a legislature of one house, elected by the states regardless of population, and with a plural executive elected by Congress.

The compromise reached after a month's debate gave the states equal representation in the Senate while maintaining the national principle—representation by population—in the House. This was an important result, not merely because it became the basis of the American government but also because it saved the Convention from dissolution. Yet it is possible to argue that, important though it was as a reconciliation of federal and national principles, it was designed to meet a dilemma—the rivalry of great and small states—that was largely illusory. Maryland, a small state, and Virginia, a large one, shared on the Chesapeake a common economy of tobacco plantations and slave labor. Similarly, Connecticut and Massachusetts were alike in their commercial interests. The rivalry of state against state has never been as important in American history as the clash of sections.

The other compromises were at the time less important but were subsequently to become matters of controversy, largely because they reflected economic and sectional tensions. The first concerned the method whereby slaves were to be counted for both representation and taxation. The Northern states wanted slaves excluded from representation, since they were neither citizens nor voters, but included for tax purposes, since they were property. This Yankee subtlety the South could not appreciate. The result was the adoption of the so-called three-fifths compromise whereby a slave was counted as three fifths of a person for both purposes. But this solution was not the result of a compromise in the Convention. It had first been proposed as an amendment to the Articles in 1783 and had been ratified by eleven states before the Convention met. There was here material for future trouble, as there was, also, in the South's fear that Congress might use the commerce power to interfere with the importation of slaves or to levy export duties on her staple products.

That these problems did not arouse the excitement then that they were to do in 1828 or 1861 was due precisely to the legalism and practicality of the delegates. Indeed, the coincidence of the publication of Madison's notes in 1840 with the rise of the slavery question gave an impression that it had been a major issue in 1787. It was not. As John Rutledge put it, "Religion and humanity have nothing to do with the question. Interest alone is the governing principle with nations. . . . If the Northern States consult their interests, they will not oppose the increase of slaves, which will increase the commodities of which they will become the carriers." They did consult their interests and a series of agreements followed: no interference with slave importation until 1808; Congress to be granted the power to regulate foreign and interstate commerce but, to protect the South, all treaties to require for ratification a two-thirds vote of the Senate; Congress to be forbidden to levy export taxes. But none of these matters was very controversial. The most bitter attack on slavery at the Convention came in fact from a Virginian.

On the final problem, the shape and the power of the federal government and its popular base, there was less controversy and less need for compromise, for the Fathers spoke and thought with remarkable unanimity. They declared that the Constitution was the supreme law of the land. The Tenth Amendment, declaring that the powers not expressly delegated to the federal government stayed with the states, has received so much attention that one is apt to minimize that to the Founders the central feature was the creation of this supreme power, as expressed in Article VI, Section 2. The new government should be strong, unlike the Congress of the Articles, and should be clearly sovereign. It was to be national rather than federal. It should act not on the states but on the people. It should legislate for all individuals in all the states. It should be empowered to levy taxes and to coin money; to declare war and make peace; to regulate commerce between the states; it should be able to admit new states on terms of absolute equality with the old; and, not least, have authority to make all laws "which shall be necessary and proper" in order to execute its powers (Art. I, Sec. 8). The states issue of paper money and legislation impairing the obligation of contracts were prohibited. The new government was something more than a "firm league of friendship" between the states. In many ways it was at once the apogee of the Revolution and its Thermidor.

Accompanying this firmness were expression of opinion critical of democracy that recalled the debate of 1744–76. Democracy was, said Gerry, the worst of all evils. The people, said Sherman, "should have as little to do as may be about the government." And Hamilton went further than most in devising plans for an executive sitting for life, indirectly elected and with an absolute veto on legislation; for a senate for life also chosen indirectly; and for a three-year assembly. Despite these views, there was nevertheless a political caution; Federalism as thus voiced did not go unopposed. Franklin, though he spoke little and was thought by some to be senile, noted that "some of the greatest rogues he was ever acquainted with were the richest rogues." Mason became overtly critical. And so again compromise was reached: a House to be elected directly, the suffrage being governed by the state suffrage; the Senate elected indirectly by the state legislatures; the President elected still more indirectly, by a cumbrously chosen electoral college. The last was the most academic device of all in an otherwise very practical document. It was hit upon in the closing stages of the Convention by a special committee set up to settle a number of questions on which agreement had not been reached. It survives now, emasculated by the growth of political parties, as a curious relic of eighteenth-century political mechanics. The judiciary was to be appointed by the President, subject to senatorial approval but quite beyond popular control.

Yet in all the rich variety of their processes of election, the three branches of government were nicely balanced one against the other. They were to be equal, coordinate, and, so far as could be contrived, harmoniously interlocked. None could for long be seized by either democrats or potential tyrants. The strong government so patiently manufactured was still as weak and as divided as could safely be managed. The very first Article, like the Articles being "amended," took pains to list at length the powers that the federal government did not have. Least of all did the Fathers attempt, either explicitly or implicitly, to define the government. The omissions again are significant; and wars and near wars were to be needed to resolve the question whether they were building a nation or a federation, and just what "We the people" implied.

The nation has been built, in 1787 as since, not by federal or judicial enactment, but by the common life lived and chosen by its members. This, too, the Fathers sensed; paper constitutions, they knew, had to be brought to life. They produced, therefore, a short document—four thousand words in length after four hundred hours of debate through a hot summer—whose ambiguities and vagueness it was left to the future to clarify. As Madison said, ambiguity was the price of unanimity. They wrought well, not primarily because they were constitutionalists—they were after all overturning one with some casualness—but because they had supreme faith in their own handiwork, in the new country, in the revolution they had led to victory, and in the future they glimpsed of their own resources and fortune. They were politicians of whom some were scholars, like Madison; some creative thinkers, like Hamilton; some, and not the least important, party managers and manipulators like John Beckley of Philadelphia; and like good politicians they had faith, most of all, in themselves. It was for the politicians that Franklin spoke on the last day of the Convention. There had been criticism of the omission of a Bill of Rights, defining the area in which an individual lived a life free from governmental constraint. There was criticism of the powers given to the central government. There was talk of summoning yet another and more representative Convention. Franklin met these challenges in a famous and characteristic plea:

> I confess that there are several parts of the Constitution which I do not at present approve, but I am not sure I shall never approve them. For having lived long, I have experienced many instances of being obliged by better information or fuller consideration, to change opinions even on important subjects, which I once thought right but found to be otherwise. It is therefore that, the older I grow, the more apt I am to doubt my own judgment and to pay more respect to the judgment of others. . . . Thus I consent, sir, to this Constitution because I expect no better, and because I am not sure that it is not the best . . . On the

> whole, sir, I cannot help expressing a wish that every member of the Convention who may still have objection to it, would with me, on this occasion, doubt a little of his own infallibility, and to make manifest our unanimity, put his name to this instrument.

The major problem, however, on which compromise would be all but impossible, was the ratification of the Constitution. This involved a public debate outside the State House in Philadelphia and the approval of popularly elected state conventions. As we have seen, the Convention was, although in name only, amending the Articles. To do so required the unanimity of all thirteen states. In the absence of Rhode Island this was clearly unattainable. The Convention therefore took the highhanded view that the new document would become effective when ratified by nine states in specially summoned conventions.

The debate in the country was far more bitter than that in Philadelphia, and much less amenable to control. It was now that the "democratic" issue was most clearly raised and in the course of the debate that faction and party first appeared. Yet the opposition to the new document did not challenge its main themes; the Republic and its balanced government were fully accepted. Nor could it provide a clear leadership: Randolph hesitated and became a Federalist; Hancock in Massachusetts was won over by the expectation of rewards; Samuel Adams was impressed by the support for the Constitution he found among the shipwrights of Boston at a carefully arranged meeting at the Green Dragon, and by the final compromise to include in it a Bill of Rights. The central theme of the Anti-Federalists was the fear of an encroachment on the rights of the states and on "liberty." This fear was stronger in the larger and more "democratic" states than in the smaller. The Delaware convention ratified promptly and unanimously; New Jersey a little less promptly but also unanimously. It took Pennsylvania a month of debate and some rather rough practices to come to accept it. It did so by 46 votes to 23; but the minority claimed that in the elections of delegates only 13,000 freemen voted out of 70,000 entitled to do so; here was still a sharp divergence between the interests of Federalist Philadelphia and Anti-Federalist western Pennsylvania. In Massachusetts the Federalist victory was narrow; 19 votes out of 355. Not until June 1788 did the ninth state, New Hampshire, give its approval. At that point it was not clear that the two key states, Virginia and New York, had agreed to support the Constitution. In fact, Virginia had approved it by a narrow majority of ten votes, 89 to 79, before learning of the action of New Hampshire. New York's majority was even smaller—30 to 27—when it came to its decision in July.

This result in New York was once again evidence of Alexander Hamilton's energy, political flair, and persuasive power. At Philadelphia he had been in a minority in his delegation; he attended only occasionally and his theories of centralization made him suspect. His colleagues, Yates and Lansing, who had finally withdrawn from the Convention on the grounds that it had exceeded its authority, were friends of George Clinton, governor of the state and a leading Anti-Federalist. Clinton expressed his fears in a series of articles under the pen name Cato. New York's politics were personal and peculiar, and they were largely the mercantile politics of the City of New York. It commanded the trade of the whole country, and in 1787—as in 1776 and earlier—it preferred neutrality or even independence to coming down on the wrong side. To these motives of fear, of cupidity, and of commercial risk and profit as well as of public spirit, Hamilton appealed in the series of eighty-five essays that became, along with Madison's and Jay's, the *Federalist Papers*. There was small hope, he believed, for the future of the country so long as the government was powerless and was scorned by foreign trades, so long as it was handicapped by varied and conflicting state laws and currencies, and so long as it was incapable of paying its own debts or compelling the states to meet theirs. He won the New York convention to his views by the sheer force of his arguments.

The victory in New York was narrow. The nation as a whole, had it been polled individually, might well have been opposed to the Constitution. Charles A. Beard's figures, suspect though they now are, showed that only one in four of the adult males voted for delegates to the state ratifying conventions; probably not more than one in six of them ratified it. Hamilton thought that four sevenths of the people of New York were against the Constitution. Neither Rhode Island, which submitted it to its town meetings, nor North Carolina adopted the Constitution until the new government was in operation, when they had little choice. The extent of the opposition led seven states to accompany acceptance by a series of amendments, and in the first session of the new Congress twelve of these were agreed upon and submitted to the states. Ten were ratified and became the Bill of Rights. This was a concession by the Federalist leaders to their critics.

The Constitution was drafted and enacted by a group of determined men, very much a minority among their fellows and acting without legality; so it had been with the Revolution, and so it is with most great developments in human history. Neither the document nor the methods whereby it was made the fundamental law were the work of a majority; nor were they tributes to democracy, still an ideal of the future. The Federalists were nationalists; in nothing were they so skillful as in the name they chose, for their intention was unitary rather than federal. They were led by two masterful politicians, Hamilton and Madison. If Hamilton appears, in print as in his subsequent legislation, an apologist for the economic royalists, it is impossible not to see in his handiwork, as in his consistent purpose, a policy that had about it, at this stage at least, courage, foresight, and idealism. If Madison supplied the scholarship and the draftsmanship, Hamilton provided the drive and combative power that were even more necessary.

Of all aspects of the Revolutionary period, the motives that led to the drafting of the Constitution have become the most controversial. As the United States grew and prospered, it was natural that the Constitution as its basic law should become revered, and that its Founding Fathers should be seen as men of remarkable wisdom. This view was natural but has not gone uncontested in American history. The crisis of 1814, the Civil War of 1861, and the controversies over the legality of the New Deal were indications that the compromises of 1787 had not been final solutions for all problems. There has been in fact no "consensus," to use today's fashionable word, on the central theme of the American story—whether it is a *plures* or a *unum,* a federation or a centralized nation. Yet once the Civil War was won and nationalism was triumphant, Hamilton emerged as the patron saint of the American entrepreneur, and the Constitution was seen once more as a work of great prescience. It came to win approval abroad in the eloquent encomiums of Gladstone and of Bryce. Nationalist historians such as Bancroft praised it still more lavishly. John Fiske, writing in 1888, accepted the Federalist arguments of a century before, to compose his study of *The Critical Period* and to portray the Founders as inspired and dedicated men who had brought order and security out of chaos.

It was natural that there should be a reaction from this patriotic view. And of it Charles Beard became the spokesman. Product of a Midwest that was then passing through the Populist and Progressive phase and of British politics in its Fabian heyday, Beard's *Economic Interpretation of the Constitution* (1913) was, as much as Fiske's book, a product of its time. To use a phrase used six years before by one of Beard's mentors, J. Allen Smith, in his *The Spirit of American*

Government, Beard saw the Constitution as "a reactionary document," or at least as one that was counterrevolutionary. It was the product, Smith had said, not of democracy but of men who feared democracy, a "scheme of government . . . planned and set up to perpetuate the ascendancy of the property-holding class leavened with democratic ideas." Or, as Burke had said of 1688, it was a revolution not made but prevented.

Beard argued, as did Merrill Jensen later, that the Federalists, the conservatives or nationalists of their day, had exaggerated the weakness of government in the decade before 1787, and that Fiske et al. had accepted their partisan indictments as statements of permanent truth. He pointed to the many fears the Federalists expressed of "democracy," their provisions guarding contracts and debts, their concern with a strong judiciary and the separation of powers as checks on majority rule. And he substantiated his argument by a massive analysis of the economic interests of the Founders, drawing heavily on the Treasury Department on lines that anticipated the cumulative-biography approach of Sir Lewis Namier toward British eighteenth-century politics. Not one of the Founders, he argued, was a farmer or an artisan; and five sixths of them stood to gain from the Constitution, since they owned securities or slaves or land for speculation. Far from being disinterested men, the patriots who came to the rescue of their country, Washington and Randolph, James Wilson and Rufus King, Oliver Ellsworth and Alexander Hamilton, Robert Morris and John Dickinson, had such a large stake in its property and society that the document they drafted was inevitably biased toward their own economic interest. Their motive was the safeguarding of property rights. The value of their bond holdings appreciated by some $40 million when supported by the credit of the new government. Moreover, they were not popularly chosen and were a small but highly influential group. By controlling elections and manipulating conventions they put through an undemocratic document to which the majority of Americans were in fact opposed.

If Beard's analysis represents a piece of historical debunking, an expression in fact of militant Jeffersonian populism, it was brilliantly done and has left a profound mark on all subsequent writing on this period. It stimulated many state-by-state analyses; it greatly influenced the attitude of all later writers, some of whom, like V. L. Parrington, made contributions to American historical writing quite as significant as Beard's; it reinforced the trend toward the "new" and social emphasis in historical writing, evidence in the work of Carl

Becker, J. Franklin Jameson, and Arthur Schlesinger, Sr.; and, not least, many of the Founding Fathers at last emerged as explicable and human figures. They were not only human, they were capitalists and speculators. Beard was seeking to portray what he called the true "inwardness" of the Constitution. This was needed, he thought, expressly because the document gives no outward recognition of any economic groups in society, mentions no special privileges, and, as he puts it, "betrays no feelings." "Its language is cold, formal and severe." It could hardly be said to be either cold or noncontroversial after he had written.

The extent of Beard's impact is best evidenced by the scale on which his work has recently been attacked. For it was equally bitterly censured in his own time, not only for its economic determinism, but for its demonstration that a work believed to be of near-divine ordering had been in fact the product of a very mundane self-interest. And much of the criticism then made was as weighty as that of our own day. E. S. Corwin in 1914 criticized Beard's exaggerations and faulted his figures; and he pointed out that one of the biggest property-owners of the Convention was Elbridge Gerry, who refused to sign the Constitution and opposed its adoption. R. L. Schuyler, in his excellently balanced study of the Constitution, while accepting that the two main groups were based principally on economic interests, stresses that there were many other motives; among the Federalists it was impossible to exclude patriotism, the wish to see the new country playing a dignified role in international affairs, the belief that only a strong and vigorous government would preserve the Union, experience in and respect for the Army rather than the Continental Congress; among critics, there was fear for liberty, strong state-right sentiments, and much sectional jealousy. The leaders, it was pointed out, were as much lawyers as businessmen and speculators; they were politicians also playing for power. It was Franklin who spoke of the Untied States as a "Nation of Politicians," and none could speak of the profession with more authority. Yet they were also, in some measure, idealists. They were affected, says Charles Warren, "by pride in country, unselfish devotion to the public welfare, desire for independence, inherited sentiments and convictions of right and justice."

Economic determinism is persistent and unfashionable in the United States. And in recent years a new political attack has been launched on Beard's interpretation of the Constitution. Robert E. Brown has examined Beard's thesis in great detail and denied not only its validity but the research on which it was based. The records that Beard used date, he has argued, from several years after the Constitutional Convention. The holdings of the Founding Fathers were in land far more than in securities. If their property was adversely affected by the situation before 1787, so were the property interest of the great majority of people, for the ownership of property was widespread. If they were selected by their state legislatures rather than popularly elected, such a method was the constitutional form under the Articles. If a man refrained from voting for delegates to the ratifying convention, this was more from indifference, and therefore presumably from contentment with the status quo, than from disfranchisement. And if both the Founders and the people acted as they did, it was as much for reasons of conviction as for reasons of economic self-interest.

The same author in his *Middle-Class Democracy and the Revolution in Massachusetts 1691–1780* argues that there was no large working class denied the vote in Massachusetts and that the farmers in the western part of the state had as full representation in the legislature as the merchants of the east. Massachusetts, he believes, was already a democratic state. And even more bravely he holds that the same arguments can be sustained for Virginia. Not all the latest research accords with this interpretation, and it would indeed be revolutionary if similar views were to obtain of the Southern states. But the emphasis is clear.

It has been driven home even more ruthlessly by Forrest McDonald in a name-by-name analysis of the Fathers and of the states, proving that they represented agriculture far more than commerce or securities, that many of them were lawyers with many varied clients to represent, and that their interest were far more diverse than Beards's categories revealed. Clearly, there was no sharp division between the interest of real and personal property.

At this point one is tempted to recall Louis Hartz's remark: "But after all is said and done Beard somehow stays alive, and the reason for this is that, as in the case of Marx, you merely demonstrate your subservience to a thinker when you spend your time attempting to disprove him." What the critics are asserting, however, is partly the superiority of recent research to Beard's avowedly "fragmentary" methods, and still more the viewpoint of the mid-twentieth century. The Fathers, they remind us, were patriots after all, men with principles as well as pocketbooks. If they represented property, they spoke for many constituents, for there were many property owners. They sought to create a strong government not only, and perhaps not mainly, to curb democracy but also to create a new nation and preserve the gains of the Revolution. For they had pride in both achievements. The fashion today is to revere the Constitution almost as did Bancroft and Fiske, and to see it as conserving a society that had already gone far toward becoming a property-owning democracy. The most remarkable characteristic of the political theory of the Revolution, says Clinton Rossiter, was "its deep-seated conservatism." "The American future was never to be contained in a theory," writes Daniel Boorstin. "The Revolution was . . . a prudential decision taken by men of principle rather than the affirmation of a theory." Beard, despite his errors, has, it seems, been legitimized; the Founders were not selfish; they were only wise. The United States has come a long way, not only since 1776, but since 1913.

In his *Politics and the Constitution in the History of the United States,* William W. Crosskey goes much further and contends that the members of the Convention were in fact seeking deliberately to create a unitary national government which would have the power of direct legislation in the fields of commerce and welfare. The power to regulate commerce in its eighteenth-century usage included, he contends, the whole range of economic activity. The Supreme Court was to be a national judicial body which would create a uniform system of national law. In his view, the Fathers were unsympathetic to state rights and sought salvation in the centralizing of power. Moreover, the "United States," he holds, existed as a body politic before the states acquired what was, wrongly, called "sovereignty." This is an interpretation that has not yet won general acceptance.

Does any consensus emerge, then, from these conflicting views?

In contrast with the states of contemporary Europe, American society of 1787 was small in numbers, reasonably unified, and strongly democratic. If there were classes, they were much closer to each other than in Europe, and careers in America had long been open to talents, before the phrase became a slogan of European revolution. There was, as the French troops saw, a much greater degree of economic equality than in Europe. There prevailed in America what Franklin called a "happy mediocrity." If there were conservatives and radicals, they were not yet completely aligned in 1787, and not recruited from the same groups in every state. As Oscar and Mary Handlin have shown, the Federalists and Anti-Federalists of 1788 in Massachusetts do not correspond either politically or socially with the conservatives and radicals of a decade before. Opinion was in flux. The revolutionary Patrick Henry ended up a conservative. Wealthy landowner George

Mason was a radical who feared aristocracy, yet he opposed the suggestion that the President be directly elected, on the unradical grounds that "it would be as unnatural to refer the choice of a proper character for chief magistrate to the people, as it would to refer a trial of colours to a blind man"; the people, he said, had not "the requisite capacity to judge." And the proposal that the chief executive should be directly elected was made by the conservative jurist James Wilson. Randolph, who helped to draft the constitution, refused to sign it, then campaigned for its ratification on his return to Virginia. Individuals can rarely be reduced to a pattern either of economic or of any other determinism. Nor indeed can states. The wealthy states like New York and Virginia hesitated longest over adoption. As Washington noted, the opposition to the Constitution came from "the men of large property in the South," not from "the genuine democratical people of the east."

Americans in 1787 were engaged in a great debate on government that had been in progress at least since the Albany Plan of 1754—if not since 1620 itself—of which the *Federalist Papers* and the Constitution were in a sense merely the latest expression. It is impossible to accept the gloomy view of V. L. Parrington when he says that little abstract political speculation accompanied the making and adoption of the Constitution, for the *Federalist Papers* are a classic statement of the issues that the Fathers faced, and of the ideals of the Whig style of politics. They enshrined a century and a half of experience, and much reflection on classical parallels.

But, in one sense, Beard and Parrington are right. The Fathers were lawyers and practical men, dealing with the problems of their day. They had discovered that, with Britain now removed and themselves facing acute local problems and frontier threats, there was need in America for a strong native executive power and for a President who was also Commander-in-Chief. A reading of Professor Farrand's compilation of the views of the framers of the Constitution reveals clearly that they saw their task as that of correcting the weakness of the Articles. But the appeals they were making were to interests much wider than Beard seems to have realized: to the public creditor, certainly, but also to the soldier, paid in bounty land that he could not obtain without a strong government, or in paper scrip that was almost worthless; to citizens as well as speculators in the West, who alike wanted protection from Indians and from foreign intrigues; to merchants trading abroad as well as manufacturers and workers seeking economic protection and security. "An assembly of the states, alone, by the terror of its power, and the fidelity of its engagements, can preserve a perpetual peace with the nations of Europe.'' The words were ''Harrington's'' in *The American Museum,* June 1787. There were very many who by 1787 had a stake in America's stability and its future, who in Hamilton's words were ''anxious for the respectability of the nation.'' America was, he said, a ''representative democracy''; Americans were, in other words, good Whigs.

Equally, the Founders accepted the other dominant aspect of their world, that it was one of sectional interests. Federalism was not an invention but the translation into political form of geographic and economic facts, an expression of social and political reality. Not the least of the miracles wrought in Philadelphia was the settlement of the rivalry between small states and large—an issue that never again became a major problem. Localism remained, of course, a major issue. There was, in 1787, still little sentiment of nationalism to buttress the work of the architects in Philadelphia. And there was great variation. The democratic upthrust that occurred in Pennsylvania was not in evidence in Delaware or Maryland.

The greatest achievement, however, less willed by the Fathers' reason than product of their century and a half of political experience, was popular sovereignty and the principle of representation. As Gordon Wood has brilliantly demonstrated, given the need for a strong central government, whether for economic, nationalist, or idealistic reasons, or perhaps because they were simply persuaded of its necessity, both their history and their revolution taught them that it would be acceptable only if its roots went deep in some formula of consent. The higher the pyramid the deeper must be the local roots and the broader the base. In this sense, what Federalists and Anti-Federalists accepted as common ground was far more striking than the controversy between them. There was no Thermidorean reaction; it was not needed. The men of property formed a party, although only slowly; they sought a stronger union than many, perhaps the majority, may have wanted. They sought it, however, as conservators of the Revolution. They came to Philadelphia from thirteen distinct states, but many had found in the Army a forcing-house of nationalism. The strongest statement heralding Federalism had come from Washington in June 1783, in his last circular as Commander-in-Chief. It was a plea for ''An indissoluble Union of the States under One Federal Head.'' As Washington had again made plain at Newburgh, the Federalists were as dedicated to republicanism as their opponents. They accepted, even accentuated, the separation of powers: they erected barriers against potential executive tyranny with quite as much zeal as the radicals. They did so, however, less from principle or from a reading of Montesquieu or Locke than from practice: it was but the form of colonial government, of governor versus assembly, to which they were accustomed.

Equally, the "democratic" movement was far removed from Jacobinism. There was no need for any cry of "The land to the peasants," for the land was abundant and was already fairly extensively owned; and few would have accepted the term *peasant*. The seizure of Loyalist land was the closest approximation in American history to the expropriation of the expropriators. They did not need to go further. They were not expropriators but inheritors. And their faith in what men could do with their own property made some of them also—not always successfully—entrepreneurs.

To some aspects of the modern state, of course, almost all Americans in 1787 were quite blind. Some of their modern admirers approve of their "principles." But what were they? They were far from explicit in 1787. It is easier to define them negatively; for they knew more clearly what they were against than what they were for. They were hostile to tyranny, in all its forms—of one man or of many, hostile to the concentration of authority in any one man or institution, hostile to any unbalanced government. The essence of their fears was seen in the bills of rights, incorporated in the state constitutions and by 1790 in the federal document. The liberties for which they had fought were listed there, and the written documents gave them precise form, protection, and, over the years, increasingly sanctity. But despite all its revolutionary advance, there is much that is missing, much that the Constitution did not say. It was not clear where lay the power to regulate industry, as Crosskey shows. Nothing was said on the acquisition of new territories, as Jefferson was to find. Political parties were not mentioned, apparently not even foreseen, despite the threat of faction. Least of all was anything said or glimpsed of the rights of a member state to secede from the new Union.

This is, however, but to say that the Constitution was drafted by politicians seeking to settle, if not to solve, the problems of their own age. "Experience must be our only guide," said John Dickinson. "Reason may mislead us." The work of lawyers, and of men influenced by their own British traditions, the strength of the document was its realism. There was little evidence in it of humanitarian sentiments and no nonsense about a world crusade. "Symbols of a world revolution," says Louis Hartz, "the Americans were not in truth world revolutionaries.'' Those with foreign experience, like Paine and Franklin, and those without it alike accepted the wisdom of isolation. Nearly all the constitutions, state and federal, contained some statement about equality, but none of them suggested crusading for it abroad—or at home. There was little concern with the rights of man, and when Rufus King did use the phrase, it was in a less exciting fashion than the French. There was no stress on tolerance; indeed, many ''democrats'' were markedly intolerant men; in Pennsylvania and in the back country clearly so. None of them proclaimed the abolition of slavery or the granting of equal rights, in law or suffrage, to women as well as men. Some Protestants sought to limit the rights on non-Protestants. In Pennsylvania the radicals tried to curb the free expression of opinion. And by equality what was meant was equality before the law, not social justice or economic rights.

Extensive property-owning, then, meant a wide franchise; this in itself did not produce democracy. *Democracy* as a term was little used and in general greatly feared. It was a term completely absent from the Declaration of Independence and from the state and federal constitutions. Even Jefferson avoided it. Nor was a majority vote seen as a safeguard against tyranny. In the form of unicameral legislatures it was particularly feared. Under the Constitution there was to be, locally and at the center, a series of checks on arbitrary power, whether the power came from above or below. Elections were to be as indirect as possible, to allow time for reflection and for passions to cool. Few of the constitution-makers had any faith in simple majority rule.

The great debate of 1787 was successful in its outcome expressly because both groups held so many postulates and so many fears in common. There were men of property, as Beard argued, in the Federal convention. There were many more outside it, as Brown argues. The Revolution over, all now had much to conserve.

8

Tecumseh, the Shawnee Prophet, and American History

R. David Edmunds

The Anglophobia besetting the United States in the last few years before the War of 1812 was heightened by the famous Tecumseh Rebellion in 1811. R. David Edmunds sheds new light on the other half of the rebellion's leadership, the mysterious Prophet. Clearly the rebels were led by two gifted men.

High upon a graphite pedestal overlooking "the Yard" at the United States Naval Academy at Annapolis stands a bronze statue of an Indian warrior. Midshipmen passing in and out of Bancroft Hall traditionally salute the statue before taking examinations in the hope that the renowned warrior's medicine will assist them during the tests. Most midshipmen, if asked whom the statue represents will reply that it is a replica of Tecumseh, the famous war chief of the Shawnees. In reality, however, the statue was never intended to be Tecumseh. It represents Tamenend, a chief among the Delawares.

The midshipmen's incorrect identification of the bronze figure is not surprising, for Americans have long regarded Tecumseh as one of their foremost Indian heroes. He is one of the few militant Indian leaders who was almost universally praised by his white contemporaries. During the War of 1812 both British and American officers spoke highly of the Shawnee, and since his death his image has grown accordingly. Eulogized by historians, Tecumseh has achieved an almost legendary status. His biographers have presented an Indian of superhuman qualities; and Alvin M. Josephy, in his volume *The Patriot Chiefs*, entitles his chapter on the Shawnee as "Tecumseh: The Greatest Indian."

Reprinted from "Tecumseh, the Shawnee Prophet, and American History," by R. David Edmunds, *Western History Quarterly*, 14 (1983), pp. 261–76. By permission of R. David Edmunds.

If the white observers and historians have been laudatory in their description of Tecumseh, they have been universal in their condemnation of his brother Tenskwatawa, the Shawnee Prophet. Both British and American leaders denounced the holy man as a "pretender" and a "coward," and historians have enlarged upon such qualities to present an image of a charlatan who manipulated the tribesmen for his own purposes. While Tecumseh's political and military movement is pictured as logical and praiseworthy, the Prophet represents the darker side of Indian life. A religious fanatic, Tenskwatawa is presented as riding his brother's coattails to a position of minor prominence.

Unquestionably, the Shawnee brothers emerged to positions of leadership during a period of great stress for Native Americans. Although the Treaty of Greenville supposedly had drawn a line between Indian and American lands in Ohio, the treaty was ignored. Frontier settlement continued to advance north from the Ohio valley, threatening the remaining Indian land base in the region. Meanwhile, white hunters repeatedly trespassed onto Indian lands to hunt game needed by the tribesmen, and by the first decade of the nineteenth century game was becoming scarce. The fur trade declined in a similar manner, and after 1800 many warriors were hard pressed to provide for their families. Not surprisingly, the Indians retaliated by stealing settlers' livestock, and the resulting clashes produced casualties on both sides. Obviously, both Indians and whites suffered, but losses were much larger among the natives. Governor William Henry Harrison of Indiana admitted that "a great many of the Inhabitants of the Fronteers (*sic*) consider the murdering of the Indians in the highest degree meritorious," while Governor Arthur St. Clair of the Northwest Territory reported that "the number of those unhappy people (the Indians) who have been killed since the peace at Greenville . . . is great enough to give serious alarm for the consequences."

Much of the Indian-white conflict was triggered by alcohol. Frustrated over their declining political and economic status, beleaguered tribesmen drowned their sorrows in frontier whiskey. Although illegal, alcohol was in plentiful supply, and brawls resulting from the Bacchanalia spread social chaos throughout the Indian villages. Once-proud warrior quarreled among themselves or abused their kinsmen, while others retreated into drunken stupors. Some Shawnees, weakened by their dissipation, fell victims to influenza, smallpox, and other diseases. Others sat passively in their lodges, bewildered by the changes swirling around them. Meanwhile, the clans—traditional kinship systems designed to regulate and provide cohesiveness among the separate Shawnee villages—were unable to cope with the multitude of problems besetting the tribe.

Overwhelmed by the chaos within their villages, the Shawnees pondered the causes. Although many tribesmen realized that the majority of their problems emanated from outside sources such as loss of lands, economic deterioration, injustice, and alcohol, others suspected darker elements and probed inward, examining the fabric of tribal society. Predictably, traditional Shawnees concluded that much of their trouble resulted from witchcraft, for the fear of witches and their evil power permeated Shawnee culture, and neighboring tribes believed the Shawnees to have a particular affinity for sorcery and the supernatural.

The basis for such fear lay deep in tribal tradition. The Shawnees believed that in the dim past, when they first crossed the Great Water in search of their homeland, they had been opposed by a huge water serpent who represented the evil powers in the universe. Although their warriors had killed the serpent, witches had saved part of its body, which still held a potent and malevolent power. Contained in medicine bundles, this evil had been passed down through the ages and was used by witches to spread disorder throughout the tribe.

The balance between order and chaos formed a focal point for Shawnee cosmology. The Shawnees believed they were a people chosen by the great power in the universe—"the Master of Life"—to occupy the center of the earth and bring harmony to the world. For their assistance, the Master of Life provided the Shawnees with a sacred bundle possessing powerful medicine that could be used for good. He also gave the tribe a series of laws regulating their personal conduct. If the Shawnees cherished the bundle, and used its medicine properly, and if they followed the sacred laws, they would prosper and their world would be orderly. But if witches gained the ascendancy, or if the Shawnees relinquished the ways of their fathers, their lives would be full of turmoil. In the years following the Treaty of Greenville, many traditional Shawnees believed that the witches had gained the upper hand.

Not surprisingly, many associated the American with these forces of evil. The Shawnees believed that the sea was the home of the Great Serpent—the embodiment of disorder. Their forefathers had always warned that pale-skinned invaders might emerge from the water to disrupt the harmony of the Shawnee homeland. Since the Americans had first appeared on the eastern seashore, many tribesmen were certain the invaders were the children of the serpent, intent upon the

Indians' downfall. In 1803 Shawnees at Fort Wayne informed Indian agents that their ancestors had stood on the eastern seashore, watching as a strange ship came over the horizon.

> At first they took it to be a great bird, but they soon found it to be a monstrous canoe filled with the very people who had got the knowledge which belonged to the Shawnees. After these white people had landed, they were not content with having knowledge which belonged to the Shawnees, but they usurped their lands also—But these things will soon end. The Master of Life is about to restore to the Shawnees their knowledge and their rights and he will trample the Long Knives under his feet.

And even Black Hoof, a government chief committed to the American cause, admitted, "The white people has spoiled us. They have been our ruin."

Yet the same chaos that threatened the tribesmen also produced a man who promised them deliverance. Known as Lalawethika ("The Noisemaker" or "Loud Mouth"), the man had been born in 1775 on the Mad River in Eastern Ohio. Prior to Lalawethika's birth, his father had been killed by the Americans and his mother had abandoned him when he was only four years old. Raised by a sister, his childhood had been overshadowed by two older brothers, Chiksika and Tecumseh. Lalawethika never excelled as a hunter or a warrior, and during his adolescence he became an alcoholic. Following the Treaty of Greenville he lived in a small village headed by Tecumseh, where he unsuccessfully aspired to the status of shaman. But in April 1805 this alcoholic ne'er-do-well experienced a vision that changed his life and propelled him to the forefront of Indian leadership.

While lighting his pipe from the fire in his lodge, Lalawethika collapsed, falling into a coma so deep his wife and neighbors believed him to be dead. As his wife began her mourning song he astonished his family by first stirring, then regaining consciousness. Visibly shaken, he informed the gathered onlookers that indeed he had died and had visited heaven, where the Master of Life had shown him both an Indian paradise and a hell where eternal fires lay in wait for sinful tribesmen. Alcoholics like himself suffered the most, for molten lead was poured down their throats until flames shot out their nostrils. Amidst much trembling, Lalawethika vowed to renounce his former ways and never again drink the white man's whiskey. No longer would he be known as Lalawethika. Henceforward he would be called Tenskwatawa—"The Open Door"—a name symbolizing his new role as a holy man destined to lead his people down the narrow road to paradise.

In the following months Tenskwatawa experienced other visions and enlarged upon his doctrine of Indian deliverance. Much of his teachings addressed the decline of traditional moral values among the Shawnees and other tribes. Tenskwatawa claimed he "was particularly appointed to that office by the Great Spirit" and that his "sole object was to reclaim the Indians from bad habits and to cause them to live in peace with all mankind." While he continued to denounce whiskey as "poison and accursed," he also condemned the violence that permeated tribal society. He urged warriors to treat each other as brothers, to stop their quarreling, and to refrain from striking their wives and children. Husbands and wives should remain faithful to each other, and marriages should be monogamous. Shawnee warriors currently married to more than one "might keep them," but such marriages displeased the Master of Life.

Convinced that his forefathers had enjoyed a happier existence, the new Shawnee Prophet attempted to revitalize some facets of traditional tribal culture. Indeed, much of Tenskwatawa's teaching was nativistic in both tone and content. He asked his followers to return to the communal life of the past and to renounce all desire to accumulate property as individuals. Those tribesmen who hoarded their possessions were doomed, but others who shared with their kinsmen, "when they die are happy; and when they arrive in the land of the dead, will find their wigwams furnished with everything they had on earth." He also instructed them to use only the food, implements, and dress of their fathers. Pork, beef, and mutton were unclean, and the tribesmen were instructed to eat only the game they killed in the forests. Neither were the Indians to eat bread, but only corn, beans, and other crops raised by their ancestors. Stone or wood implements should replace metal tools, and although guns could be used for self-defense, the warriors were to hunt with bows and arrows. With the exception of weapons, all items of American manufacture were to be discarded. In a similar manner, the Indians were to dress in skin or leather clothing and were ordered to shave their heads, leaving only the scalp lock of their forefathers. False gods should be forgotten, but the tribesmen should pray to the Master of Life, asking that he return fish to the streams and game to the forest. To assist his disciples, Tenskwatawa provided them with sacred "prayer sticks." The sticks were inscribed with pictographs illustrating certain spirits who would help the tribesmen in their supplications. If the Shawnees were faithful and their hearts pure, the Master of Life would restore order, the earth would be fruitful, and they would prosper.

While Tenskwatawa attempted to revitalize some part of Shawnee culture, he condemned others. He warned that many of the traditional dances and ceremonies no longer had any meaning and offered new ones in their place. He also instructed his followers to throw away their personal medicine bundles, which he claimed had been powerful in the past, but no longer possessed the potency needed to protect the Shawnees from the new dangers that threatened them. Tenskwatawa alone spoke for the Master of Life, and only those tribesmen who subscribed to the new faith would ever know happiness. But his disciples would be rewarded above all men, for they alone would eventually "find your children or your friends that have long been dead restored to life."

If the Prophet condemned some of the old religious practices, he was particularly suspicious of those tribesmen who held religious beliefs differing from his own. At best those shamans or medicine men who opposed his doctrine were misguided fools. At worst they were witches, in league with the Great Serpent to spread disorder among the tribes. And the Prophet did not limit his accusations to religious leaders. For the holy man, religion and politics were the same. He had been chosen by the Master of Life to end the chaos in the Shawnee world. All those who opposed him also opposed the Master of Life. Therefore, he was particularly suspicious of tribesmen who were becoming acculturated or who had been converted to Christianity. Such men also were suspect of witchcraft. Unless they repented, they too should be destroyed.

Tenskwatawa's distrust of those Indians who adhered to American values reflected his general condemnation of the Long Knives. He informed his followers that the Master of Life had made the British, French, and Spanish, but the Americans were the children of the Great Serpent. In his visions Tenskwatawa had seen the Americans take the form of a great crab that crawled from the sea, and the Master of Life had told him, "They grew from the scum of the great water when it was troubled by the Evil Spirit. And the froth was driven into the woods by a strong east wind. They are numerous, but I hate them. They are unjust. They have taken away your lands, which were not made for them." Only if the Indians rejected the Americans would order ever be restored to the Shawnee world. The Prophet instructed his people to cease all contact with the Long Knives. If they met an American in the forest, they might speak to him from a distance, but they should avoid touching him or shaking his hand. They were also forbidden to trade Indian foods to their white neighbors, for these provisions were the special gifts of the Master of Life, to be used by his children, not the spawn of the Serpent. Tenskwatawa instructed his disciples to cut their ties with frontier merchants, and "because the (the Americans) have cheated you," the Indians were to pay "no more than half their credits." Moreover, Indian women married to American men should return to their tribes, and the children of such unions were to be left with their fathers.

The new faith soon spread to other tribes, who like the Shawnee were unable to adjust to the great changes sweeping around them. By the autumn of 1805 warriors from the Delaware and Wyandots were traveling to Greenville, Ohio, where the Prophet had established a new village. There Tenskwatawa converted the visitors, then sent them back to proselytize their home villages. The Delawares proved particularly susceptible to the new religion, and during the late winter of 1806 they accused about one dozen of their tribesmen of witchcraft. In March 1806 the Prophet journeyed to the Delaware villages, where he examined the captives, exonerating some, but condemning others. The Delawares eventually burned four of their kinsmen before the witch-hunt terminated. Predictably, all those burned were converted Christians whose acculturation made them more suspicious.

The witch-hunt among the Delawares frightened Moravian missionaries associated with the tribe and brought a storm of protest from government officials. During the spring of 1806 Harrison wrote to the Delawares denouncing the Prophet and asking, "If he is really a prophet, ask him to cause the sun to stand still—the moon to alter its course—the rivers to cease to flow—or the dead to rise from their graves. If he does these things, you may believe that he has been sent from God."

Ironically, Harrison's challenge played into Tenskwatawa's hands. In the spring of 1806 several astronomers had traveled through Indiana and Illinois locating observation stations to study an eclipse of the sun scheduled to occur on June 16. Although Harrison either ignored or forgot about the event, the Prophet remembered. Among the Shawnees such an eclipse was known as a "Black Sun," an event surrounded with dread and portending future warfare. Accepting Harrison's challenge, in early June Tenskwatawa surprised even his closest followers by promising to darken the sun. On June 16, while his disciples and skeptics both assembled in his village, the Prophet remained secluded in his lodge throughout most of the morning, but as the noon sun faded into an eerie twilight he stepped forth exclaiming, "Did I not speak the truth? See the sun is dark!" He then assured his audience that he would restore the sun's former radiance, and as the eclipse ended even those tribesmen who still remembered him as Lalawethika, the drunken loudmouth, now were convinced of his medicine.

Following the eclipse, the Prophet's influence spread rapidly. During the summer of 1806 Kickapoos from the Wabash visited his villages, were converted, and by the following summer their towns in eastern and central Illinois had become seedbeds for the new religion. Early in 1807 large numbers of Potawatomis and Ottawas from the Lake Michigan region traveled to Greenville and then carried the new faith back to the western Great Lakes. One of the Ottawas, Le Magouis, or "the Trout," became a special envoy for Tenskwatawa and journeyed into upper Michigan where he taught the Prophet's doctrines to the Chippewas. The results were phenomenal. At Chequamegon Bay hundreds of Chippewas gathered opposite Madeline Island to "dance the dances and sing the songs" of the new deliverance. Subscribing to the Prophet's instructions, they threw their medicine bags into Lake Superior and made plans to visit the holy man in Ohio. In the following months so many tribesmen were enroute to the Prophet's village that white traders found most of the Chippewa towns along the southern shores of Lake Michigan deserted. The Menonimees, Sacs, and Winnebagos also were swept up in the religious frenzy, and during the summer of 1807 they trekked to Greenville in large numbers.

Unable to comprehend the religious nature of the movement, American officials at first believed that Tenskwatawa was only a figurehead controlled by more traditional chiefs among the Shawnees. During 1807 several groups of American agents arrived at the Prophet's village to investigate the character of the new movement. After meeting with Tenskwatawa, most of the envoys agreed that the holy man was the dominant Indian leader in the village. Moreover, the Prophet was able to persuade them that his religion posed no threat to the government. But Harrison and other officials refused to admit that the movement was an indigenous uprising, resulting from desperate conditions among the Indians. Instead, they charged that the prophet was actually a British agent, intent upon raising the tribes against the United States.

Yet the British were as mystified about Tenskwatawa as were the Americans. During the summer of 1807 British agents were active among the Indians of Michigan and Wisconsin, but they remained suspicious of the Prophet. Although they invited the Shawnee to visit them in Canada, he refused. In response, William Claus, Deputy Superintendent of Indian Affairs for Upper Canada, warned other Indians to avoid him, speculating that the holy man might be working for the French.

The large numbers of Indians who journeyed to Tenskwatawa's village enhanced his prestige, but they also alarmed white settlers in Ohio. Moreover, the influx of tribesmen exhausted Tenskwatawa's food supply, and he was hard pressed to feed his followers. In November 1807 the Potawatomis suggested that he withdraw from Greenville and establish a new village on the Tippecanoe River in Indiana. The new site would be much less exposed to white influence and was located in a region where game was more plentiful. Therefore, in April 1808 the Prophet and his followers abandoned Ohio and moved to Prophetstown.

The withdrawal to Indiana temporarily removed Tenskwatawa from white scrutiny, but his logistical problems continued. Since Prophetstown was located further west, it was more accessible to potential converts, and during 1808 and 1809 Indians flocked to the new village in numbers surpassing those who had visited him at Greenville. Although the villagers planted fields of corn and scoured the surrounding countryside for game, they could not feed the multitude. To obtain additional food, the Prophet brazenly turned to the Americans. In June 1808 he sent a delegation of warriors to Harrison assuring the governor of his peaceful intentions and asking for provisions. The Indians were so persuasive that Harrison sent food to Prophetstown and invited Tenskwatawa to meet with him in Vincennes. Two months later, in August 1808, the Prophet and his retinue arrived at Vincennes and spent two weeks conferring with Harrison. The governor was astonished at "the considerable talent of art and address" with which Tenskwatawa mesmerized his followers. Moreover, the holy man's pleas of friendship toward the United States were so convincing that Harrison provided him with additional stores of food and gunpowder and reported to his superiors that his earlier assessments of the Shawnee were in error, for "the influence which the Prophet has acquired will prove advantageous rather than otherwise to the United States."

Tenskwatawa was also able to hoodwink John Johnston, the Indian agent at Fort Wayne. In May 1809 he met with Johnston, and although the agent previously had expressed misgivings about the

Prophet's motives, Tenskwatawa assured him of his friendship. The Shawnee spent four days, denying "in the most solemn manner, having any views inimical to (the Americans') peace and welfare." Indeed, when the conference ended, Johnston, like Harrison, exonerated the holy man from all charges and reported, "I have taken much pains and have not been able to find that there existed any grounds for the alarm."

But the facade of friendship was too fragile to last. Although the Prophet feigned goodwill toward the government, he could not control his followers, many of whom were less devious in their relations with the United States. As Indian depredations spread along the Wabash Valley, Harrison became convinced of the Shawnee's duplicity. During the summer of 1809 Tenskwatawa again visited with the governor in Vincennes, but this time Harrison was less hospitable. Tenskwatawa's protestations of friendship had little impact, and Harrison informed the War Department that his suspicions of the Prophet "have been strengthened rather than diminished in every interview I have had with him since his arrival." Moreover, by the summer of 1809 Harrison was making preparations for the Treaty of Fort Wayne, and he assumed that such a transaction would terminate any pretense of amity between the government and the holy man.

Harrison was correct. The treaty of Fort Wayne, signed in September 1809, ceded over three million acres in Indiana and Illinois to the United States. Negotiated by friendly chiefs among the Miamis, Delawares, and Potawatomis, the treaty was adamantly opposed by Tenskwatawa. In response, he redoubled his efforts to win new disciples. Messengers were sent to the Ottawas and Potawatomis, and many Wyandots who earlier had shunned the new faith now were converted to the Prophet's teachings. Once again Harrison received reports that the Indians were burning witches, and friendly chiefs among the Miamis and Piankashaws complained that warriors long faithful to the government now were flocking to Prophetstown.

Concerned over the new upsurge in the Prophet's influence, Harrison sent informers to the Tippecanoe and invited Tenskwatawa to again meet with him in Vincennes, but the holy man refused. He also ignored an invitation by the governor to travel to Washington and meet with the president. Instead, he informed Harrison that the recent treaty was illegal and threatened to kill all those chiefs who had signed it. He also vowed that the lands would never be settled by white men and warned Harrison to keep American settlement south of the mouth of the Vermillion River.

The Treaty of Fort Wayne ended any pretense of cooperation between Tenskwatawa and the government. By 1810 the lines were drawn. Tenskwatawa and his movement were unequivocally opposed to American expansion, and in the years following the treaty the anti-American sentiment was both transformed and intensified.

Tecumseh's role in the formation of this movement was entirely a secondary one. He subscribed to the new faith and lived with the Prophet at Greenville, where he assisted his brother in meeting the delegations of both Indian and white visitors. Tecumseh sometimes spoke in council upon such occasions, but no more so than Blue Jacket, Roundhead, or other Indians prominent in the village. In 1807 he accompanied a group of tribesmen who met with Governor Thomas Kirker of Ohio, but in this instance he spoke in defense of his brother, convincing the governor that the Prophet and his movement were no threat to peace. Although primary materials from this period are full of references to the Prophet, almost none mention Tecumseh. Most accounts of Tecumseh's activities during these years are from the "reminiscences" of American observers recorded decades later.

Indeed, Tecumseh did not challenge the Prophet's position of leadership until 1810, two years after the move of Prophetstown and five years after the religious movement's beginnings. During 1808 Indians continued to flock to Prophetstown to see the holy man, not his brother; and in that year it was the Prophet, not Tecumseh, who met with Harrison at Vincennes. In the summer of 1808 Tecumseh did visit Malden seeking supplies for the Indians at Prophetstown, but he made no claims to leadership; and British accounts of the visit, which are quite specific in listing other Indians' names, refer to him only as "the Prophet's brother," not as Tecumseh, a chief among the Shawnees.

The springboard to Tecumseh's emergence was the Treaty of Fort Wayne. From Tecumseh's perspective it was obvious that the religious emphasis of his brother could no longer protect the remaining Indian land base. During the summer of 1809 he visited a few Indian villages in Illinois, but after the treaty Tecumseh took a new initiative and began to travel widely, emphasizing a political and military solution to the Indians' problems. The tribesmen should still adhere to the new religion, but they should abandon their old chiefs who remained friendly to the Americans. Instead, all warriors should politically unite under Tecumseh, for in his own words, "I am the head of them all . . . I am alone the acknowledged chief of all the Indians."

Therefore, for two years—in 1810 and 1811—Tecumseh traveled extensively among the Indians of the West. During these years he met twice with Harrison, who reported to his superiors that Tecumseh now had emerged as "really the efficient man—the Moses of the family." In this period Tecumseh slowly eclipsed the Prophet's position of leadership, but ironically as the character of the Indian movement changed, its appeal to the tribesmen declined. In 1810 and 1811 parties of warriors recruited by Tecumseh temporarily joined the village at Prophetstown, but their numbers never approached the multitude of Indians who earlier had flocked to the Prophet. And although the Prophet no longer dominated the movement, he continued to exercise considerable influence. For example, his ability to convince his followers that they could easily obtain a victory over the Americans contributed to their ill-fated attack upon Harrison's forces at the Battle of the Tippecanoe in 1811. Obviously, after the battle the Prophet's influence was broken, and Tecumseh remained the dominant leader of the battered movement. But Tecumseh's preeminence was of short duration, for he was killed less than two years later, on October 5, 1813, at the Battle of the Thames.

It is evident, therefore, that the Prophet, not Tecumseh, was the most important figure in the emergence of the Indian movement prior to the War of 1812. Tecumseh used the widespread religious base earlier established by his brother as the foundation for his unsuccessful attempt to unite the tribes politically and militarily. Although the Prophet has been pictured as either a charlatan or a religious fanatic whose teachings seem quite bizarre, such an appraisal reflects an ethnocentric bias. He certainly seemed logical to the Indians, and for several years he exercised a widespread influence throughout the Old Northwest. In retrospect, such a phenomenon is not surprising. In times of oppression native American peoples have often turned to a religious deliverance. The Shawnee Prophet fits into a historical pattern exemplified by the Delaware Prophet, Handsome Lake, Wovoka, and the Ghost Dance, and many others. Indeed, Tecumseh's emphasis upon political and military unification was much less typical than the Prophet's messianic nativism.

Why then has Tecumseh emerged as "the Greatest Indian"? The answer is obvious. If white Americans could design an "ideal Indian," they would have designed Tecumseh. His concepts of political and military unification under a centralized leadership appealed to whites because it was what *they* would have done. His solution had much less appeal to native Americans who had little tradition of either centralized leadership or of pan-Indian confederacies in response to American expansion. White Americans also praised Tecumseh's intervention in behalf of prisoners, but such intervention reflected European concepts of warfare more than those practiced by native Americans. Much of traditional Indian warfare was based upon vendetta, and prisoners expected the worst. Indeed, captured warriors took pride in their ability to withstand torture and laugh in the faces of their captors.

White Americans have championed Tecumseh because he, more than any other Indian, exemplifies the American or European concept of the "noble savage": brave, honest, a true "prince of the forest"—natural man at his best. Since his death, his American and British contemporaries and later historians have continued to embellish his memory with qualities and exploits that have added to his image. Many of the attributes and incidents were apocryphal (for example, his reputed love affair with the white woman, Rebecca Galloway, or the assertion that his skin was of a lighter hue than other Indians), but they only strengthened what Americans wanted to believe and have been incorporated into his biographies. Even his death added to the romantic appeal of the man. He fell, fighting to the last, in the Battle of the Thames—the red Armageddo. And his body was not among the dead on the field, but buried mysteriously by his followers in the forest. In contrast, the poor Prophet survived the war, was exiled in Canada, returned to the United States, was removed to the West, and in 1836 died an inglorious death in Kansas.

This reassessment does not mean that Tecumseh was not a remarkable man. Indeed, he was a brave and farsighted leader who sacrificed his life for his people. But the real Tecumseh stands on his own merits. He does not need the romantic embellishments of ethnocentric historians. Tragically, the Tecumseh who has emerged from the pages of history is, in many respects, a "white man's Indian."

9

Creation of a New Political and Legal Order

James Henritta and Gregory Nobles

Just as the new United States struggled to gain world recognition and political independence, the country also strived mightily to achieve an effective political and legal system. In this path breaking synthesis of current research, James Henritta and Gregory Nobles weave together the fabric of the emerging order that becomes America.

In 1787, the Pennsylvania physician and Patriot Dr. Benjamin Rush observed:

> The American war is over, but this is far from being the case with the *American Revolution.* On the contrary, nothing but the first act of the great drama is closed. It remains yet to establish and perfect our new forms of government.

By 1820, American political leaders had met Rush's challenge and devised three "new forms of government."

First, the Federalists led by Alexander Hamilton used the framework provided by the Constitution to create a strong national government. When Hamilton employed governmental powers to assist merchants and to establish a national system of public credit, James Madison and Thomas Jefferson contested his policies. To oppose Hamilton's Federalists, they founded the Democratic-Republican political party. From 1794 to 1816, these two parties struggled for control of the national government; each wanted to use governmental power to assist the social groups that it represented.

Second, state governments quickly and purposefully created a mercantilist (or state-directed) economic system. They established new institutions, such as banks, to provide credit for merchants and traders. To assist farmers and planters, northern and southern legislatures encouraged the construction of turnpikes and canals that would provide cheap and reliable transport. Between 1790 and 1820, state governments created an impressive financial and transportation infrastructure, thereby unleashing a massive expansion of the market economy. The states' policies, like those of Hamilton, favored capitalist entrepreneurs to the detriment of ordinary citizens and prompted political unrest.

Third, American political leaders created new institutions that expanded the "rule of law." Lawyers played an important role in this process; they drafted the new state constitutions and won election to legislative offices in increasing numbers. In addition, the hierarchically organized state judicial systems that enforced criminal statutes and adjudicated civil disputes were devised and staffed by lawyers. Along with the United States Supreme Court, these state courts gave direction to the emergent market economy.

Thus, the years between 1790 and 1820 were among the most creative in the history of the United States. In less than a single generation, leaders divised new institutions that significantly changed the character of American political, economic, and legal life. The "great drama" envisioned by Rush came to pass, but the plot was more complex and troubled than he had supposed. Each of the new institutions was "republican," created by the authority of the sovereign people. Yet wealthy or ambitious Americans exercised considerable control over these organizations, giving them an aristocratic, or elitist, character. Consequently, the creation of a republican polity both unleashed the energy of the American people and revived the social conflicts of the revolutionary era.

A National Fiscal System

The creation of a national system of public credit produced a rapid (and unexpected) division among the framers of the Constitution. Alexander Hamilton of New York and James Madison of Virginia were the main protagonists in this political drama. The son of a wealthy Virginia planter, Madison attended the College of New Jersey (Princeton University) and, between 1784 and 1787, served in the Virginia Assembly. An idealistic, conservative Patriot, Madison was astounded by the "crudeness" of his fellow state legislators who seemed to have only "a particular interest to serve." He tried repeatedly to beat back measures of a "popular cast," such as an "itch for paper money." Madison was unable to prevail on the state level, but did succeed at the constitutional convention in transferring control over many financial issues to the national government. It was his belief that on a national level policies would be determined by "individuals of extended views and of national pride."

Madison got more than he bargained for. As expected, the Electoral college created by the Constitution chose George Washington as the first president of the new government of the United States. A committed nationalist, Washington deliberately chose his cabinet advisors from all regions and the most important states. Thomas Jefferson and Edmund Randolph, both Virginia planters, became secretary of state and attorney general, respectively; Henry Knox of Massachusetts served as secretary of war; and Alexander Hamilton of New York became secretary of the treasury. All were men of "national pride." But Hamilton had an especially purposeful "extended view" of the destiny of the United States. Soon he and Madison were bitter political enemies.

Alexander Hamilton was born on the Caribbean island of Nevis in 1753. Abandoned by his father, an unsuccessful Scottish merchant, Hamilton was raised by his mother, the daughter of a French Protestant physician. In 1772, he enrolled at Kings College (Columbia University) in New York and joined the Patriot movement. During the war, Hamilton served as a trusted military aide to Washington. He then married into the aristocratic Schuyler family of New York and quickly adopted the social values of the elite. Mobilizing New York landlords, merchants, and creditors, he sought to defend the "security of property" by putting "men in the Legislature whose principles were not of the *leveling kind.*" To guarantee rule by "the rich and well-born," Hamilton advocated an elective monarchy at the constitutional convention.

As secretary of the treasury in Washington's administration, Hamilton used his brilliant talents to enhance the power of wealthy families within American society. His strategy had two interrelated elements. First, Hamilton augmented the power of the national government by creating a new system of public finance. Second, he designed this fiscal system to increase the wealth of the mercantile and creditor classes, thereby winning their support for the new national government.

Hamilton's fiscal system had four parts: redemption, assumption, funding, and credit. As secretary of the treasury, Hamilton submitted legislation in 1791 to redeem the war securities issued by the Continental Congress. He proposed payment of the full face value of the certificates to their present owners. As a congressman from Virginia,

Madison opposed Hamilton's scheme as unjust, pointing out that merchants and speculators owned a substantial majority of the $70 million of outstanding Continental securities. These securities had been bought as speculative investments for only a fraction of their original value. Madison proposed that the soldiers, farmers, and investors who had first owned these certificates receive a portion of the redemption fund. The House of Representatives defeated Madison's proposal by a vote of 36 to 13. Some members thought that Madison's plan was too complex. Other congressmen stood to benefit personally from Hamilton's scheme; no fewer than twenty-nine of the sixty-four members of the House held securities themselves.

Madison rose again to oppose Hamilton's "assumption" scheme. The secretary of the treasury wanted the national government to assume and pay off the war debts of the several states. Virginia and several other states opposed assumption. They had already taxed their citizens heavily to retire most of their war debts, and did not want to pay the debts of other states. Moreover, many southerners knew that northern speculators had bought up much of the remaining southern war debt. In fact, forty-seven nonresidents owned $3.2 million of the $8 million in securities still owed by Virginia, North Carolina, and South Carolina. A mere thirteen individuals or firms, mostly located in New York City, controlled nearly $2 million of these securities.

Hamilton made a deft move to win southern support for this monumental financial manipulation. In return for Virginias' support for assumption in the House of Representatives, the secretary of the treasury agreed to move the national capital to a new "federal' district to be laid out along the banks of the Potomac River, between Maryland and Virginia. Despite this accord, many political leaders from the southern states openly questioned the wisdom of Hamilton's financial policies.

Hamilton did nothing to quiet the fears of southerners or northern farmers. He declared his intention to create a permanent national debt. To fund the annual interest on the debt, Hamilton imposed two sets of national taxes. First, he secured legislation increasing the tariffs on imported goods. Once again southern planters protested, for they wanted low-priced British goods. Second, Hamilton placed substantial excise taxes (of up to 25 percent) on whiskey and other domestically produced goods. These internal taxes reminded many Americans of the Stamp Act imposed by Prime Minister Grenville in 1765. They also rekindled doubts concerning the extent of the authority bestowed upon the national government by the Constitution. As Patrick Henry of Virginia had warned at the time, "Your rich snug, fine, fat, Federal offices—The number of collectors of taxes and excises will outnumber anything from the States." Farmers in western Pennsylvania refused to accept these taxes and forcefully resisted national authority in the Whiskey Rebellion of 1794.

Meanwhile, Hamilton proposed legislation creating the First Bank of the United States—the final part of his fiscal edifice. He hoped that the bank would expand the credit available to merchants and assist the government in the collection of tax revenues. Astounded by the bank bill, Secretary of State Thomas Jefferson joined Madison in active opposition to Hamilton's program. "The incorporation of a Bank," Jefferson argued, was not "delegated to the United States by the Constitution." Reading the Constitution in a "strict" manner, Jefferson pointed out that a national bank was "not among the powers specially enumerated" and was not "*necessary* and proper for carrying into execution the enumerated powers." He therefore urged President Washington to veto the bank bill.

In reply, Hamilton endorsed a "loose" reading of the Constitution. The word "*necessary,*" he told Washington, "often means no more than *needful, requisite . . . useful.*" "If the *end* be . . . within any of the specified powers, and if the measure have an obvious relation to that *end,*" he told the president, "it may safely be deemed to come within the compass of the national authority." Because of his own nationalist sympathies, Washington endorsed Hamilton's position on the bank. Likewise supporting the secretary of the treasury on the issue of excise taxes, Washington dispatched 15,000 United States troops to repress the Whiskey Rebellion.

Backed by the president and a majority of the Congress, Hamilton had created an impressive system of public credit, the revenue measures to fund it, and a national army to uphold it. Many southern planters and backcountry farmers soon realized that Hamilton's financial program favored northern mercantile interests at the expense of their agricultural economies.

The First Party System

Hamilton's policies led to the creation of what historians call the "First Party System." Initially, Madison and Jefferson worked within the existing political institutions to defeat Hamilton's designs. They vigorously pressed their point of view on the president, and they organized an opposition "faction" within Congress. When these meas-

TABLE 9.1 Hamilton's Public Credit Policy, 1792

National Government Debt		
Redemption:	Foreign Debt	$11.7 million
	Domestic Debt	42.4 million
Assumption:	State Debts	21.5 million
	TOTAL DEBT	$75.6 million

Annual Revenue		*Annual Expenditures*	
Custom Duties	$4.4 million	Interest on Debt (at 6%)	$4.6 million
Excise Taxes	0.4 million	Operating Expenses	1.0 million
Miscellaneous	0.8 million		
TOTAL REVENUE	$5.6 million	TOTAL EXPENSES	$5.6 million

Hamilton created a permanent debt to tie merchant capitalists (who owed government securities) to the new Federal regime. He supported customs and excise duties to pay the substantial annual interest on the debt.

ures failed, the two Virginians became political innovators. As the election of 1794 approached, they created a political party, the Democratic-Republicans, to win support among the people. In response, Hamilton's supporters formed the Federalist party.

The social roots of the two parties extended deep into the history of the revolutionary era. Many backcountry farmers who had campaigned for democratic state constitutions after 1776 and who supported the Antifederalist cause in 1787 flocked to the Democratic-Republican banner. And Federalists drew part of their strength from creditors and merchants who led the movement for a strong national Constitution. As a result of the French Revolution, which broke out in 1789, these struggles between political parties took a more ideological form. Chanting the French republicans' slogan of "liberty, equality, and fraternity," American Democratic-Republicans condemned Hamilton's "aristocratic" economic policies and his pro-British foreign policy. For their part, Federalists attacked the "levelling" principles of the French republicans and their repression of Christian churches. Federalists used their control of the national government to give diplomatic support to Britain in its war against the First French Republic. In the Jay Treaty of 1795, Federalists patched up existing disputes with Britain over western lands and maritime rights.

To secure a majority in the national legislature, both parties organized on the state and local levels. By 1796, Federalist and

TABLE 9.2 Party Outlooks Compared

Federalist	*Democratic-Republican*
Support for merchants and manufacturers	Aid to artisans and western farmers
Rule by a well-born elite	Rule by an elite of talent
Vote restricted to property-owners	Democratic franchise
A strong judiciary	A strong legislature
A powerful national government	A limited national government
A permanent debt financed by wealthy	Elimination of national debt
Pro-British foreign policy	Pro-French foreign policy

Democratic-Republican "legislative caucuses" existed in every state. These caucuses nominated candidates for each congressional district, influenced the selection of senators, and provided institutional support for local politicians.

The first party system dramatically changed the structure of American politics. Before 1794, the political system had been basically "cellular" in nature. Each New England town, or Middle Atlantic and southern county, elected its own officials on the basis of social status or personal abilities. Voters similarly chose local notables to represent their interests in the colonial or state assemblies and in the new national Congress.

After 1794, party affiliation became as important as social prestige in determining the outcome of many elections. "The novel doctrine of new-fashioned republicans . . . that characters should be tried at the bar of public opinion" was "senseless jargon" complained one New England Federalist, who favored the old system of rule by local notables. Nonetheless, Federalists sought to turn ideological principles and party identity to their advantage. "Our combination is to preserve principle," one Federalist asserted, and another party leader accused Democratic-Republicans of seeking "to obtain office, and change the customs and habits of the country." Many voters supported men for office because they stood for a certain set of economic and social policies.

The first party system encompassed the entire society within a single political framework. Federalists confronted Democratic-Republicans in each of the traditional local "cells," breaking down the fragmented character of the old political world. The party system endangered the position of many of the traditional power brokers—the ministers, merchants, planters, and landlords who had connected separate communities to the wider world. Some of these established leaders were politicians by instinct; they found it easy to campaign for office. Many local notables remained committed, emotionally and intellectually, to the older world of deferential politics. They refused to seek the votes of their social "inferiors" or to engage in public debates with the lawyers who became leaders of many local party organizations. Thus, the first party system partially undermined the old system of deferential politics and created a new institutional structure of power and prestige.

This struggle between Federalists and Democratic-Republicans led to a series of major political crises that nearly destroyed the American union. In the election of 1796, Federalist John Adams of Massachusetts succeeded Washington as president. Adams ignored the continued seizure of American merchant ships by Britain yet undertook an undeclared naval war against France in response to similar actions. To suppress domestic criticism of this pro-British foreign policy, the Federalists enacted the Naturalization, Alien, and Sedition Acts of 1798. These acts curbed the voting rights of recent immigrants, many of whom were Democratic-Republicans, and made it illegal to conspire "with intent to oppose any measure or measures of the government of the United States."

Led by Thomas Jefferson, the Democratic-Republicans exploited popular discontent with foreign war and domestic repression. Winning the support of southern planters, western farmers, urban artisans, and ambitious northeastern politicians, Jefferson won election to the presidency in 1800. In a symbolic effort to restore national unity, Jefferson declared in his first inaugural address, "We are all Republicans, We are all Federalists."

The new president's attempt to end the party system was premature. The two parties drew their support from different regions and social groups, and espoused fundamentally divergent policies. On coming into power, the Democratic-Republicans ended internal excise taxes, reduced the size of the army and the national debt, and enacted a new Land Act to encourage rapid settlement of the west. Federalists opposed all these measures, but without success, for Democratic-Republicans held majorities in both houses of Congress.

Jefferson was reelected in 1804, only to face renewed attacks on American merchant vessels by the warring nations of Europe. To force France and, especially, Britain to respect American ships as "neutral traders," the president endorsed legislation imposing an embargo on American shipping. The embargo of 1807 rekindled the fires of party politics. Federalist merchants readily accepted the risks of wartime trade because the potential profits were immense. They assailed the embargo as "unfeeling and odious," a direct attack on the economy of New England and the seaport cities, and they campaigned strenuously to oust the Democratic-Republicans from office.

Despite the Federalists' opposition, James Madison won the presidency in 1808. By leading the nation into war against Great Britain, he triumphed again in 1812. Federalists vigorously opposed the War of 1812. Led by Daniel Webster of New Hampshire, they refused to lend money to the national government or to supply it with troops. It was only in 1815, with the end of the War of 1812 and the French Revolution in Europe, that the political passions generated by the workings of the first party system gradually cooled.

Political parties had not appeared by design. Colonial political leaders had consistently condemned "factions" as dangerous to the safety of the state. The ideology of classical republicanism was hostile to the concept of groups of self-interested politicians; it celebrated "virtuous" leaders who ruled on behalf of the entire people. As a result, neither the state constitutions nor the Constitution of 1787 mentioned parties or sanctioned their appearance. By creating disciplined political organizations, Federalists and Democratic-Republicans deliberately circumvented the checks and balances built into the new republican institutions of government. The inherently antirepublican character of bitterly contending parties alarmed most politically minded Americans. "If I could not go to heaven but with a party," Jefferson declared, "I would not go there at all."

On the other hand, parties were the logical result of another aspect of republican thought, the doctrine of popular sovereignty. Ultimate power in the new American republic lay in the hands of the people, and parties were the only way that the populace could be mobilized for effective action. American politics had not yet become "democratic," since most Federalist and Democratic-Republican leaders assumed that the people would defer to their views. However, the first party system partially undermined the elitist-controlled political system established by the Constitution. It created a new institutional structure that arrayed factions of elites against one another and forced them to appeal for popular support. At the same time, party organizations united the ordinary citizens of the American republic and provided them with a conscious sense of membership in the political order and a measure of electoral power.

The Structure of Politics

The battles over Hamilton's fiscal system and Jefferson's foreign policy took place in a new national political arena. Between 1775 and 1789, the states had been the units of representation in the Confederation government. To exert pressure on the national level, interest groups had to influence a state's delegation to the federal congress. As a result, the state legislatures controlled politics both within their own boundaries and for the nation as a whole.

The Constitution dramatically changed this structure of power. Property-owning white adult males in every state voted, either directly or indirectly, for members of the Electoral College. In turn, these electors selected the president of the United States. More important, voters in each congressional district directly elected a member of the House of Representatives, the lower house of the national legislature. State legislatures still retained a significant role in the selection of the central government. Some legislatures chose members of the Electoral College and (until the passage of the Seventeenth Amendment of the Constitution in 1912) all of them elected members of the United States Senate. In spite of this, the Constitution did shift the locus of power away from the state legislatures. "The powers given to the federal body for imposing internal taxation will necessarily destroy the state sovereignties," William Findley of Pennsylvania prophesied in 1788, "for there cannot exist two independent sovereign taxing powers in the same community, and the strongest will, of course, annihilate the weaker."

The imposition of excise taxes and the vigorous suppression of the Whiskey Rebellion of 1794 demonstrated the immense potential power of the national government. The war crisis with France in 1798 pointed out the ability of the national government to quell ordinary political dissent as well. Using the federal courts, the Adams administration indicted dozens of Democratic-Republicans for seditious libel. Federalist judges assisted prosecutors in obtaining guilty verdicts and sentenced numerous Democratic-Republican newspaper editors to lengthy jail terms. Jefferson and many other Democratic-Republicans thought the New England Federalists were using the national government to rule in an arbitrary and tyrannical manner. "We are completely under the saddle of Massachusetts and Connecticut," Jefferson wrote to his friend John Taylor, "[and] they ride us very hard, cruelly insulting our feelings as well as exhausting our strength and substance."

Jefferson and Madison anonymously drafted resolutions for passage by the Kentucky and Virginia legislatures. These resolutions attacked the Sedition Acts as contrary to the First Amendment to the Constitution, which protected the rights of freedom of speech and freedom of the press. Equally important, the resolutions claimed substantial sovereign powers for the states. The limits of the powers of the national government had already been clarified in the ten amendments to the Constitution that had been ratified in 1791. Proposed in response to Antifederalist criticisms, these amendments protected the rights of citizens; the Tenth Amendment declared that "powers not delegated to the United States by the Constitution, nor prohibited by it to the States, are reserved to the States respectively, or to the people."

Jefferson went further than that in the Kentucky Resolutions; he asserted that the national government was a "compact" constituted by the "several states" and that "whensoever the General Government assumes undelegated powers, its acts are unauthoritative, void, and are of no force." In the Virginia Resolutions, Madison asked other states to concur with the Virginia legislature "in declaring, as it does hereby declare, that [such] acts . . . are unconstitutional." The political intent of these resolutions was clear. Madison and Jefferson were using their influence in the states controlled by the Democratic-Republicans to contest Federalist authority on the national level.

The Federalists adopted a similar strategy during the administrations of Jefferson and Madison. Jefferson's view of America's destiny was very different from that of Hamilton. He dreamed of a society filled with families of yeoman farmers and independent artisans. To open new lands for southern tenant farmers and hard-pressed new England freeholders, Jefferson advocated the rapid settlement of the west. He drafted the Land Ordinance of 1784, which called for the creation of new western states and banned slavery within their bounds.

As president, Jefferson pursued this vision of an expanding commercial agricultural society. Early in his administration, the Spanish government first threatened to restrict American use of the Mississippi River and next secretly transferred the vast territory of Louisiana to France. Jefferson wrote to a friend:

> There is on the globe one single spot, the possessor of which is our natural and habitual enemy. It is New Orleans, through which the produce of three-eighths of our territory must pass to market, and from its fertility it will ere long yield more than half of our whole produce and contain more than half of our inhabitants.

In 1803, Jefferson purchased New Orleans and the entire territory of Louisiana from the French government, at the time headed by Napoleon I. By this magnificent diplomatic coup, the president moved the western boundary of the United States from the Mississippi River to the Rocky Mountains, nearly doubling the nation's land area.

The legality of the Louisiana Purchase was as doubtful as that of the creation of the First Bank of the United States and the Sedition Acts, for the Constitution did not specifically provide for the acquisition of new territories. The political implications of this acquisition were equally controversial, since it threatened the eastern-oriented Federalist party with the permanent loss of power. "We rush like a comet into infinite space," warned Fisher Ames, a prominent New England Federalist, on learning of the purchase. "The western states, multiplied in number, and augmented in population," predicted Federalist Harrison Gray Otis, "will control the interest of the whole." To avoid domination by southern and western Democratic-Republicans, Massachusetts Federalist Timothy Pickering advocated separation from "the *aristocratic democrats* of the South" and the breakup of the Union.

The embargo of 1807 and the War of 1812 gave new force to the separatist sentiments that were prevalent in New England. "We have always been led to believe that a separation of the States would be a great evil," the editor of the Newburyport, Massachusetts *Centinel* observed in 1813, "[and] we still think it an evil." "But rather than prosecute the present war . . .," he continued, "we think it by far the least of two evils." Like Madison and Jefferson in 1798, these Federalists argued that the United States was simply a collection of "several independent confederated republics."

To defend the interests of their party, states, and region, New England Federalists called the Hartford Convention in 1815 [met in 1814, ed.]. Resisting the advice of Pickering and other secessionists, the convention endorsed seven constitutional amendments. These amendments would give the New England states an effective veto over certain important issues: an affirmative vote by two-thirds of the states would be required before the national government could impose an embargo, declare an offensive war, or admit new states into the Union. Even as it sought compromise, the convention declared that in cases of "deliberate, dangerous" violations of state sovereignty or popular liberties, "it is not only the right but the duty of such a state to interpose its authority for their protection."

In 1800, Jefferson's victory had ended the threat of southern secession from the Union. In 1815, the conclusion of a peace treaty with Great Britain quashed the plans of separatists in New England. Yet these threats to the Union were serious, for they showed that many Americans had not accepted the national structure of politics created by the Constitution in 1787. Accustomed to the primacy of local and state politics, they refused to accept the authority of the president and Congress when it seriously affected their interests.

The legacy of these early confrontations between state and national sovereignty was twofold. After 1815, most American political leaders advocated a very limited role for the national government in order to avoid similar constitutional controversies. Where national action was necessary, such as in the origination of tariff policies or the admission of new states into the Union, politicians carefully balanced the interests of the various regions and of powerful social groups. These cautious strategies preserved the Union until the conflict over the expansion of slavery prompted the secession of most southern states. Then, in the Civil War, the paramount authority of the national government was confirmed by force of arms.

State Mercantilism

Beginning in the 1780s, American governments—national, state, and local—systematically promoted economic development. This effort resembled the mercantilism of European nations in that it involved the use of political authority to mobilize the society's resources. Both republican ideology and economic necessity justified this political intervention. "The establishment of useful manufacturers is closely connected with the public weal," the New York legislature declared in 1790, as it granted a loan to a pottery factory. Mercantilist assumptions determined American economic policy for the next half-century. Chief Justice Black of Pennsylvania declared in a court decision in 1853:

> It is a grave error to suppose that the duty of a state stops with the establishment of those institutions which are necessary to the existence of government. . . . To aid, encourage, and stimulate commerce, domestic and foreign, is a duty of the sovereign, as plain and universally recognized as any other.

Aid to business enterprises took various forms. Following the ratification of the Constitution, the United States government embarked on a program of economic nationalism. The Tonnage Act, passed by

Congress in 1789, closely resembled the British Trade and Navigation Acts. To encourage the American shipping industry, the Tonnage Act restricted the transport of goods between American ports to vessels owned by United States citizens. In addition, it levied a special duty of 50 cents a ton on goods imported in foreign-built or foreign-owned ships.

Congress also passed a series of tariff acts that placed duties on imported goods. Like the despised Townshend Duties of 1767, these acts were designed primarily to raise revenue. Unlike that earlier British legislation, they did so with great success. Tariffs provided two-thirds of the income of the national government between 1790 and 1860. In addition, tariff legislation assisted the growth of American industry. By 1794, import duties on shoes and various other foreign manufactured items reached 20 percent of the goods' value. These protective duties subsidized domestic manufacturers (at the public's expense) by raising the price of imported goods.

State governments fostered economic development with even greater dedication. In the thirty years from 1789 to 1819, state legislatures issued more than 2500 charters to business corporations. These charters gave corporations a defined legal existence, enabling them to enter into contracts and to attract capital from private investors. At first, legislatures granted corporate charters selectively, directing private resources primarily into transportation projects. Of the 326 charters issued before 1800, 207 (or 63 percent) were for the construction of turnpikes, bridges, and canals. By 1812, the Commonwealth of Pennsylvania had chartered 55 turnpike companies, New York had granted articles of incorporation to 57 such companies, and Massachusetts to 105. In many cases, these charters guaranteed monopoly rights over certain routes in order to encourage an adequate level of investment.

Governmental participation in the construction of canals was much more extensive than the mere granting of legal privileges. The amount of capital required to build a canal was enormous. Only in eastern New England, with its densely concentrated population, was the prospect of profit imminent enough to attract a sufficient number of private investors. Elsewhere, state governments took the initiative, concluding that canal building was a worthwhile endeavor in the long term because it would open up interior regions for settlement and for trade. Pressed by George Washington and other influential planters, the Maryland and Virginia legislatures created the Potomac River Canal Company in 1785 and appropriated state funds for construction.

Subsequently, other states poured massive amounts of public funds into canal projects. Of the total investment of $132 million in the canals of the trans-Appalachian region between 1815 and 1860, state governments arranged for $117 million through grants, bond issues, or taxation. This use of public financing permitted the rapid settlement of the states of the Ohio River Valley.

The Commonwealth of Pennsylvania took the most active role of all the states in assisting economic development. In 1809, its legislature granted a loan to private individuals to construct a steel mill. Other ventures outside the field of transportation quickly followed. Arguing simply that "works of public importance deserve public encouragement," the commonwealth invested in a variety of mixed public and private enterprises. By 1844, the state government was part-owner of more than 150 companies.

Purposeful government intervention gave public direction to American economic development. In addition, government-financed projects increased the rate of investment, of capital accumulation, and of western settlement. The Erie Canal, financed and constructed by the state government of New York, was the crowning achievement of state mercantilism. The building of this magnificent canal, connecting the Hudson River and Lake Erie, required an immense importation of laborers (thousands of Irish immigrants) and capital resources from Europe. The end of the Napoleonic Wars had dramatically reduced the borrowing needs of European governments and created, as Governor Clinton of New York correctly discerned, "a vast disposable capital in Great Britain." New York pledged public taxes to guarantee its canal bonds, and British investors poured millions of dollars into the project.

By the time of its completion in 1825, the Erie Canal had already helped to make New York City the largest and wealthiest American city. Most trade with the Great Lakes' states of Ohio, Indiana, and Illinois moved along the canal, as did tens of thousands of bushels of wheat grown on the fertile lands between Albany and Buffalo. No fewer than 900,000 settlers already lived in these upstate counties of New York. Most of them had migrated from New England, where two centuries of rapid population growth had diminished the size of farms and depleted the fertility of the soil. Expansion into the interior of North America gave these farmers—and the society as a whole—access to new and more productive natural resources. Thus, the construction of canals, in conjunction with other state mercantilist activities, spurred the rapid economic development of the new American republic.

Mercantile Capitalism

Even as the state governments used public taxes to attract capital from foreign investors, they encouraged the creation of an extensive privately owned domestic banking system. Before 1776, there were no banks in America. Merchants formed business partnerships or obtained private loans to finance commercial or manufacturing enterprises. During the War of Independence, leading merchants transformed these informal credit arrangements into formal banking institutions. The president of the Bank of North America wrote from Philadelphia in 1784:

> When the bank was first opened here, we established our books on a simple mercantile plan, and this mode . . . pointed out by experience alone, has carried us through so far without a material loss or even mistake of any consequence.

By 1791, when Congress established the First Bank of the United States, state-chartered banks existed in New York, Massachusetts, Maryland, and Pennsylvania. Merchants controlled most of these institutions, using them primarily as a source of short-term credit to pay for imported goods. By 1795, there were twenty-one banks in the United States, and by 1812, there were ninety. By that time, state-chartered banks held more than $15 million in gold and silver. In addition, they had more than $52 million out in loans or circulating as negotiable bills of credit. The First Bank of the United States provided monetary stability for this private banking system. It accepted bank notes in payment of tariffs and then presented them for redemption in specie, forcing the state-chartered banks to maintain adequate reserves.

The existence of this complex banking system indicated that the United States had entered a new stage in its financial development. Money, markets, and rational economic behavior were all to be found in America prior to 1776, but the real center of financial power and decision making lay in England and Scotland. Colonial merchants relied on British sources of credit and lacked the institutions to mobilize capital for noncommercial ventures. Partly as a result of the weakness of the American credit system, a highly developed market economy existed only in the seaport cities and among tidewater planters.

By 1800, however, business corporations, complex credit institutions, and new forms of economic enterprise were playing a more extensive role in American life. Again, governments took the lead. To encourage technological innovation, the United States government created the Patent Office. By registering an invention with the office, a citizen could obtain the exclusive right to manufacture, sell, or use it. This establishing of a government-protected property right fostered an outpouring of mechanical ingenuity; the number of patents increased from an average of 20 per year between 1790 and 1795 to 200 per year between 1808 and 1824.

Early nineteenth-century American merchants began developing new types of financial institutions. Around 1800, the merchant house of Alexander Brown and Sons of Baltimore cut back in trade in commodities, such as wheat exports and textile imports. Instead, the Browns started to specialize in "paper" transactions, becoming financial brokers. They charged merchants a fee of 2 percent for buying bills of exchange drawn on foreign banks; then they redeemed the bills in Europe or used them to speculate in the international money market. In Philadelphia, the firm of S. and M. Allen and Sons provided another specialized financial service. The Allens organized a system of state-authorized lotteries to raise capital for public institutions, such as schools, and for private transportation and manufacturing ventures. Because they tapped the small savings of thousands of Americans, lotteries were both popular and successful. The number of offices run by the Allens grew from three in 1809 to sixty in 1827.

Previously, small merchant firms had stood at the center of the American commercial system. Such firms handled a wide array of business—trade, insurance, money lending—as the situation demanded. These diversified merchant entrepreneurs were pushed off the center of the economic stage by a wide variety of specialized bankers, brokers, and commodity traders. These financial specialists had less range and versatility than eighteenth-century merchants, but were no less audacious. Moreover, firms like those of the Browns and Allens became more accomplished practitioners of their trades because they devoted all their energies to a narrow field. With this division of labor, the American financial system advanced to a more efficient level.

The overall effect of the new system of banks, financial institutions, and state mercantilist enterprises was the encouragement of a sustained process of economic growth. Public corporations attracted massive amounts of foreign capital for large-scale transportation projects. By the 1820s, Europeans had invested $80—90 million in the United States, and this amount reached $200–250 million by the 1820s. This foreign capital permitted the rapid settlement of the trans-Appalachian west. At the same time, the new system of domestic banking provided short-term credit for merchants and amassed funds for the expansion of the shoe, textile, ship-building, and iron industries.

This accumulation of foreign and domestic capital promoted a substantial increase in national prosperity. The per capita wealth of American citizens had returned to its prewar level by 1790. After that, the rapid growth of the population (from 3.9 million in 1790 to 9.6 million in 1820) strained productive capacity, resulting in a slow growth in per capita wealth. Finally, in the 1820s and 1830s, the positive effects of a generation of institutional development and capital accumulation became apparent. Per capita wealth soared from an index figure of 67 in 1820 to 100 in 1840.

Although government intervention expanded the total wealth of American society, it also increased the extent of economic inequality. In 1775 and in 1790, the top 10 percent of the wealthholders in New England and the Middle Atlantic states owned about 50 percent of the society's resources; by 1840, their share had increased to 70 percent. Economic development had greatly augmented the fortunes of the wealthier citizens: the merchants, manufacturers, and capitalist financiers. Farmers, artisans, and workers enjoyed much more modest rises in their standards of living. By 1840, their relative position in the economic order had worsened significantly.

Thus, the American system of state mercantilism was not socially neutral. Legislatures directly rewarded innovative entrepreneurs and achievement-oriented capitalists by giving them special charters, funneling public money through their hands, and perfecting a legal framework designed to suit their needs. In many cases, the managers of public enterprises were also private investors in the same companies; they acted to promote their personal interests as much as the common good. State mercantilism obtained gains in the gross national product at the cost of a growing inequality in the distribution of wealth.

Most public leaders defended these policies as contributing to the "commonwealth" of the society—which they did. Some contemporaries took a more critical view, however. They argued that state mercantilism, and especially the creation of privileged capitalist corporations, undermined the republican principles of liberty and equality for which Americans had fought in 1776. Pointing to the growing inequality of wealth, these critics warned of the disparities in social status and political power that would inevitably follow. "In this country," a Pennsylvanian argued, "sovereignty is vested in the people themselves, and whatever power is granted to corporations, is so much abstracted from the people themselves." This criticism of state mercantilism had as much validity as the argument in its defense. In the name of economic development, the system of state governmental assistance to private business enterprise had enhanced the power of merchants, manufacturers, and other wealthy Americans.

Lawyers and the Rule of Law

In the twentieth century, wars for national independence have often produced authoritarian political regimes. In some new nations, charismatic leaders rely on their personal authority to rule in an arbitrary fashion. Elsewhere, military regimes use armed force to suppress political dissent. In still other new nations, privileged social groups mask their authoritarian rule behind the facade of representative institutions.

The American War of Independence yielded a different result. The governments established during the war adhered, in most respects, to the "rule of law." Authoritarian institutions existed only in the southern states, where white slaveowners continued to control the lives of blacks in an arbitrary and essentially lawless manner. Otherwise, the American people repudiated monarchical and other nonrepresentative forms of authority. In 1812, Chief Justice Theophilus Parsons of the Massachusetts Supreme Court declared in *Ainslie v. Martin:*

> This people . . . considered the several aggressions of their sovereign on their essential rights as amounting to an abdication of his sovereignty. The throne was then vacant; but the people, in their political character, did not look after another family to reign; nor did they establish a new dynasty; but assumed to themselves, as a nation, the sovereign power. . . . Thus the government became a republic.

This fortuitous result reflected the traditional predominance of legally defined political procedures. In the half-century before 1776, the colonists had created broadly based representative assemblies that routinely enacted new laws and amended old ones. Long before they became republics in name, American governments were republican in fact.

In the colonial period, the American settlers had also gradually developed court systems to adjudicate criminal, personal, and economic disputes. Merchants, planters, and land speculators frequently used these courts to enforce written contracts, extract payment from debtors, and uphold property titles. At times, backcountry farmers, impoverished tenants, and hard-pressed artisans assailed this legal regime as unjust and oppressive. "There should be no Lawyers in the province," proclaimed angry North Carolina Regulators, and debtors in New Jersey attacked lawyers as "Private Leaches, sucking out our very Hearts Blood." These protests were to no avail. The court system, along with the legal profession that staffed it, became an ever more important part of colonial life.

The emergence of an influential American bar paralleled the evolution of a legally oriented political culture. "How greatly elevated, above common People, and above Divines is this Lawyer," young John Adams noted after listening to a leading member of his profession. Lawyers commanded impressive fees and pursued elegant lifestyles. John Tabor Kempe, who became attorney-general of New York in 1759, realized a yearly income of £880 from his private law practice, and William Livingston averaged nearly £700 a year during his twenty-four years at the New York bar. Lawyers' incomes were more modest in country areas, where the volume of lucrative commercial transactions was lower. Yet Waightsill Avery, a backcountry Virginia and North Carolina lawyer, received £164 in fees in one six-month period, making him one of the more affluent residents of this newly settled region.

To solidify their wealth and prestige, established lawyers challenged the competence of untrained "pettifoggers." In Virginia, the House of Burgesses enacted legislation requiring that men "learned in the law" license new practitioners. New York lawyers formed a bar association in 1748; by the 1760s, this association demanded that a prospective lawyer either serve a five-year apprenticeship or attend college and then work as a clerk in a law office for three years. Subsequently, Boston lawyers set a hefty minimum apprenticeship fee of £100, intended both to increase their incomes and to keep the profession small and exclusive.

Lawyers exercised their newfound authority during the Revolution. At state constitutional conventions, they translated general republican principles into precise legal language. The resulting documents often reflected the concerns or enhanced the authority of the legal profession. The Massachusetts Constitution of 1780, for example, contained a clause that gave the general court "full power and authority . . . to make, ordain, and establish . . . reasonable orders, laws, statutes, and ordinances." Although legislative supremacy was a key republican principle, the doctrine of judicial review was more problematic. Yet the above clause also declared that laws must not be "repugnant or contrary to this Constitution," thus raising the prospect that courts might review (and reject) legislative enactments.

The decision to consider both constitutions and legislation as "law" created a single, but at the same time complex, web of political and legal authority. To further complicate things, eleven of the thirteen states followed the example of the New Jersey Constitution of 1776s stating that the "common law of England . . . as . . . practiced in the Colony, shall still remain in force." Only those trained in law could sort out the complexities in the three sources of authority: constitutional provisions, legislative statutes, and common law precedents. The United States Constitution of 1787 added yet another dimension to the intellectual problem of the location of legal authority by specifying the ultimate primacy of national law. The so-called supremacy clause declared that the

> . . . Constitution, and the laws of the United States which shall be made in pursuance thereof . . . shall be the supreme law of the land: and the judges in every State shall be bound thereby, anything in the Constitution or laws of any State to the contrary notwithstanding.

The rule of law was a simple concept, but its implementation would have intricate and far-reaching consequences.

The rule of law formed the basis for an increase in the number and the power of lawyers. There were 24 lawyers for every 10,000 residents in Massachusetts in 1775 and in 1790, but 70 lawyers per 10,000 by 1810 and 87 by 1820. In South Carolina, the proportion of lawyers to residents doubled from 19 per 10,000 in 1771 to 40 per 10,000 by 1820. The legal profession became the most important single source of political leaders, especially for the higher levels of government. Of the 764 lawyers in Massachusetts before 1810, no fewer than 338 (or 44 percent) won election to office. By 1820, even though lawyers made up less than 1 percent of the adult male population, they constituted 15 percent of the representatives in the Massachusetts legislature and 35 percent of the senators. Even more striking, 63 percent of all United States congressmen from Massachusetts between 1789 and 1839 were trained as lawyers.

The growing political power of the legal profession alarmed both backcountry farmers and wealthy gentlemen. Amos Singletary, an Antifederalist farmer in Sutton, Massachusetts, warned that lawyers supporting ratification of the Constitution of 1787 "expect to get into

Congress themselves . . . and get all the power and money into their own hands, and then they will swallow up all us little folk, like the great leviathan.'' Using the elevated language of republican political theory, Antifederalist Dr. Nathaniel Ames (brother of archconservative federalist Fisher Ames) arrived at a similar conclusion. ''The making of lawyers [into] legislators,'' he argued in 1799, ''seems to defeat the grand principle of keeping the Legislative Department distinct and separate from the Judiciary.''

In various states, popular distrust of lawyers had led to the enactment of laws to diminish the influence of the legal profession. In Massachusetts, an ''Act for Rendering Processes in Law Less Expensive'' placed most court actions initially in the hands of local justices of the peace, and a ''Referee Act'' encouraged the settlement of civil suits through arbitration. Reflecting popular sentiment, many Jeffersonian Democratic-Republicans supported efforts to simplify the common law and to reduce educational requirements for the practice of law.

The attack on the elitism of the legal profession drew support from upwardly mobile individuals as well as from democratic reformers. Over the years, the legal profession had become an exclusive and self-perpetuating caste. Only wealthy families could afford to send their sons to college to qualify them for the bar, and the costly apprenticeship system similarly discriminated against those from the middle and lower ranks of society. To correct this social bias, most states reduced the educational standards for admittance to the bar. By the 1820s, the composition of the American legal profession was more democratic than ever before.

In *Democracy in America* (1835), however, Alexis de Tocqueville described the legal profession as ''the most powerful existing security against the excesses of democracy.'' The French aristocrat's conclusion was somewhat flawed, for he associated primarily with established Federalist lawyers during his visit to America and did not fully appreciate the new diversity of the profession. But Tocqueville correctly discerned that the American judicial system had become a hierarchical and authoritarian institution. Until the early nineteenth century, for example, juries of ordinary men decided questions of *law* as well as of *fact*. Then, rather suddenly, judges assumed the authority to tell juries which law to apply in a given case and how to interpret the law. If a jury brought in a verdict that did not follow that interpretation, a judge would often declare the verdict ''contrary to the law'' and therefore void. This judicial aggressiveness was in part due to the publication of decisions rendered on appealed cases by the supreme courts of the various states. By "declaring" the law, these printed decisions promoted uniformity throughout the court system. The influential work *Commentaries on American Law* (4 volumes, 1826–1830) by Chancellor James Kent of New York similarly imparted a new degree of predictability to court decisions, as local judges and lawyers argued and decided cases on the basis of precedents cited by the eminent jurist.

Democratic reformers contested the centralization of power in the hands of judges and especially their reliance on common law principles. These reformers demanded the codification of the common law in legislative statutes to ensure the primacy of republican political institutions. As Ohio lawyer John Milton Goodenow argued in the *The Principles of Maxims of American Jurisprudence* (1819), "the judge . . . is *governed* himself by *positive* law, and executes and enforces the will of the supreme power, which is the will of THE PEOPLE." Nonetheless, the judicial system had created a legal elite, which had the power to influence American social and economic development.

Law and Economic Process

Judges recognized that law was less a sacred body of immutable truths than the product of political power and will. Just as the state governments enacted mercantilist legislation to assist economic development, judges increasingly interpreted statutes and common law rules in an "instrumentalist" fashion. If courts strictly adhered to precedent, a judge of the New York Supreme Court declared in 1799, "we must hope of little improvement in our commercial code. A single decision, though founded on mistake, would become of binding force, and by repetition, error might be . . . heaped on error." Therefore, "we are at liberty," another New York high court judge argued in 1802, "to adopt such a construction as shall most subserve the solid interests of this growing country."

John Marshall, Chief Justice of the United States Supreme Court from 1801 to 1835, embraced judicial activism and legal instrumentalism. As a Federalist, he gave these doctrines a conservative and nationalistic twist. In *Marbury v. Madison* (1803), Marshall declared that the Supreme Court could decide the constitutionality of congressional legislation. Two decades later, in *Cohens v. Virginia* (1821), the chief justice ruled that verdicts of state courts could be appealed to the Supreme Court. These decisions were indicative of both the increasing centralization of the judicial system and its role as the arbiter of constitutional legitimacy.

Marshall's conservatism became evident in a series of decisions regarding property rights. Most state constitutions contained "Bills of Rights" that protected the property, religious beliefs, and personal liberty of their citizens from arbitrary governmental actions. The Fifth Amendment to the Constitution similarly prohibited the national government from depriving citizens of their liberty or property without "due process" of law. These guarantees were both procedural and substantive. In procedural terms, the court system resolved disputes in a legal forum that was fairly free from political interference and private passion. And certain substantive rights were established, which even representative governments could not infringe.

Marshall interpreted these constitutional guarantees to give maximum protection to existing (or "vested") property rights. Article I, Section 10, of the Constitution barred the states from enacting any "law impairing the obligation of contracts." In the case of *Fletcher v. Peck* (1810), Marshall ruled that a land grant made by the Georgia legislature constituted such a contract. Therefore, he asserted, the original grant could not be cancelled by a subsequent legislature, even though it had been obtained through fraud and bribery. Similarly, in *Dartmouth College v. Woodward* (1819), Marshall declared that the royal charter of 1769 gave the college "corporate powers and privileges." Hence, he ruled that the New Hampshire legislature could not change the charter to make the college into a public university.

The *Dartmouth College v. Woodward* decision had far-reaching economic implications. By equating charters with contracts, Marshall extended the contract clause of the Constitution so as to protect corporations as well as individuals. As Chancellor Kent pointed out, the decision threw "an impregnable barrier around all rights and franchises derived from the grant of government." Using this decision, turnpike, canal, and banking corporations avoided regulation by the state governments that originally had chartered them. "The government must control these institutions," the attorney for the state of New Hampshire warned, "or they shall control the government."

Judges with republican political philosophies heeded this warning. On the whole, they were less concerned with protecting vested property rights than encouraging economic development. In 1795, for example, the Massachusetts legislature enacted the Mill Dam Act. This legislation allowed owners of grain and textile mills to flood adjacent farming lands if they paid an annual rent. Although the act deprived farmers of the use of their lands without their consent and "without due process of law," it was upheld by the Massachusetts Supreme Judicial Court. In *Stonewell v. Flagg* (1914), the court barred farmers from using normal legal procedures, such as a suit at law for trespass, to reclaim the use of their flooded property. It was "the design of the legislature . . . to favor the owners of mills," Chief Justice Parker proclaimed, "as the law is, so we must declare it."

These judges followed legal philosophies that contrasted sharply with Marshall's support for vested property rights. In *Palmer v. Mulligan* (1805), a New York mill-owner attempted to use common law principles (which gave priority to the first user of a resource) to prevent the construction of another mill on the same river. Denying his petition, the New York Supreme Court declared that monopolies based on doctrines of prior use were contrary to the "public" interest, "which always [benefits from] . . . competition and rivalry."

The conflict among the legal philosophies of various influential judges indicated the central importance of the legal system in the American economy. State governments intervened continuously in economic affairs, enacting legislation that favored some social groups at the expense of others. Lawyers and judges acted similarly, protecting the economic rights of their clients and giving their own definitions to rights of property. What they claimed was the public interest was in fact a fragmented and competing set of private rights.

The evolution of contract law clearly showed the increasing primacy of individual goals in legal doctrine and in economic reality. In the 1790s, some lawyers and judges, such as Francis Dana and Theophilus Parsons of Massachusetts, argued that "the existing rights of the public" should not be infringed by private contracts. In fact, some jurists of the time still supported the older "equitable" theory of contract, which permitted courts to intervene to ensure a fair result even in agreements between two private parties. "It would be a great mischief to the community, and a reproach to the justice of the country," Chancellor Desaussure of South Carolina argued in 1817, "if contracts of very great inequality, obtained . . . by the skillful management of intelligent men, . . . could not be examined into, and set aside."

Gradually, the equitable theory of contract gave way to a "will" theory, which upheld private bargains made by individuals, regardless of their intrinsic justice. The single case of *Seymour v. Delancey*, decided differently by two courts, dramatically exemplifies this transition in legal doctrine. In 1822, Chancellor James Kent of New York refused to uphold a contract exchanging two farms for two town lots.

''The village lots were not worth half the value of the country farms,'' he wrote, and such a ''hard bargain'' was not ''fair and just.'' Two years later, a higher state court reversed Kent's verdict. This court argued that the parties had freely entered into the transaction and were in the best position to determine its fairness. ''Purchases are constantly made upon speculation,'' the court pointed out, ''[and] the value of real estates is fluctuating.'' Hence, it concluded, courts should intervene in private contracts only when there was ''flagrant and palpable'' fraud.

This innovation in legal theory, in combination with changes in the laws of property and negligence, facilitated the expansion of the market economy and the triumph of a capitalist system of business ethics. In *The Wealth of Nations* (1776), the Scottish economist Adam Smith posited the existence of an ''invisible hand'' that brought buyers and sellers previously unknown to one another together in large-scale markets and regulated their transactions. In fact, Smith's ''invisible hand'' consisted of the legal rules of contracts and of the courts that enforced them. Therefore, the newly powerful judicial system created the institutional and ideological foundation of the emergent market economy.

The creation of the legal foundation of a capitalist society was a major achievement of the years between 1790 and 1820. With the national government, the systems of public finance, the political parties, and the policies of state mercantilism, it formed a new institutional matrix. This new and complex political framework would shape the identities and aspirations of millions of Americans in the materialistic and nationalistic world of the nineteenth century.

10

Through the Prism of Folklore

Sterling Stuckey

Only in recent years have historians discovered the value of studying folklore to get a picture of slave attitudes and acts of rebellion. By using common perceptions and symbols expressed in Spirituals and folk tales, the slaves consistently outwitted their white "masters." Sterling Stuckey analyzes the nature of these communications.

It is not excessive to advance the view that some historians, because they have been so preoccupied with demonstrating the absence of significant slave revolts, conspiracies, and "day to day" resistance among slaves, have presented information on slave behavior and thought which is incomplete indeed. They have, devoted very little attention to trying to get "inside" slaves to discover what bondsmen thought about their condition. Small wonder we have been saddled with so many stereotypical treatments of slave thought and behavior.

Though we do not know enough about the institution of slavery or the slave experience to state with great precision how slaves felt about their condition, it is reasonably clear that slavery, however draconic and well supervised, was not the hermetically sealed monolith—destructive to the majority of slave personalities—that some historians would have us believe. The works of Herbert Aptheker, Kenneth Stampp, Richard Wade, and the Bauers, indicate that slavery, despite its brutality, was not so "closed" that it robbed most of the slaves of their humanity.

It should, nevertheless, be asserted at the outset that blacks could not have survived the grim experience of slavery unscathed. Those historians who, for example, point to the dependency complex which slavery engendered in many Afro-Americans, offer us an important insight into one of the most harmful effects of that institution upon its

Reprinted from "Through the Prism of Folklore: The Black Ethos in Slavery," *The Massachusetts Review*, 1968, by permission of *The Massachusetts Review*, Inc.

victims. That slavery caused not a few bondsmen to question their worth as human beings—this much, I believe, we can posit with certitude. What is at issue is not whether American slavery was harmful to slaves but whether, in their struggle to control self-lacerating tendencies, the scales were tipped toward a despair so consuming that most slaves, in time, became reduced to the level of "Sambos."

My thesis, which rests on an examination of folk songs and tales, is that slaves were able to fashion a life style and set of values—an ethos—which prevented them from being imprisoned altogether by the definitions which the larger society sought to impose. This ethos was an amalgam of Africanisms and New World elements which helped slaves, in Guy Johnson's words, "feel their way along the course of American slavery, enabling them to endure. . . ." In short, I shall contend that the process of dehumanization was not nearly as pervasive as Stanley Elkins would have us believe; that a very large number of slaves, guided by this ethos, were able to maintain their essential humanity.

II

Frederick Douglass, commenting on slave songs, remarked his utter astonishment, on coming to the North, "to find persons who could speak of the singing among slaves as evidence of their contentment and happiness."

> They (spirituals) are the music of an unhappy people, of the children of disappointment; they tell of death and suffering and unvoiced longing toward a truer world, of misty wanderings and hidden ways.

Though few historians have been interested in such wanderings and ways, Frederick Douglass, probably referring to the spirituals, said the songs of slaves represented the sorrows of the slave's heart, serving to relieve the slave "only as an aching heart is relieved by its tears."

Sterling Brown, has observed: "As the best expression of the slave's deepest thoughts and yearnings, they (the spirituals) speak with convincing finality against the legend of contented slavery." Rejecting the formulation that the spirituals are mainly otherworldly, Brown states that though the creators of the spirituals looked toward heaven and "found their triumphs there, they did not blink their eyes to trouble here." . . . these songs, in Brown's opinion, "tell of this life, of 'rollin' through an unfriendly world!" To substantiate this view, he points to numerous lines from spirituals: "Oh, bye and bye, bye and bye, I'm going to lay down this heavy load"; "My way is cloudy"; "Oh, stand the storm, it won't be long, we'll anchor by and by". To those scholars who "would have us believe that when the Negro sang of freedom, he meant only what the whites meant, namely freedom from sin," Brown rejoins:

> Free individualistic whites on the make in a prospering civilization, nursing the American dream, could well have felt their only bondage to be that of sin, and freedom to be religious salvation. But with the drudgery, the hardships, the auction block, the slave-mart, the shackles, and the lash so literally present in the Negro's experience, it is hard to imagine why for the Negro they would remain figurative. The scholars certainly did not make this clear, but rather take refuge in such dicta as: "the slave never contemplated his low condition."

"Are we to believe," asks Brown, "that the slave singing 'I been rebuked, I been scorned, done had a hard time sho's you bawn,' referred to his being outside the true religion?" Sometimes, in these songs, we hear slaves relating to divinities on terms more West African than American. The easy intimacy and argumentation, which come out of a West African frame of reference, can be heard in "Hold the Wind."

> When I get heaven, gwine be at ease,
> Me and my God *gonna do as we please.*
>
> Gonna chatter with the Father, argue with the Son,
> *Tell um 'bout the world I just come from.* (Italics added.)

If there is a tie with heaven in those lines from "Hold the Wind," there is also a clear indication of dislike for the restrictions imposed by slavery.

If slaves could argue with the son of God, then surely, when on their knees in prayer, they would not hesitate to speak to God of the treatment being received at the hands of their oppressors.

> Talk about me much as you please, (2)
> Chillun, talk about me much as you please,
> Gonna talk about you when I get on my knees.

To be sure, there is a certain ambiguity in the use of the word "chillun" in this context. The reference appears to apply to slaveholders.

The spiritual, *Samson,* as Vincent Harding has pointed out, probably contained much more (for some slaves) than mere Biblical implications. Some who sang these lines from *Samson,* Harding suggests, might well have meant tearing down the edifice of slavery. If so, it was the ante-bellum equivalent of today's "burn baby burn."

> He said, "An' if I had-'n my way,"
> He said, "An' if I had-'n my way,"
> He said, "An' if I had-'n my way, I'd tear the build-in' down!"
>
> He said, "And now I got my way, (3)
> And I'll tear this buildin' down."

Both Harriet Tubman and Frederick Douglass have reported that some of the spirituals carried double meanings. Whether most of the slaves who sang those spirituals could decode them is another matter. It seems to me that slaves, as their folktales make eminently clear, used irony repeatedly, especially with animal stories. Their symbolic world was rich. Indeed, the various masks which many put on were not unrelated to this symbolic process. It seems logical to infer that it would occur to more than a few to seize upon some songs, even though created originally for religious purposes, assign another meaning to certain words, and use these songs for a variety of purposes and situations.

At times slave bards created great poetry as well as great music. One genius among the slaves couched his (and their) desire for freedom in a magnificent line of verse. After God's powerful voice had "Rung through Heaven and down in Hell," he sang, "My dungeon shook and my chains, they fell."

In some spirituals, Alan Lomax has written, Afro-Americans turned sharp irony and "healing laughter" toward heaven, again like their West African ancestors, relating on terms of intimacy with God. In one, the slaves have God engaged in a dialogue with Adam:

> "Stole my apples, I believe."
> "No, marse Lord, I spec it was Eve."
> Of this tale there is no mo'
> Eve et the apple and Adam de co'.

Douglass informs us that slaves also sang ironic seculars about the institution of slavery. He reports having heard them sing: "We raise de wheat, dey gib us de corn; We sift de meal, dey gib us de huss; We peel de meat, dey gib us de skin; An dat's de way dey take us in." Slaves would often stand back and see the tragicomic aspects of their situation, sometimes admiring the swiftness of blacks:

Run, nigger, run, de patrollers will ketch you,
Run, nigger run, it's almost day.
Dat nigger run, dat nigger flew;
Dat nigger tore his shirt in two.

In the ante-bellum days, work songs were of crucial import to slaves. As they cleared and cultivated land, piled levees along rivers, piled loads on steamboats, screwed cotton bales into the holds of ships, and cut roads and railroads through forest, mountain, and flat, slaves sang while the white man, armed and standing in the shade, shouted his orders. Through the sense of timing and coordination which characterized work songs well sung, slaves sometimes literally created works of art. These songs not only militated against injuries but enabled the bondsmen to get difficult jobs done more easily by not having to concentrate on the dead level of their work. "In a very real sense the chants of Negro labor," writes Alan Lomax, "may be considered the most profoundly American of all our folk songs, for they were created by our people as they tore at American rock and earth and reshaped it with their bare hands, while rivers of sweat ran down and darkened the dust."

Ol' massa an' ol' missis,
Sittin' in the parlour,
Jus' fig'in' an' a-plannin'
How to work a nigger harder.

Missus in the big house,
Mammy in the yard,
Missus holdin' her white hands,
Mammy workin' hard (3)
Missus holdin' her white hands,
Mammy workin' hard.

Old Marse ridin' all time,
Niggers workin' round,
Marse sleepin' day time,
Niggers diggin' in the ground, (3)
Marse sleepin' day time,
Niggers diggin' in the ground.

Courlander tells us that the substance of the work songs "ranges from the humorous to the sad, from the gentle to the biting, and from the tolerant to the unforgiving." The statement in a given song can be metaphoric, tangent or direct, the meaning personal or impersonal. Pride on their strength rang with the downward thrust of axe—

When I was young and in my prime, (hah!)
Sunk my axe deep every time, (hah!)

Blacks later found their greatest symbol of manhood in John Henry, descendant of Trickster John of slave folk tales:

A man ain't nothing but a man,
But before I'll let that steam driver beat me down.
I'll die with my hammer in my hand.

Though Frances Kemble, an appreciative and sensitive listener to work songs, felt that "one or two barbaric chants would make the fortune of an opera," she was on one occasion "displeased not a little" by a self-deprecating song, one which "embodied the opinion that "twenty-six black girls not make mulatto yellow girl,' and as I told them I did not like it, they have since omitted it," What is pivotal here is not the presence of self-laceration in folklore, but its extent and meaning. While folklore contained some self-hatred, on balance it gives no indication whatever that blacks, as a group, liked or were indifferent to slavery, which is the issue.

To be sure, only the most fugitive of songs sung by slaves contained direct attacks upon the system. Two of these were associated with slave rebellions. The first, possibly written by ex-slave Denmark Vesey himself, was sung by slaves on at least one island off the coast of Charleston, South Carolina, and at meetings convened by Vesey in Charleston. Though obviously not a folksong, it was sung by the folk.

Hail! all hail! ye Afric clan,
Hail! ye oppressed, ye Afric band,
Who toil and sweat in slavery bound
And when your health and strength are gone
Are left to hunger and to mourn,
Let independence be your aim,
Ever mindful what 'tis worth.
Pledge your bodies for the prize.
Pile them even to the skies!

The second, a popular song derived from a concrete reality, bears the marks of a conscious authority:

You mought be rich as cream
And drive you coach and four-horse team,
But you can't keep de world from moverin' round
Nor Nat Turner from gainin' ground.

And your name it mought be Caesar sure,
And got you cannon can shoot a mile or more,
But you can't keep de world from moverin' round
Nor Nat Turner from gainin' ground.

The introduction of Denmark Vesey, class leader in the A.M.E. Church, and Nat Turner, slave preacher, serves to remind us that some slaves and ex-slaves were violent as well as humble.

It is also well to recall that the religious David Walker, who had lived close to slavery in North Carolina, and Henry Highland Garnett, ex-slave and Presbyterian minister, produced two of the most inflammatory, and vitriolic, polemics America has yet seen. There was theological tension here, loudly proclaimed, a tension which emanated from and was perpetuated by American slavery and race prejudice. This dimension of ambiguity must be kept in mind, if for no other reason than to place in bolder relief the possibility that a great many slaves and free Afro-Americans could have interpreted Christianity in a way quite different from white Christians.

Even those songs which seemed most otherworldly, those which expressed profound weariness of spirit and even faith in death, through their unmistakable sadness, were accusatory, and God was not their object. If one accepts as a given that some of these appear to be almost wholly escapist, the indictment is no less real. Thomas Wentworth Higginson came across one—". . . a flower of poetry in that dark soil," he called it.

I'll walk in de graveyard, I'll walk through de graveyard,
    To lay dis body down.
I'll lie in de grave and stretch out my arms,
    Lay dis body down.

There seems to be small doubt that Christianity contributed in large measure to a spirit of patience which militated against open rebellion among the bondsmen. Yet to overemphasize this point leads one to obscure a no less important reality: Christianity, after being reinterpreted and recast by slave bards, also contributed to that spirit of endurance which powered generations of bondsmen, bringing them to that decisive moment when for the first time a real choice was available to scores of thousands of them.

When that moment came, some slaves who were in a position to decide for themselves did so. W. E. B. DuBois re-created their mood and the atmosphere in which they lived.

> There came the slow looming of emancipation. Crowds and armies of the unknown, inscrutable, unfathomable Yankees; cruelty behind and before; rumors of a new slave trade, but slowly, continuously, the wild truth, the bitter truth, the magic truth, came surging through. There was to be a new freedom! And a black nation went tramping after the armies no matter what it suffered; no matter how it was treated, no matter how it died.

The gifted bards, by creating songs with an unmistakable freedom ring, songs which would have been met with swift, brutal repression in the antebellum days, probably voiced the sentiments of all but the most degraded and dehumanized. Perhaps not even the incredulous slavemaster could deny the intent of the new lyrics. "In the wake of the Union Army and in the contraband camps," remarked Sterling Brown, "spirituals of freedom sprang up suddenly. . . . Some celebrated the days of Jubilo: 'O Freedom; O Freedom!' and 'Before I'll be a slave, I'll be buried in my grave!', and 'Go home to my lord and be free,' " And there was: "No more driver's lash for me. . . . Many thousand do.' "

DuBois brought together the insights of the poet and historian to get inside the slaves:

> There was joy in the South. It rose like perfume—like a prayer. Men stood quivering. Slim dark girls, wild and beautiful with wrinkled hair, wept silently; young women, black, tawny, white, and golden, lifted shivering hands, and old and broken mothers, black and gray, raised great voices and shouted to God across the fields, and up to the rocks and the mountains.

Some sang:

> Slavery chain done broke at last, broke at last, broke at last,
> Slavery chain done broke at last,
> Going to praise God till I die.
>
> I did tell him how I suffer,
> In de dungeon and de chain,
> *And de days I went with head bowed down,*
> And my broken flesh and pain,
> Slavery chain done broke at last, broke at last, broke at last.

Whatever the nature of the shocks generated by the war, among those vibrations felt were some that had come from Afro-American singing ever since the first Africans were forcibly brought to these shores. DuBois was correct when he said that the new freedom song had not come from Africa, but that "the dark throb and beat of that

Ancient of Days was in and through it.'' Thus, the psyches of those who gave rise to and provided widespread support for folk songs had not been reduced to *tabulae rasae* on which a slave-holding society could at pleasure sketch out its wish-fulfillment fantasies.

We have already seen the acute degree to which some slaves realized they were being exploited. Their sense of the injustice of slavery made it so much easier for them to act out their aggression against whites (by engaging in various forms of ''day to day'' resistance) without being overcome by a sense of guilt, or a feeling of being ill-mannered. To call this nihilistic thrashing about would be as erroneous as to refer to their use of folk lore as esthetic thrashing about. For if they did not regard themselves as the equals of whites in many ways, their folklore indicates that the generality of slaves must have at least felt superior to whites morally. And that, in the context of oppression, could make the difference between a viable human spirit and one crippled by the belief that the interests of the master are those of the slave.

When it is borne in mind that slaves created a large number of extraordinary songs and greatly improved a considerable proportion of the songs of others, it is not at all difficult to believe that they were conscious of the fact that they were leaders in the vital area of art—giving protagonists rather than receiving pawns. And there is some evidence that slaves were aware of the special talent which they brought to music. Higginson has described how reluctantly they sang from hymnals—''even on Sunday''—and how ''gladly'' they yielded ''to the more potent excitement of their own 'spirituals.' '' ''They soon found,'' commented Alan Lomax, ''that when they sang, the whites recognized their superiority as singers, and listened with respect.'' He might have added that those antebellum whites who listened probably seldom understood.

What is of pivotal import, however, is that the esthetic realm was the one area in which slaves knew they were not inferior to whites. Small wonder that they borrowed many songs from the larger community, then quickly invested them with their own economy of statement and power of imagery rather than yield to the temptation of merely repeating what they had heard. Since they were essentially group rather than solo performers, the values inherent in and given affirmation by the music served to strengthen bondsmen in a way that solo music could not have done. In a word, slave singing often provided a form of group therapy, a way in which a slave, in concert with others, could fend off some of the debilitating effects of slavery.

The field of inquiry would hardly be complete without some mention of the slave tales. Rich in quantity and often subtle in conception, these tales further illumine the inner world of the bondsmen, disclosing moods and interests almost as various as those found in folksongs. That folk tales, like the songs, indicate an African presence, should not astonish; for the telling of tales, closely related to the African griot's vocation of providing oral histories of families and dynasties, was deeply rooted in West African tradition. Hughes and Bontemps have written that the slaves brought to America the ''habit of storytelling as pastime, together with a rich bestiary.'' Moreover, they point out that the folk tales of slaves ''were actually projections of personal experiences and hopes and defeats, in terms of symbols,'' and that this important dimension of the tales ''appears to have gone unnoticed.''

Possessing a repertoire which ranged over a great many areas, perhaps the most memorable tales are those of Br'er Rabbit and John. Br'er Rabbit, now trickster, ladies' man and braggart, now wit, joker and glutton, possessed the resourcefulness, despite his size and lack of strength, to outsmart stronger, larger animals. ''To the slave in his condition,'' according to Hughes and Bontemps, ''the theme of weakness overcoming strength through cunning proved endlessly fascinating.'' John, characterized by a spiritual resilience born of an ironic sense of life, was a secular high priest of mischief and guile who delighted in matching wits with Ole Marster, the ''patterollers,'' Ole Missy, and the devil himself. He was clever enough to sense the absurdity of his predicament and that of white people, smart enough to know the limits of his powers and the boundaries of those of the master class. While not always victorious, even on the spacious plane of the imagination, he could hardly be described as a slave with an inferiority complex. And in this regard it is important to note that his varieties of triumphs, though they sometimes included winning freedom, often realistically cluster about ways of coping with everyday negatives of the system.

Slaves were adept in the art of storytelling, as at home in this area as they were in the field of music. But further discussion of the scope of folklore would be uneconomical, for we have already seen a depth and variety of thought among bondsmen which embarrasses stereotypical theories of slave personality. Moreover, it should be clear by now that there are no secure grounds on which to erect the old, painfully constricted ''Sambo'' structure. For the personalities which lay beneath the plastic exteriors which slaves turned on and off for white people were too manifold to be contained by cheerful, childlike images. Slave folklore, on balance, decisively repudiates the thesis that Negroes *as a group* had internalized "Sambo" traits, committing them, as it were, to psychological marriage.

III

It is one of the curiosities of American historiography that a people who were as productive esthetically as American slaves could be studied as if they had moved in a cultural cyclotron, continually bombarded by devastating, atomizing forces which denuded them of meaningful Africanisms while destroying any and all impulses toward creativity. One historian, for example, has been tempted to wonder how it was ever possible that "*all* this (West African) native resourcefulness and vitality have been brought to such a point of *utter* stultification in America." (Italics added.) This sadly misguided view is, of course, not grounded in any recognition of understanding of the Afro-American dimension of American culture. In any event, there is a great need for students of American slavery to attempt what Gilberto Freyre tried to do for Brazilian civilization—an effort at discovering the contributions of slaves toward the shaping of the Brazilian national character. When such a study has been made of the American slave we shall probably discover that, though he did not rival his Brazilian brother in staging bloody revolutions, the quality and place of art in his life compared favorably. Now this suggests that the humanity of people can be asserted through means other than open and widespread rebellion, a consideration that has not been appreciated in violence-prone America. We would do well to recall the words of F. S. C. Northrop who has observed:

> During the pre-Civil War period shipowners and southern landowners brought to the United States a considerable body of people with a color of skin and cultural values different from those of its other inhabitants. . . . Their values are more emotive, esthetic and intuitive. . . . (These) characteristics can become an asset for our culture. For these are values with respect to which Anglo-American culture is weak.

These values were expressed on the highest level in the folklore of slaves. Through their folklore, black slaves affirmed their humanity and left a lasting imprint on American culture. No study of the institutional aspects of American slavery can be complete, nor can the larger dimensions of slave personality and style be adequately explored, as long as historians continue to avoid that realm in which, as DuBois has said, "the soul of the black slave spoke to man."

In its nearly two and one half centuries of existence, the grim system of American slavery doubtless broke the spirits of uncounted numbers of slaves. Nevertheless, if we look through the prism of folklore, we can see others transcending their plight, appreciating the tragic irony of their condition, then seizing upon and putting to use those aspects of their experience which sustain in the present and renew in the future. We can see them opposing their own angle of vision to that of their oppressor, fashioning their own techniques of defense and aggression in accordance with their own reading of reality and doing those things well enough to avoid having their sense of humanity destroyed.

Slave folklore, then, affirms the existence of a large number of vital, toughminded human beings who, though severely limited and abused by slavery, had found a way both to endure and preserve their humanity in the face of insuperable odds. What they learned about handling misfortune was not only a major factor in their survival as a people, but many of the lessons learned and esthetic standards established would be used by future generations of Afro-Americans in coping with a hostile world. What a splendid affirmation of the hopes and dreams of their slave ancestors that some of the songs being sung in antebellum days are the ones Afro-Americans are singing in the freedom movement today: "Michael, row the boat ashore"; "Just like a tree planted by the water, I shall not be moved."

11

The Jacksonian Character

Edward Pessen

The people and attitudes of Jacksonian Americans is shrouded in the myth of the "common man." In reality the period was not nearly so egalitarian or freedom loving as popularly pictured. Edward Pessen clearly identifies the characteristics of this complex period as seen from the perspective of European travellers.

The pursuit of the essential Jacksonian continues. The elusive fellow has been interpreted as a child of the frontier, the democratic man, the product of equality, an entrepreneurial seeker after the main chance, and as a "venturous conservative" whose feet drew him irresistibly in the direction of speculative profit even as his mind held to "an ideal of a chaste republican order, resisting the seductions" of a dynamic capitalism. Nor do these explanations exhaust the list. These assessments have for the most part been arrived at through indirection, the nature of the man being inferred from the abundant evidence on his nation's behavior. The method is a sensible one and would in fact be the historian's only recourse were no other data available.

There does exist, however, a vast amount of evidence that throws a most direct light on the traits and values of Jacksonians. For not only did Americans themselves observe their fellow countrymen but an army of European, mainly English, visitors swarmed over this country during the Jacksonian era. They subsequently published hundreds of travelers' accounts in response to the great European interest in the young republic and in insatiable American curiosity about what the visitors thought of them. Covering almost every aspect of American civilization—its political, social and economic institutions and in tellectual life.

Reprinted from *Jacksonian American: Society, Personality and Politics,* (Homewood, Ill.: The Dorsey Press, 1969). Reprinted by permission of the author.

Contemporary comments about Americans fall into four not always distinct categories: emotional traits or attributes of personality; mental or intellectual traits; manners, habits or customs; and values—themselves, of course, manifested in behavior. The notorious spitting done by males chewing tobacco is a nice example of a clear-cut *habit* which is distinct from personality and mind, and can be related to values only by the too imaginative. Shrewdness, on the other hand, is a trait that cuts across all lines, reflecting personality, intelligence, and one's appraisal of the scheme of things. In any case the categorization emerged naturally from the observations of contemporaries.

The natural or unspoiled part of his person—precisely that aspect of personality least touched by the artificial or institutional environment that gave distinctiveness to his society—was the most admired feature of the Jacksonian. Dickens found that "by nature [Americans were] frank, brave, cordial, hospitable and affectionate." Marryat took time out from his censure to remark that "at bottom [Americans] are a very good tempered people." Captain Hall was amazed at how even-tempered they were, despite his faultfinding. Harriet Martineau found that westerners were the most pleasant people in the world, a judgment that George Combe would expand to include Americans from the other sections. Charles Murray believed the American people unusually hospitable and cordial, while Peter Neilson was impressed by the small but significant fact that Americans went out of their way to give directions to the traveler. Sir Charles Lyell, the great geologist, was interested above all in the country's rock formations, Cincinnati's "alluvial terraces," for example, attracting more of his attention than did its society. When he did glance up from the fossil flora, however, he noted admiringly that the human fauna behaved with propriety and a wholesome openness.

American generosity was also applauded, if not always by the American people themselves. New Englanders, Miss Martineau was advised in the nation's capital, "do good by mania." She was herself most favorably impressed by "the generous nature of their mutual services." America was the land of assorted benevolent associations, the leaders of which clearly were not themselves suffering from the abuses they sought to correct. Sophisticated critics of a later time might explain their charitableness as only neurotic do-gooding, brought on by emotional discord of one kind or another. It might be due to a too strong or a too weak father, or to the crisis following the disappearance of the traditional opportunities for their privileged class to play its accustomed paternalistic part in society. Jacksonian travelers, less inclined to be psychoanalytical, noted the absence of economic or tangible self-interest in the charitable activities of Americans, and applauded.

If Miss Martineau experienced little impoliteness, a number of the visitors complained of rudeness shown by the Americans either to them or to others. Staring was characteristic and disconcerting. Requests that the plate be passed at hotel or boarding house table often went unheeded, as was true also of requests for removal of hats in theatres. A minister was dismayed to find a church service emptying before he "had scarcely named the text." He had not yet had time to be boring. Fanny Kemble, having been offended once too often by American women who unceremoniously interrupted a nap she was taking on a river boat for no better reason than to glance at the books lying by her side, exclaimed that "no person whatsoever, however ignorant, low or vulgar, in England, would have done such a thing." She attributed such conduct to "the mixture of the republican feeling of equality peculiar to this country and the usual want of refinement common to the lower classes;" together they formed "a singularly felicitous union of impudence and vulgarity, to be met nowhere but America." Miss Kemble's theorizing cannot be confused with Tocqueville's.

The American was curious, sometimes excessively so, according to visitors who felt themselves badgered by incessant questions they not only had no wish to answer but which they considered bad form even to ask. "They cannot bear anything like a secret," was the conclusion of Marryat, one of whose confidants had advised him that the Ursuline Convent had been stormed more because of curiosity about the life behind its sealed gates than out of bigotry.

Humorlessness was allied with dullness. Since the emotions of the people were too restrained, "there is little of what is called *fun* in America," mourned Francis Lieber. Admirable but not lovable, said Hamilton. The visitors were not sure whether Calvinism or other factors were to blame for this unattractive trait. Few blamed it on the weather, as did Beaumont, but many agreed with his verdict on the Americans: "cold as ice."

The cruelty displayed so often and by so many Americans was shocking. Whether tories or liberals, the visitors—with the exception of Lyell and a few others—were repelled at both the system of slavery and at white American attitudes towards Negroes, whether slaves or free. Joseph Pickering was horrified that a respectable crowd could watch, with feelings that ranged from indifference to enthusiasm, as a colored man was burned alive. In Hartford, according to Abdy, "to pelt [colored people] . . . with stones, and cry out nigger! nigger! as they pass, seems to be the pastime of the place." Europeans were dismayed not only by racism but at the cruelty shown unfortunates. Buckingham could understand neither newspapers nor their readers in treating flippantly poverty and misery "that ought to thrill the heart with horror or melt it with pity." Hangings or public executions of any kind attracted vast crowds of "respectable" or obviously well-to-do folk, as well as the other kind. William Dean Howells' father recollected that public hangings used to fill the taverns and grog shops, as thousands of people came from all over the countryside, most of them of "respectable appearance," drawn to the spectacle by "morbid curiosity." One visitor was appalled at the sight of young women cheerfully present at a hanging in New York City.

Violence was a much-observed trait, although it was reported mainly in the south and on the frontier. Personal quarrels occur everywhere but Americans seemed ready to mutilate one another for reasons that Europeans found incredible. In Kentucky one man came near to killing another for opening a coach window. As shocking as the ridiculous reasons for fighting were the extreme forms it took. Stabbing, shooting, gouging out of eyes, biting off of nose or ears were not uncommon. Frontier violence was not too surprising, but what amazed visitors was the proneness of "respectable men" of some standing to throw themselves savagely on someone who had inadvertently provoked them.

Less frightening if not more attractive was the selfishness of Americans. Tocqueville was aware that they could be public-spirited, but he found no one more dedicated to the gratification of his own physical wants than the American. (In his explanation, public-spiritedness was self-interest sensibly pursued.) The bad manners sometimes displayed at the dinner table were regarded by some as nothing more than the behavior of men so preoccupied with satisfying their own wants of the moment that they either ignored requests by others for food or else gave them inferior portions. Combe concluded that there was something in his training that led the American to the ignoble feeling that the purpose of life was nothing more than the satisfaction of "his own good pleasure."

Americans as individuals were wanting in self-confidence. The word "insecure" was not yet the vogue in those happy times but, if it were, it would have been applied to a people who, every day and in every kind of company, asked the visitor, "What do you think of us upon the whole?'' Miss Martineau felt it was not a serious flaw but she admitted that like Captain Hall, she had suffered through innumerable variations on ''the perennial question: 'How do you like America?' ''Hamilton found this ''restless and insatiable appetite for praise, which defies all restraint of common sense,'' one of the ''most remarkable features'' of the American character. Lieber, who came here to stay because he was so delighted with this country, reports being asked, ''Do you think it as fine as the Rhine?''—''What, sir?''—''The Hudson.'' He describes his figurative gnashing of teeth, ''when you enjoy on a hot day a glass of cool, sparkling cider of the best kind, and an officious acquaintance . . . seeing the praise of the liquid in the expression of your face, asks you: ''Now, tell me, is not it equal to any champagne?' The taste is gone at once.'' In Tocqueville's memorable words, the Americans ''unceasingly harass you to extort praise, and if you resist their entreaties, they fall to praising themselves. It would seem as if, doubting their own merit, they wished to have it constantly exhibited before their own eyes.'' They were also insecure amongst one another, according to Abdy, whose explanation of their preoccupation with external appearance or conspicuous display anticipates the better known theories of Tocqueville and Veblen.

Marryat advised those who came after him: do not find fault with them if you seek their hospitality. Tudor referred to the ''extraordinary sensibility to the slightest appearance of dispraise'' as a ''puerility'' which had he ''not witnessed on a thousand occasions (he) . . . should have believed utterly incredible.'' They *demanded* praise. ''Such an unhappily sensitive community surely never existed in this world,'' wrote Fanny Kemble in her journal. An American woman had told her, ''I hear you are going to abuse us dreadfully; of course, you'll wait till you go back to England and then shower it down upon us finely.'' The prediction was not inaccurate, for Miss Kemble did in fact ''shower it down'' upon them, finely. It was hard to insult Americans, however, for as Dickens noted, they quickly cited their newness as a country as the excuse for all faults. When the occasion demanded it, Americans could display a very thick skin, indeed, which made them immune to insults, let alone faint praise. ''This man [the American],'' wrote Tocqueville, ''will never understand that he wearies me to death unless I tell him so, and the only way to get rid of him is to make him my enemy for life.'' There is no better proof that when it suited him an American could make himself impervious to criticism than in the friendly reception he gave the book that contains those devastating words.

"The most striking circumstance in the American character," wrote Captain Hall, "was the constant habit of praising themselves." Insecurity and thin skin seemed to go hand in hand with boastfulness. Only a few observers mistook the latter trait for arrogance but almost all of them found it unattractive. Lieber, like Miss Martineau, believed that this "national contentment" was an innocent blemish, in part a simple response to the criticisms of foreigners. She did feel, however, that much of this boasting was absurd, and that combined with the insatiable hunger for flattery, was "the most prominent of their bad habits." It was agreed that Americans, in view of their achievements, had much to be vain about but need they be so wearisome about it? Americans of every sort, in all sections and of every social order, praised to the heavens their weather, their rivers, the speed of their railroads, their political system, their orators, even their roads—which were notoriously bad or at the least discomfiting to a normal human anatomy—and, of course, themselves. Only America had anything worth seeing, according to Mr. Wenham, a typical villager in Cooper's *Home As Found.* An Englishman, to his consternation, read in an American geography text that "the English tongue is spoken in greater purity of idiom and intonation with us (in America) than in Great Britain."

Americans could make a virtue of necessity. That a slaughterhouse was situated in the midst of a residential district, was praised to Mrs. Trollope as an example of the antiaristocratic quality of American society. If Marryat was right, that "Americans are the happiest people in the world in their own delusions" Tocqueville had a logical explanation for it. "As the American participates in all that is done in his country, he thinks himself obliged to defend whatever may be censured in it; for it is not only his country that is then attacked, it is himself. The consequence is that his national pride resorts to a thousand artifices and descends to all the petty tricks of personal vanity."

The boasters were also invertebrate complainers. Harriet Martineau was amazed to hear complaints even against "the confoundedly prosperous" state of the country, not to mention every other variety of phenomenon—with the exception of land, the only thing exempt from abuse. They were particularly enthusiastic in denouncing the people of sections other than their own, invariably describing them to foreigners as the *real* culprits, whatever the ascribed fault. In Marryat's flamboyant description, easterners "pronounce the southerners to be choleric, reckless, regardless of law, and indifferent as to religion; while the southerners designate the eastern states as a nursery of over-reaching pedlars . . . ; Boston turns up her erudite nose at New York; Philadelphia . . . looks down upon both, while New York . . . swears the Bostonians are a parcel of puritanical prigs, and the Philadelphians a would-be aristocracy." " 'Hatred' is not too strong a term for their sectional prejudice," concluded Miss Martineau.

In matters of the mind, the American was above all practical. In Tocqueville's view, his spirit was "averse to general ideas; it does not seek theoretical discoveries." In politics Americans were interested in men more than principles, immediate outcomes and success rather than long-range consequences or ethics. Anti-intellectualism was due in part to an aversion for the nonutilitarian character of the speculative thinking that was done by the learned. Americans therefore preferred newspapers to great literature and were more capable of mechanical invention than of theoretical scientific innovations. The New Englander only represented an exaggeration of a national quality in being "content when he feels a grievance to apply a remedy," or in dealing with "the business of common life [with] . . . practical good sense." Their "fertility of resource," in Martineau's phrase, clearly stemmed from their preoccupation with immediate and tangible problems.

Americans were clever but not profound. Their minds were quick enough in dealing with a practical or a commercial issue, but ostensibly incapable of appreciating or coping with intellectual problems of a fundamental sort. Nurture triumphed over nature in this instance, since shrewdness was a characteristic of the American mind largely because it was so admired an ideal in the American scheme of things. The most sympathetic observers conceded not only that an unattractive cunning characterized their thinking, but that New Englanders, believed to be its arch practitioners, were generally admired for their gift. "Smart dealings" or a shrewdness which "gilds over many a swindle and gross breach of trust," were extolled, as was "every fresh display of low trickery." They smiled approvingly at a "clever villain's witty rogueries." Commercial shrewdness or "commercial frauds" were "generally dignified by the name of intelligence." Pickering expressed a typical judgment when he said that "shrewdness was (one of) the . . . most striking features in the character of an American." If they were not profound, they pretended to be, according to Lieber. He was disturbed at the descent into "verbose and therefore unfelt" cant indulged in by Americans who pretended to a depth of feeling they did not truly have. Cooper and a number of the visitors felt they were shallow. Their skewed sense of values testified to this. "Hint to them that they eat peas with a knife, and they are highly enraged; tell them that their conduct to the 'niggers' is inhuman and unmanly, and they laugh in your face," reported Abdy. Tocqueville's conclusion was that their paltry concerns and preoccupations turned them ultimately into paltry men. "They strain their faculties to the utmost to achieve paltry results, and this cannot fail speedily to limit their range of view and to circumscribe their powers."

They were not gifted conversationalists. Urbane visitors and Americans alike were unhappy with a conversational style that was composed in part of bombast, swearing—if not in "the more polished circles"—a solemnity and dullness particularly ridiculous in view of the lightness of its content, and at the other extreme from their hyperbole, an incommunicativeness that was equally characteristic, particularly in the northeast. The laconic style was not a trait of the strong, silent man from the west but rather of a shrewd, selfish, opportunistic man of the city. Mrs. Trollope has given us a verbatim transcript of a marvelous conversation between two New Englanders she overheard while on a boat. It is a bravura example of an art of discourse in which the speaker reveals nothing of importance as he in turn darts questions, probing for weaknesses in his opponent's defenses:

> Well, now, which way may you be traveling?
> I expect this canal runs pretty nearly west.
> Are you going far with it?
> Well, now, I don't rightly know how many miles it may be.
> I expect you'll be from New York?
> Sure enough I have been at New York, often and often.
> I calculate, then, 'tis not there as you stop?
> Business must be minded, in stopping and in stirring.

"So they went on," she writes, "without advancing or giving an inch, 'till I was weary of listening." The harsh conclusion of a number of observers was that though Americans talked at great length they said nothing that was worth hearing.

Americans loved scandal and were quick to believe the worst. Hamilton was amazed that "no villainy is too gross or too improbable to be attributed to a statesman in this intelligent community." A distaste for aristocracy undoubtedly explained in part the delight in the exposure of foibles, actual or alleged. Hone's diary entry for September 22, 1837, reads "*Libels.* Everybody complains of the success which attends the publications of libels on private character; everybody condemns the depravity of the times in which, and the community by which they are encouraged. Everybody wonders how people can buy and read those receptacles of scandals, the penny papers, and yet everybody does encourage them."

A well-known modern theory postulates as the characteristic type of the early 19th century, an inner-directed American, marching to his own music, living his life according to his own and his family's notions as to how it should be lived. Observers during the Jacksonian era saw a very different American, indeed.

Whether the phrase "tyranny of the majority" was too strong, as some of Tocqueville's contemporaries thought it was, there was no doubt that in small things as in large, Americans guided their behavior by the anticipated reactions of their neighbors to it.

Combe was struck that in matters of great moral significance, men feared to affirm what they knew was the right, because of fear of majority opinion.

Mrs. Trollope's book had publicized certain uncouth American habits and customs. She was shortly to be immortalized, since subsequent visitors observed that the cry, "a trollope! a trollope!" went up from American audiences when one of their number happened to be caught in that public slouching that had so offended their critical visitor. Americans slouched in theatres, they slouched in church, they were even discovered slouching when attending sessions of the Supreme Court. At one theatrical performance, Mrs. Trollope had found "the bearing and attitudes of the men perfectly indescribable; the heels thrown higher than the head, the entire rear of the person presented to the audience, the whole length supported on the benches, are among the varieties that these exquisite posture-masters exhibit." Their subsequent attempts to police offenders indicate that Mrs. Trollope's description was not exaggerated. Like a famous statesman of more than a century later who used his shoe in part to show his scorn of the traditional diplomacy and the breeding associated with it, it seems fairly clear that some Americans slouched to political purpose, in their case to display indifference or contempt for the manners of an aristocratic society. Fortunately Mrs. Trollope's strictures had effect and Americans came to see ordinary civility as devoid of social implication.

Americans were great chewers of tobacco and, what was worse, notorious spitters. Poor Miss Kemble discovered that to her "profound disgust," gentlemen too did it. On board a boat, "it was a perfect shower of saliva all the time." Almost every user of public conveyances sounded variations on the theme. "Copious spitting" was the rule. In boarding houses and hotels after a meal, an orgy of spitting would commence—although less fastidious types did not wait for the meal to end. In homes, too, spitting "was incessant, the carpet serving as a receptacle . . . when boxes were not within immediate reach." Even among the upper classes, men of otherwise polished manners indulged themselves, although in all fairness, Boardman observed that the refined would not spit on living room floors. Dickens was amazed that even in the nation's Capitol, in law courts, and hospitals, "in all the public places of America this filthy custom is recognized." Senators and judges were adept in the art. Americans even spit in their sleep. The visitors must have exaggerated for their comments seemed to indicate that spitting threatened to drown the country.

There was some difference of opinion as to whether or not they were drunkards but there was agreement that Americans drank to excess. "Why do they get so confoundedly drunk?" asked Marryat. But Stuart denied that they did, claiming he saw only twelve drunkards during the course of three years. Mrs. Felton's explanation was that Americans drank so much from the time of infancy on, that "by the time they arrive at the years of maturity they become . . . habituated to the practice." She did believe, however, that the excessive number of fires in this country was due largely to the carelessness of people who had imbibed too heavily. To Buckingham as to many others, the love of liquor was one of the great evils ruining the country. Liquor was to be found everywhere, and as Tocqueville noted, at most reasonable rates. He agreed with Hall that its prevalence here was due to the inordinate influence of the common man. Senators were thus afraid to tax so popular a commodity. Jacksonian candidates plied their constituencies with quantities of fiery liquid. Vigne believed that the absence of a law of primogeniture was a major cause of the evil, elder sons burying their disappointments in brandy. Attending a meeting of the Worcester Temperance Society, Baldwin was dismayed to find that all members "drank very freely of cyder . . . of the very worst sort." What must they have drunk in the privacy of their homes?

Drinking went hand in hand with gambling. Oliver found incessant gambling on river boats. Southern boat trips featured all night bouts of drinking and gambling. The latter custom was also closely aligned to speculation. The Jacksonian era was characterized by what

Miss Martineau called a "speculative mania." It would not have been, had the American people not been ready to gamble on the prospects of great future gains. "Everybody is speculating, and everything has become an object of speculation," wrote Chevalier. Shirreff, who liked to believe the best of the Americans, discovered in the west that "speculators have . . . brought up, at high prices, all the building ground in the neighborhood." Back in the east, in 1836, "if two persons were seen conversing in the street of New York . . . in nineteen instances out of twenty, you would have overheard 'lots' and 'thousands of dollars' as the sole topics of their discourse." In *Home As Found,* Cooper includes conversations that appear to be satirical exaggerations of the speed at which the price of a lot could appreciate and speculative fortunes be made. A Hone diary entry for January 14, 1835, when the bubble was still short of the bursting point, shows that truth was the source of Cooper's fiction. Unbelievable appreciation of the price of real estate did occur.

America the land of plenty was admired but American eating habits were not. Observers held that most Americans were gluttons or something close to it. They were accused of eating huge quantities of poorly prepared food with the manners and perhaps the charm of certain barnyard animals. In fairness to the critics, they did concede that their evidence was based not on what went on in American homes but outside of them. There seemed to be a touch of sour grapes in some of the envious comment of the visitors. This country had an unbelievable abundance of the most admired foods, particularly meats, fowl, and dairy products, easily available to ordinary persons. The visitors copied down menus with great relish; in fact they reported nothing so fully or so vividly. Since Horace was not above reporting in some detail the menu of heroic Roman feasts, perhaps a detailed report on Jacksonian delicacies, as contemporaries observed them, will be forgiven.

Visitors were disconcerted most by the American style at the dinner table. Speed and silence were the rule. Huge amounts were swallowed at breakneck speed; woe to the man who dawdled. The "extraordinary rapidity" with which food was gorged or "pitchforked down" fascinated some observers, although Miss Martineau was disquieted at the "celerity" of the American attack. Even more depressing was the absence of that pleasant talk that gave charm to a table or, in the words of the ancients, turned feeding into dining. The stillness of death was one common metaphor used to describe the atmosphere at the American table; another spoke of animal gratification.

Marryat expressed the popular belief that the American "eats his meals with the rapidity of a wolf," in order to rush to his business or practical affairs. And yet it was also noted that on some occasions Americans rushed through a meal in order to do nothing better than to lounge, chew, and spit in another room.

The consensus was that the American was unrefined. Murray found middle-class Americans "deficient in those lighter accomplishments" which constitute charm, while Cooper bemoaned American ignorance of music—"which elevates and refines human tastes"—and in addition found his countrymen "wanting in most of the higher tastes."

High on the American's scale of values was his egalitarian belief that one man—particularly an American—was as good as any other, certainly that he should be treated like any other. White Americans simply would not be known as "servants." Those who worked in other people's homes would not be summoned by bells. The word "mister" was omitted from door plates. One visitor ran into a tailor who would not go to him to take the measure of a coat, insisting it was "not republican," and a carriage driver who complained that the travelers on his coach "had had private meals every day and not asked him to the table."

Many European visitors and, for that matter, Americans, were not particularly charmed by the American stress on egalitarianism, believing as did Cooper and Hone that it was responsible for the sordid manners and mean quality of American life, or like Tocqueville, that because of it liberty was downgraded. They took a dim view of the glorification of that same common man whose traits they found so depressing. Other visitors also agreed with Cooper, John Quincy Adams and other Americans that for all the lip service they paid to equality, Americans in fact practised the same forms of inequality as Europeans, the one great difference being that in this country money rather than blood divided men into rigidly separated worlds. In a word, Americans were hypocrites.

The transcendent American value according to most contemporaries was materialism. The distinguishing feature of the American was his love of money. "At the bottom of all that an American does," wrote Chevalier, "is money; beneath every word, money." His sacrifices, when made, "are systematic and calculated. It is neither enthusiasm nor passion that unties his purse strings, but motives of policy . . . in which he feels his own private interests to be involved." His motto is,

"Victory or death! But to him, victory is to make money, to get the dollars, to make a fortune out of nothing. . . ."

The love of money had dismal side effects. It corrupted Americans, preoccupying them with vulgar displays of wealth or, in Miss Martineau's phrase, a "mean love of distinction." Tudor felt that it discouraged an appreciation of nature. Grund was startled to find theatre audiences who on the one hand counted the house at a performance of *Othello,* and on the other applauded Iago's admiration of a full purse. Hall blamed the love of money for all manner of American ills, including their indifference to women! How could there be time, interest or skill for pursuing the amenities in "a country where all men are engaged in one and the same engrossing pursuit—namely, that of making money (?)" DeRoss was present when "a young lady, talking of the most eligible class of life from which to choose a husband, declared that, for her part, she was all for the Commissions." His friend, a major, beamed happily until he found out that she meant commission merchants. Since the love of money was actually a love for the material things that money could buy, Dickens advised that "it would be well . . . for the American people as a whole if they loved the Real less, and the Ideal somewhat more." He agreed with Miss Martineau that nothing spoiled the American character more than their vulgar materialism.

Americans were snobs, though this trait and value was manifested mainly by the better sort or those who pretended to be, according to Miss Martineau. A New York female complained to Abdy that the marriage phrase should be, "wilt thou have this *lady,*" etc., while in Philadelphia, a sensible woman advised him that his "report on American manners and customs would be discredited or undervalued by his countrymen when it was known that [he] . . . had travelled with stage-drivers and conversed freely with working people." Great pains were taken by urban society circles to maintain the separation between them and lesser groups.

If those near the top were snobs, those below were social climbers. Vigne told a much-repeated tale: "The captain of a steamboat . . . happened to ask rather loudly, 'General, a little fish?' and was immediately answered in the affirmative by 25 of the 30 gentlemen that were present." Murray found "the tavern kept by a general, wagon wheels mended by a colonel, day laborers and mechanics are gentlemen." Lieber ridiculed the constant name changes that were designed to suggest a respectable origin. He believed that insanity was caused in America by "a diseased anxiety to be equal to the wealthiest, the craving for wealth and consequent disappointment which ruins the intellect of many."

Inevitably materialists and champions of equality had no respect for tradition. Americans "have no love for anything merely because it is old," observed Thomson. They were "so mutable, so much given to change . . . that [he] . . . had scarcely met with one who knew who his grandfather was." One visitor found something "cool and heartless," a sign of disrespect for the dead, in their funerals, performed in too great a hurry. Another was upset that the burial places of national heroes were so poorly kept. In Hall's indictment, "the unpleasant truth seems to be, that nothing whatsoever is venerated in America merely on account of its age, or, indeed on any other account. Neither historical associations, nor high public services, nor talents, nor knowledge, claim any peculiar reverence for the busy generation of the present hour."

Their disrespect for tradition merged into disrespect for law. Europeans were startled to observe a jury munching on food, the foreman announcing a verdict with his mouth full. Vigne blamed the spirit of equality for a courtroom informality in which lawyers sat casually on tables while judges spat. As a result of the growing feeling of self-importance on the part of the people, Chevalier believed, "the reverence for the laws (was) . . . wearing out with the Americans." In the case of so selfish a population, "the laws had no force when they jarred with interest."

Americans valued neither learning nor intellectual accomplishment. The attempt to limit medical practice to the trained, was resisted by Jacksonians. Tocqueville believed that "in no country in the civilized world [was] . . . less attention paid to philosophy than in the United States." Others expanded the charge to include literature and learning in general. Most visitors agreed with Mrs. Trollope that pure learning held little attraction to the American mind, the "pursuit of wealth" drawing it in other directions. Able sons were trained for business; a "poor boy who is a little hard of hearing, and rather slow of comprehension, shall go to college." Scholars were held in low repute because they commanded low incomes, the results of their intellectual efforts having little market value.

Americans seemed to have contempt for life. They blandly acquiesced in terrible steamboat accidents caused by faulty construction—"What are a few hundred persons more or less?" Hone wrote sarcastically in his diary, after a particularly terrible accident. The lust for profits overrode all other considerations, according to him. Americans were accused of manifesting an "utter want of . . . sympathy for the sufferings of others." They seemed ready on the slightest provocation to shoot or stab, particularly in the west and south. Murder was often lightly punished by the law, as was lynching. Duelists, often fighting over ridiculous alleged slights to their honor, in fact dueled not to satisfy honor but to kill. Marryat was surprised at the intensive practice by the involved parties prior to a duel. In this sense, certainly, Andrew Jackson captured very well the spirit of the times.

Some observers found glaring contradictions between American lip service and practice or between their professed and actual values, recording their judgments in a series of trenchant summaries. Americans were thus ambitious but lacking in lofty ambition. They talked up liberty but restricted its practice. They talked of lofty things in the absence of lofty feelings. Grund had been told, "in the absence of enthusiasm, which would inspire them with natural eloquence, they seek to maintain themselves at a certain elevation by pressing hard on lofty topics; having no wings, they endeavor to support themselves in the air by a *parachute*." Their principles were high but "their civilization and morals fall far below." They spoke glowingly of equality but strained to demonstrate their own exalted station. They loved change but dreaded revolution. Their bodies were in constant motion but their minds were inert. They loved to talk but had nothing to say. They were avid readers but preferred newspaper gossip to literature. They were in a constant "election fever" but cold to political principles. They had appetites but no passions. And finally, they knew how to make money but not how to spend it. This mournful catalog was dubious tribute to a people who were regarded as something less than they seemed.

The portrait of the Jacksonian drawn by his contemporary observers is of a good-natured but essentially shallow man: clever but not profound, self-important but uncertain, fond of deluding himself, living almost fanatically for the flesh (although not knowing too well how), straining every fibre to accumulate the things he covets and amoral about the methods to be used, a hypocrite who strains at gnats and swallows camels, an energetic and efficient fellow albeit a small one, who takes comfort in—as well as his standards of behavior from—numbers. It is not a very attractive picture.

What are we to make of him? There are several things he seems clearly not to be. This is no child of the frontier, neither his ways nor his values having much to do with Indian fighting. The people who lived in western towns imitated their eastern brethren, while the small minority living on the western outskirts of civilization, who were engaged in conversation by enterprising travelers, disclosed values very similar to those of their countrymen. This conformist was no inner-directed man. And there is little evidence that our Jacksonian, as he pursued the main chance, looked back longingly to a "chaste, republican" past. His thoughts were for today, while by a better, he meant a wealthier, tomorrow.

Possibly his materialism is his most significant characteristic, explaining as it does, not only his goals but so many of his ways and other values. What better explanation is there of his disinterest in the idealistic and reform movements which, while they proliferated during the era, commanded so little actual membership? What did it matter that some women felt unfulfilled or that colored persons were everywhere treated as less than human? What was it to him that his society might maldistribute status, so long as it promised to provide tangible comforts?

His values and intellectual traits appear to throw some light on his political and economic choices. Bigotry, supplemented by cruelty and cupidity, better explain atrocities against Indians and Negroes. Vanity and boastfulness made it easy for him to believe that his country—which was himself writ large—was superior to all others and could do no wrong. That much-admired pragmatic temper which rendered his mind indifferent to theories or fundamental principles, when combined with his lack of respect for learning, seemed to have a number of political consequences. For looked at one way, it was child's play for shrewd manipulators who sought his vote to convince this hard-headed, unlearned fellow that politics was a kind of simple morality play: good leaders v. bad, honest men v. dishonest, the people's friends v. their enemies. The unique American major party that was born during the era—which is many if not all things to most if not all men, which avoids or deflects crucial issues rather than meet them—is perfectly suited to the man who has neither interest in "fundamental principles" nor the wit to perceive them.

Our Jacksonian's lack of intellectual sophistication may account for his blissful unawareness of the central banking, or any other complex function, performed by the second Bank of the United States, and help explain the enthusiastic support he gave to those who would rid the nation of the monster of paper money by destroying the institution that best restrained its unlimited circulation. On the other hand, a combination of lust for gain, shrewdness and hypocrisy may have accounted for his zeal in overthrowing what he well understood to be the great obstacle to the speculative profits his dreams were made on. On a more general level, disinterest in the "principles" operating in his economy, would help explain his indifference to informed criticisms of its weaknesses, while his penchant for social climbing spurred him on to try to get what he could for himself. Finally, his conformity would explain his acquiescence even in policies he might secretly disapprove of or about which he might have qualms.

Jacksonians liked to think that Americans were different from—and of course better than—other people. Students of history, however, will have recognized many familiar traits, some of them manifested as long ago and far away as first-century Rome, whose gross new ways were so decried by spokesmen of the old patrician order. These were traits that sprang up where a booming commercial economy was emerging. It is by no means certain that there had been significant changes in this country from Washington's era to Jackson's, significant, that is, with regard to national character. Europeans, not having been here before, had no way of knowing whether change had occurred. They did, however, have that freshness of viewpoint that so often enables the foreigner to see things the native overlooks. Nothing was too commonplace for them, they took nothing for granted.

That the portrait they drew was not a very attractive one can be interpreted in ways flattering to the American psyche. (Of course such an interpretation runs the risk of itself being interpreted as a modern example of the American refusal to accept criticism.) In this country the mass of inhabitants, whether appealing or not, were at least *visible,* downright loquacious, inevitably unattractive to the urbane observers who wrote about them. My point is that the European counterpart of the Jacksonian common man was comparatively powerless and inarticulate, no object of fascination to an army of interested reporters. The American was sometimes admired, more often criticized, but in either case treated with a respect that was the more meaningful for being unspoken. Like him or not, he had to be reckoned with.

12

A Nation of Drunkards

W. J. Rorabaugh

The hard working frontier farmer, the urban day laborer, the preacher of the Word, and the most modest of females in the early nineteenth century are rarely portrayed as drunkards, but many were. In his insightful and disturbing study of American alcoholic behavior, W. J. Rorabaugh clearly demonstrates that many Americans were heavy drinkers and that alcohol was one of the most serious social problems in the young Republic.

Was early nineteenth-century America really a nation of drunkards? Certainly the clergymen who were crusading for temperance thought so, as excerpts from their sermons and addresses attest. These self-appointed moral guardians, convinced that a hearty indulgence in alcohol was commonplace, increasing, and unprecedented, were filled with apprehension, their sermons filled with despair. Intemperance, they warned, was widespread, "too obvious not to be noticed;" "so common, as scarcely to be thought criminal;" "the fashionable vice of the day." They noted, too, that the United States was among the most addicted of nations, that in this respect it had outstripped all Europe, and that "no other people ever indulged, so universally." Even more alarming in their eyes was the fact that this intemperance was spreading "wider and wider;" "like the plague;" "throughout our country;" "with the rapidity and power of a tempest." Not only did they see excessive use as the crying sin of the nation, but they believed it to be "a *growing* evil;" "*still increasing;*" until America "was fast becoming a nation of drunkards."

A similar alarm was voiced by the nation's most prominent statesmen. It was not so much the use of alcohol that worried them—they all drank to some extent—as its excessive use. George Washington, a

W. J. Rorabaugh, *The Alcoholic Republic*, New York: Oxford University Press, 1973. By permission of Oxford Press.

whiskey distiller himself, thought that distilled spirits were "the ruin of half the workmen in this Country. . . ." John Adams, whose daily breakfast included a tankard of hard cider, asked, ". . . is it not mortifying . . . that we, Americans, should exceed all other . . . people in the world in this degrading, beastly vice of intemperance?" And Thomas Jefferson, inventor of the presidential cocktail party, feared that the use of cheap, raw whiskey was "spreading through the mass of our citizens." In 1821 George Ticknor, a wealthy Boston scholar, warned Jefferson, "If the consumption of spirituous liquors should increase for thirty years to come at the rate it has for thirty years back we should be hardly better than a nation of sots." The Founding Fathers, fearful that the American republic would be destroyed in a flood of alcohol, were anguished and perplexed.

Other observers, more dispassionate but no less articulate, found American drinking habits deplorable. Foreign travellers, for instance, were surprised and shocked at the amount of alcohol they saw consumed. A Swedish visitor, Carl D. Arfwedson, reported a "general addiction to hard drinking," while a visitor from England, Isaac Holmes, noted that intoxication pervaded all social classes. It was not surprising that Basil Hall, a retired Royal Navy Captain hostile to the new nation's democratic ideals, should be "perfectly astonished at the extent of intemperance." But even the sympathetic English reformer, William Cobbett, deplored American tippling. "I almost wished," he wrote, "that there were Boroughmongers here to *tax* these drinkers."

The more discerning visitors observed that while heavy drinking was widespread, public drunkenness was not common. This fact led William Dalton to suggest that Americans better deserved the appellation of tipplers than of drunkards. Infrequency of conspicuous drunkenness, however, was not inconsistent with an extensive overuse of alcohol. As a shrewd Scot by the name of Peter Neilson pointed out, the nation's citizens were "in a certain degree *seasoned,* and consequently it [was] by no means common to see an American *very* much intoxicated." In other words, as a result of habitual heavy drinking Americans had developed a high degree of tolerance for alcohol. Even so, in the opinion of Isaac Candler, Americans were "certainly not so sober as the French or Germans, but perhaps," he guessed, "about on a level with the Irish."

American travellers expressed similar views. They found "a great want of economy in the use of spirituous liquors," noted that drunkenness was "everywhere prevalent," and pronounced the quantity of alcohol consumed to be "scandalous." The well-travelled Anne Roy-

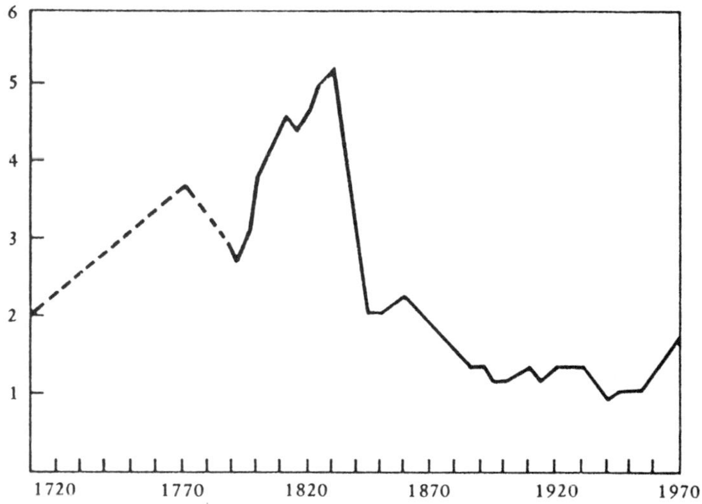

Chart 1.1. Annual consumption of distilled spirits (i.e., rum, whiskey, gin, brandy) per capita, in U.S. gallons.

all, who spent much of her life crisscrossing the country in stage coaches, wrote, "When I was in Virginia, it was too much whiskey—in Ohio, too much whiskey—in Tennessee, it is too, too much whiskey!"

It was the consensus, then, among a wide variety of observers that Americans drank great quantities of alcohol. The beverages they drank were for the most part distilled liquors, commonly known as spirits—whiskey, rum, gin, and brandy. On the average those liquors were 45 percent alcohol, or, in the language of distillers, 90 proof. It was the unrestrained consumption of liquors of such potency that amazed travellers and alarmed so many Americans. And there was cause for alarm. During the first third of the nineteenth century the typical American annually drank more distilled liquor than at any other time in our history.

A brief survey of American alcohol consumption from the colonial period to the present will help us put the early nineteenth century in proper perspective. As Chart 1.1 shows, during the colonial period the annual per capita consumption of hard liquor, mostly rum, reached 3.7 gallons. After the Revolution, because of decreased trade with the West Indies, high import duties on West Indian rum and on the West Indian molasses from which New England rum was made, and a new tax on domestic whiskey, the consumption of distilled liquors declined by one-quarter. But by 1800, prosperity, improved distilling technology, the growing popularity of whiskey together with illicit and therefore untaxed distilled spirits had combined to raise per capita consumption to the 1770 level. Then, between 1800 and 1830, annual per capita consumption increased until it exceeded 5 gallons—a rate nearly triple that of today's consumption. After 1830 the temperance movement, and later on high federal taxation discouraged the drinking of distilled beverages. Annual per capita consumption fell to less than 2 gallons, a level from which there has been little deviation in more than a century.

In addition to distilled spirits, Americans drank weaker fermented beverages: beer (5% alcohol), hard cider (10%), and wine (18%). Colonial beer consumption was negligible, except for home brewed 'small beer,' which was only one percent alcohol. Until 1850 annual per capita consumption of commercial beer at no time reached 2 gallons, and it was not until after the Civil War that it rose dramatically toward today's rate of more than 18 gallons. But hard cider was a different matter. Pre-Revolutionary cider consumption, heaviest in the apple country from Virginia northward, was probably as high if not higher than in the early nineteenth century. In fact, so much cider was drunk that colonial Americans probably ingested more alcohol from that beverage than from their much more potent rum. And even with the increased popularity of distilled spirits after 1800, the annual per capita consumption of hard cider was 15 or more gallons. It continued until the 1830s to account for a significant proportion of all the alcohol Americans imbibed. Hard cider disappeared only after the leaders of the temperance movement succeeded in persuading farmers to cut down their apple trees. Wine consumption was and always has been relatively light. In 1770 the typical American annually drank only one-tenth of a gallon; between 1770 and 1870 less than a third of a gallon; and even today less than one and a half gallons.

From the quantity of each beverage drunk and the percentage of alcohol in each, it is a simple matter, of course, to compute the total amount of alcohol consumed. As Chart 1.2 shows, in 1770 the annual per capita intake of alcohol from all sources was 3.5 gallons. In the years following the Revolution the amount declined as the consumption of spirits declined. But after 1800, as the quantity of spirits consumed increased, the total quantity of alcohol consumed from all sources increased until it reached a peak of nearly 4 gallons per capita in 1830. This rate of consumption was the highest in the annals of the United States. After reaching this peak, consumption fell sharply under the influence of the temperance movement, and since 1840 its

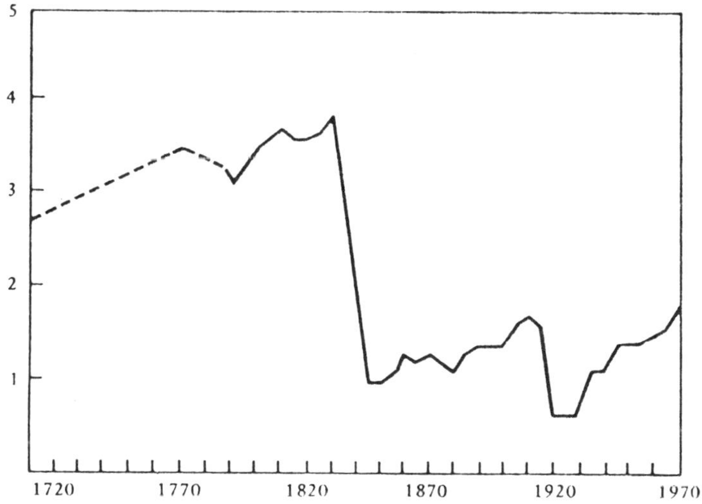

Chart 1.2. Annual consumption of alcohol contained in all alcoholic beverages per capita, in U.S. gallons.

highest levels have been under 2 gallons—less than half the rate of consumption in the 1820s.

Drinking in the young nation was obviously hearty, not to say excessive. However, the charge made by alarmed clergymen and statesmen that in this respect America had outstripped every other nation was exaggerated. A comparison of the annual per capita intake of alcohol in the United States with that in other countries during the early nineteenth century shows that Americans drank more than the English, Irish, or Prussians, but about the same as the Scots or French, and less than the Swedes. The nations with high consumption rates tended to share certain characteristics. Except for France, where wine predominated, the remaining heavy drinking countries, Scotland, Sweden, and the United States, were distilled spirits strongholds. These nations were agricultural, rural, lightly populated, and geographically isolated from foreign markets; they had undercapitalized, agrarian, barter economies; they were Protestant. In all three cheap, abundant grain fed the distilleries. By contrast, consumption was low in Ireland and Prussia because their economies lacked surplus grain and, hence, could not support a high level of distilled spirits production. In England high spirits taxes had encouraged the populace to switch from whisky and gin to beer. Although early nineteenth-century Americans did not drink more than relatively affluent Europeans of that era, by modern standards they drank a lot. A recent survey of alcohol consumption in ten European countries shows only France with a higher per capita consumption than the American rate during the early nineteenth century and shows five countries drinking at less than half that rate.

So the typical American was drinking heartily, but not all Americans drank their share. It is impossible to obtain an exact accounting, but the American Temperance Society estimated that during each year of the late 1820s nine million women and children drank 12 million gallons of distilled spirits; three million men, 60 million gallons. At this high point the average adult male was imbibing nearly a half pint a day. Few, however, were average. It was calculated that half the men drank 2 ounces a day; one-quarter (''habitual temperate drinkers''), 6 ounces; one-eighth (''regular topers, and occasional drunkards''), 12 ounces; and another eighth (''confirmed drunkards''), 24 ounces. Thus, half the adult males—one-eighth of the total population—were drinking two-thirds of all the distilled spirits consumed.

While men were the heartiest topers, women were not fainthearted abstainers. Little, however, can be learned about either the reputed 100,000 female drunkards or the more numerous women who consumed from one-eighth to one-quarter of the nation's spirituous liquor. The subject received scant attention because it was ''too delicate'' to be discussed. The ideal of femininity did discourage tippling, for a woman was supposed to show restraint consistent with virtue, prudence consonant with delicacy, and a preference for beverages agreeable to a fragile constitution. The public was not tolerant of women drinking at taverns or groceries, unless they were travellers recovering from a day's arduous journey. Then the ladies might be permitted watered and highly sugared spirituous cordials.

The concept of feminine delicacy led women to drink alcohol-based medicines for their health; many who regarded spirits as ''vulgar'' happily downed a highly alcoholic ''cordial or stomachic elixir.'' Furthermore, there were some social occasions when it was proper for women to imbibe freely and openly. For example, eastern ladies drank in mixed company at society dinners, suppers, and evening parties; and at pioneer dances the ''whiskey bottle was . . . passed pretty briskly from mouth to mouth, exempting neither age nor sex.'' A surprised Frances Kemble learned that New York ladies who visited the public baths were ''pretty often'' supplied with mint juleps. Still, because a woman had to conform, at least outwardly, to the social precepts of the day, she was most likely to drink in the privacy of her own home. There she could suit herself. The usual roles of male and female were reversed when temperance reformer Edward Delavan called upon Dolly Madison. After the teetotaling Delavan declined a drink, the flustered hostess declared that "such an example was worthy of imitation" and proceeded to mix herself a toddy.

Southern slaves, like women, drank less than their share of liquor. Masters usually provided watered spirits as a work incentive during harvest time, and many allowed their bondsmen a three-day spree at Christmas. The law, however, generally prohibited blacks from drinking at other times. This prohibition was only partially effective. Blacks in some districts were reputed to be a majority of tavern customers, and slaves often found that they could acquire liquor by bartering their own garden vegetables or hams purloined from the master. One Warrenton, North Carolina man complained that on Sunday afternoon the streets were "infested with drunken negroes staggering from side to side." This observer concluded that custom was "stronger than law." Defiance of the liquor laws led to tougher statutes. North Carolina, for example, in 1798 prohibited retailers from selling alcohol to slaves if their owners objected; in 1818 forbade slaves from vending liquor; and in 1833 forbade them from buying spirits under any condition. But these legal restraints against slaves drinking were less effective in discouraging consumption than was the plantation system under which there was neither the opportunity to obtain liquor nor the money to buy it. As Eugene Genovese has pointed out, the slaves' principal drinking problem was the drinking of their masters.

White males were taught to drink as children, even as babies. "I have frequently seen Fathers," wrote one traveller, "wake their Child of a year old from a sound sleap to make it drink Rum, or Brandy." As soon as a toddler was old enough to drink from a cup, he was coaxed to consume the sugary residue at the bottom of an adult's nearly empty glass of spirits. Many parents intended this early exposure to alcohol to accustom their offspring to the taste of liquor, to encourage them to accept the idea of drinking small amounts, and thus to protect them from becoming drunkards. Children grew up imitating their elders' drinking customs. Boys who played 'militia' expected the game to end, like their fathers' musters, with a round of drinks. Adolescents perceived drinking at a public house to be a mark of manhood. Sometimes the swaggering young male made a ridiculous picture. "It is no uncommon thing," wrote one man, "to see a boy of twelve or fourteen years old . . . walk into a tavern in the forenoon to take a glass of brandy and bitters. . . ." Men encouraged this youthful drinking. Many a proud father glowed when his son became old enough to accompany him to the tavern where they could drink as equals from the same glass.

The male drinking cult pervaded all social and occupational groups. A western husbandman tarried at the tavern until drunk; an eastern harvest laborer received daily a half pint or pint of run; a southern planter was considered temperate enough to belong to the Methodist Church if he restricted his daily intake of alcohol to a quart of peach brandy. A city mechanic went directly from work to the public house where he stayed late and spent his day's wages. Alcohol was such an accepted part of American life that in 1829 the secretary of war estimated that three-quarters of the nation's laborers drank daily at least 4 ounces of distilled spirits. Liquor was so popular that the army dared not bar the recruitment or reenlistment of habitual drunkards. If such a policy were adopted, warned the surgeon general, the army might have to be disbanded. The middle classes were scarcely more sober. Attorneys disputed with physicians as to which profession was the more besotted. Even more shocking was the indulgence of clergymen. One minister who considered himself temperate systematically downed 4 glasses of spirits to help him endure the fatigues of Sunday. At Andover Seminary, one of the most important centers of temperance activity, students regularly drank brandy toddies at the local tavern. Perhaps this practice was necessary to prepare would-be ministers for keeping up with their future congregations.

Drinking by these enthusiastic topers was done in a variety of places, including, of course, taverns. Although the original purpose of public houses had been to provide travellers a place to obtain refreshment, most localities had so few travellers that tavern owners found it necessary for their economic survival to attract local customers to the bar. Even so, the typical early nineteenth-century tavern recorded fewer than fifty visits a week. Half of these trips were made by the same four or eight men, the regulars who gathered every day or two around the potbellied stove to talk about the crops and weather, to argue politics, to quarrel and fight over insults, and, of course, to drink. They usually treated, that is, each man bought a half pint of whiskey, which was passed around the room. Since every man was expected to treat in turn, by evening's end each had drunk half a pint. With so few regulars, the solvency of most public houses depended upon the Saturday trade, when as many as twenty men might gather to drink a half pint apiece. It appears that the typical man patronized a public house once a week, that these visits provided him with 13 quarts of distilled spirits a year, and that this amount represented about one-fifth of his annual consumption.

Most liquor was drunk in the home, where whiskey and rum provided mealtime drinks, customary refresheners, and hospitable treats for guests. Fashionable people owned ornate liquor cases or elaborate sideboards that contained numerous bottles of various cordials, including mild, sweet, fruit-flavored elixirs for the ladies. Even the poorest host proffered his whiskey jug. While some of this liquor was made on the premises, bartered from neighbors, or bought at a distillery, much came from the general store, where its sale was often the most important item of business. Although some merchants curried favor with their customers by plying them with free samples of their spirits, less liquor was given away than was sold for home use. A study of one New Hampshire store's records from 1810 to 1833 showed that farmers who purchased supplies usually bought liquor along with their other purchases. During the early 1820s one-quarter of the value of this store's total sales was alcohol; typically, at that time, in a transaction that was for more than $1 and that included the sale of alcohol, distilled beverages accounted for more than half the value of the sale. A decade later less than one-tenth of the value of total sales was liquor; in a transaction over $1 that included alcohol, spirits were but one-third the value of the sale.

Leaving home, however, did not require that an American forego his favorite beverage. When journeying by stage coach, travellers could obtain liquor at the inns where the horses were changed. During one arduous seventeen-hour, sixty-six mile trip across Virginia, the stage stopped ten times, and two of the passengers had drinks at each way station: ten drinks apiece. Such habits led one foreign observer to conclude that "the American stage coach stops every five miles to water the horses, and *brandy the gentlemen!*" With the invention of steamboats, Americans were provided with yet another place to drink. Whereas stage travellers had been able to imbibe only when their vehicle rested at a wayside inn, boat passengers usually found a bar conveniently situated in the gentlemen's compartment, on the middle deck above the engine room. This arrangement is telling. The location of the bar not only discouraged female travellers from drinking; it also indicates that the bar was the boat's central feature. Of all forms of public transportation, only the steamboat focused so much attention on the bar. In part, this design reflected the owners' hopes for high profits from liquor sales; some boats were little more than floating saloons. More important is the fact that the steamboat was conceived at a time when drinking was central to American society. Boat designs that stressed bars conformed to a cultural imperative.

Americans drank not only any place but also any time. Some began to imbibe even before breakfast with an eye opener concocted of rum, whiskey, or gin mixed with bitters. In one Rhode Island factory town, laborers going to work made their way through the dawn's early light to the tavern "to take a little drop." Gentlemen adjourned from business at 11:00 A.M. for the old-fashioned equivalent of the coffee break, the 'elevens,' an occasion for partaking of spirituous liquor. When the weather was cold, they might have hot toddies made of whiskey or rum, sugar, and hot water, or hot slings made of gin, sugar, and hot water. At times a little lemon juice, cherry brandy, or bitters was added. The Virginia gentry gathered at 1:00 P.M., an hour before dinner, for the purpose of taking juleps compounded of peach brandy or whiskey, sugar, and ice. Sometimes crushed mint was added to make a mint julep. Throughout America early afternoon dinner was accompanied by hard cider or distilled spirits mixed with water; in late afternoon came another break; then supper with more refreshment. Finally, in the evening it was time to pause and reflect upon the day's events while sitting by the home or tavern fireside sipping spirits.

Americans drank on all occasions. Every social event demanded a drink. When southerners served barbecue, they roasted hogs and provided "plenty of whiskey." Guests at urban dances and balls were often intoxicated; so were spectators at frontier horse races. Western newlyweds were customarily presented with a bottle of whiskey to be drunk before bedding down for the night. Liquor also entered into money-making and business affairs. When a bargain was negotiated or a contract signed, it was sealed with a drink; auctioneers passed a whiskey bottle to those who made bids. After the harvest, farmers held agricultural fairs that ended with dinners laced with dozens of toasts. Whiskey accompanied traditional communal activities such as house-raisings, huskings, land clearings, and reaping. It was even served when women gathered to sew, quilt, or pick the seeds out of cotton.

Liquor also flowed at such public events as militia musters, elections, and the quarterly sessions of the courts. Militiamen elected their officers with the expectation that the elected officers would treat. One newly elevated colonel pledged, "I can't make a speech, but what I lack in brains I will try and make up in rum." Voters demanded and received spirits in exchange for their ballots. Electoral success, explained one Kentucky politico, depended upon understanding that "the way to men's hearts, is, *down their throats*." At trials the bottle was passed among spectators, attorneys, clients—and to the judge. If the foreman of a jury became mellow in his cups, the defendant stood an excellent chance for acquittal."

Alcohol was pervasive in American society; it crossed regional, sexual, racial, and class lines. Americans drank at home and abroad, alone and together, at work and at play, in fun and in earnest. They drank from the crack of dawn to the crack of dawn. At nights taverns were filled with boisterous, mirth-making tipplers. Americans drank before meals, with meals, and after meals. They drank while working in the fields and while travelling across half a continent. They drank in their youth, and, if they lived long enough, in their old age. They drank at formal events, such as weddings, ministerial ordinations, and wakes, and on no occasion—by the fireside of an evening, on a hot afternoon, when the mood called. From sophisticated Andover to frontier Illinois, from Ohio to Georgia, in lumbercamps and on satin settees, in log taverns and at fashionable New York hotels, the American greeting was, "Come, Sir, take a dram first." Seldom was it refused.

Early nineteenth-century America may not have been 'a nation of drunkards,' but Americans were certainly enjoying a spectacular binge.

13

Texas Must Be Ours

Robert V. Remini

The years of the Jackson presidency were marked with numerous conflicts and controversies. One of the less often mentioned controversies was over whether to annex Texas, as Jackson's old pal Sam Houston wanted, or not. Robert V. Remini describes the circumstances of the Texas question from independence to statehood.

From the moment he entered the White House in March 1829, Andrew Jackson of Tennessee turned a cold and calculating eye on Texas. Sitting in his study on the second floor of the mansion, maps strewn around the room, the white-haired, sharp-featured, cadaverous President breathed a passion for Texas that was soon shared by other Americans.

Old Hickory always believed—or so he said—that Texas had been acquired by the United States as part of the Louisiana Purchase in 1803 and then had been recklessly thrown away when "that old scamp J. Q. Adams" negotiated the Florida treaty with Spain in 1819 and agreed to the Sabine River as the western boundary of the country. The claim was questionable at the very least, but many Southerners, outraged by Northern reaction to the slavery issue during the debates over the admission of Missouri and chagrined over the institution's prohibition in the Louisiana Territory north of 36° 30′, decided to press it anyway.

The loss of Texas by virtue of the Florida treaty dismayed some Americans. It infuriated Jackson. "How infatuated must have been our councils who gave up the rich country of Texas," he wrote. Such action, in his mind, verged on treason. And why had it happened? "It surely must have been with the view to keep the political ascendence in the North, and east," he fumed, "& cripple the rising greatness of

Reprinted from "Texas Must be Ours," by Robert V. Remini, *American Heritage*, February, 1986, pp. 42–47. © 1986 by Robert V. Remini. Used with permission.

the West.'' No matter. He would attend to it at the first opportunity. And indeed he did—or tried to. ''I have long since been aware of the importance of Texas to the United States,'' he wrote a friend just a few months after taking office as President, ''and of the real necessity of extending our boundary west of the Sabine. . . . I shall keep my eye on this object & and first propitious moment make the attempt to regain the Territory as far south & west as the great Desert.''

All his attempts at acquiring Texas proved feeble, however, mostly because he had assigned a freewheeling, fast-talking, double-dealing incompetent to represent the United States in Mexico. Col. Anthony Butler made numerous ''diplomatic'' efforts to purchase Texas from Mexico, and when those failed, he turned to bribery. ''I have just had a very singular conversation with a Mexican,'' he wrote Jackson in October of 1833, and this Mexican ''has much influence with the Presidt. Genl. St. Anna.'' The Mexican had bluntly asked Butler, ''Have you command of Money?''

''Yes, I have money,'' Butler responded.

The price would be high, said the Mexican, in excess of half a million dollars. The Mexican himself required two or three hundred thousand, and Butler allowed that ''there are others amongst whom it may become necessary to distribute 3 or 4 Hundred thousand more.''

''Can you command that Sum?'' the Mexican demanded.

''Yes,'' Butler assured him.

He was wrong. ''I have read your confidential letter with care, and astonishment,'' a furious Jackson replied, ''. . . astonishment that you would entrust such a letter, without being in cypher, to the mail.'' Moreover, wrote Jackson, as he was astounded by Butler's presumption that ''my instructions authorized you to apply to corruption, when nothing could be farther from my intention than to convey such an idea.''

At length Jackson had to recall Butler. The President was discouraged not only by the diplomatic failure and the shady operations of his minister but also by the resistance of the Mexicans to his assurance that a ''natural boundary'' at the Rio Grande River would work to the mutual benefit of both nations. Such a boundary, Jackson insisted, would eliminate ''collisions'' that two peoples of ''conflicting laws, habits and interests'' were bound to have. Moreover, it would provide the Mexicans with needed cash to bolster their economy: the President was willing to go as high as five million dollars to purchase the territory. Failure of the sale was sure to encourage the many Americans who had moved to Texas over the previous ten years to establish an independent republic. And such a turn of events, the President feared, would sever the "bonds of amity and good understanding" between the United States and Mexico.

Since the early 1820s, Americans had been migrating to Texas, particularly from the South and West. Motivated to a large extent by the hard times generated by the Panic of 1819, they sought relief in Texas because the Mexicans encouraged them to settle there. Led by Moses Austin and his son Stephen F., they established an American colony in Texas and accepted Mexican authority. Slave owners from Alabama, Mississippi, and Tennessee were particularly attracted to this haven. By 1830 over twelve thousand Americans had emigrated to Texas, and Mexico, alarmed, eventually prohibited all immigration from the north.

Many Texans desired immediate annexation by the United States, especially after 1829, when slavery was forbidden throughout Mexican territory. The blatant and hostile intentions of these Texans naturally provoked the Mexicans, and Jackson's fumbling efforts to purchase the territory only exacerbated an already worsening situation. Despite his passion for Texas, the President wanted neither war with Mexico nor domestic strife over the wisdom of adding what might become another slave state. Still, he would not abandon his dream of territorial expansion. "The boundary between the U. States and Mexico," he jotted into his private memorandum book, "must be altered."

Jackson's apprehensions deepened when he learned that his old friend and protégé, Sam Houston, late governor of Tennessee, had fled to Texas after a disastrous marriage and reportedly "would conquer Mexico or Texas, & be worth two millions in two years." These were the "elusions of a distempered brain," said Jackson; Houston would never place millions before the welfare of his country, but that did not guarantee a peaceful resolution to the problem.

Perhaps, given Mexico's stiff opposition to territorial dismemberment, no one in the United States possessed the diplomatic skill to bring about the peaceful acquisition of this valuable and strategically important landmass. But certainly Jackson botched what little chance he may have had by appointing Butler and then keeping him long after Jackson had reason to believe that his minister was a scoundrel. Gen. Antonio Lopez de Santa Anna was convinced that the United States had acted dishonorably and had violated its neutrality laws by encouraging filibustering expeditions into Texas and by arming Americans to instigate revolution.

The failure of American diplomacy did indeed spur the Texans to take matters into their own hands. A war party was formed at the same time that the Mexican government was moving to centralize control over all parts of the Mexican republic, including Texas. The struggle for independence ignited in October 1835 and roared to its climax when General Santa Anna marched into Texas at the head of a five-thousand-man army. Texas proclaimed its independence on March 2, 1836, and on April 21 a Texan army commanded by Sam Houston defeated Santa Anna at the Battle of San Jacinto. Santa Anna himself was captured and forced to sign a treaty (later repudiated) recognizing Texan independence.

No American doubted that annexation by the United States would soon follow. Some Texans might have preferred to remain a republic, but probably many more desired eventual statehood.

The Mexican minister to the United States, Manuel Eduardo de Gorostiza, peppered President Jackson with angry protests. He raged against American treachery and ultimately demanded his passports. Relations between Mexico and the United States rapidly deteriorated, and within two months it appeared that war between the two countries would break out momentarily. The secretary of the Navy, Mahlon Dickerson, reported at a cabinet meeting that Com. Alexander J. Dallas had notified him that the American consul and residents at Tampico had suffered innumerable "indignities" at the hands of Mexican authorities. Moreover, American armed vessels in the area had been refused water, and their officers had been denied permission to go ashore. Worse, these authorities had threatened to put to death all Americans in Tampico in retaliation for the capture of Santa Anna.

Dickerson concluded his report. Benjamin Butler, in a letter to his wife, explained what happened next. Jackson "broke out in his most impassioned manner." He jumped to his feet, gesticulated wildly, and shook his fist at invisible enemies. It was one of the most frightening displays of the President's anger that the cabinet had ever witnessed. The members set frozen, staring; nobody dared interrupt the wild outburst.

Then, wrote Butler, Old Hickory barked, "Write immediately to Commodore Dallas & order him to *blockade* the harbour of Tampico, & to suffer nothing to enter till they allow him to land and obtain his supplies of water & communicate with the Consul, & if they touch the hair of the head of one of our citizens, tell him *to batter down & destroy their town & exterminate the inhabitants from the face of the earth!*"

The cabinet sucked in its collective breath, but said nothing. Could he be serious?

Finally, Jackson addressed his secretary of state, John Forsyth. "Have you recd., any information on this subject?"

Forsyth shook his head.

"Then let the Secy of the Navy furnish you the papers," Jackson ordered, "and do you write immediately to Mr. Gorostiza informing him of the orders we have given to Commodore Dallas, & that we shall not permit a jot or tittle of the treaty to be violated, or a citizen of the United States to be injured without taking immediate redress."

Fortunately, cooler heads on both sides prevented the extermination of the citizens of Tampico, but American-Mexican relations continued to deteriorate: Texans were doing everything possible to force U.S. recognition of their independence and eventual annexation. Commissioners dispatched to lobby in Washington were all warmly received by the president. During one such meeting Jackson turned to Special Commissioner Samuel Carson and said, "Is it true, Mr. Carson, that your Government has sent Santa Anna back to Mexico?" Carson responded that Santa Anna was indeed expected to depart shortly to assist in winning ratification of the treaty recognizing the independence of Texas.

"Then I tell you, Sir," said Jackson, "if ever he sets foot on Mexican ground, your Government may whistle; he, Sir, will give you trouble, if he escapes, which you dream not of."

Then where would be war, Carson said.

"Where is your means, Sir, to carry on an offensive war against Mexico?"

"In the enthusiasms of the American people," said Carson happily, "their devotion to the cause of Liberty are the ways and means, to defray the expenses of the War."

Jackson blanched. It was one thing for the President of the United States to threaten war, quite another for "outsiders" from Texas to presume they could manipulate this country into one. The United States had a treaty with Mexico, and the annexation of Mexican territory would most certainly be viewed around the world as a betrayal. Civilized countries would label it a brutal and aggressive act, a violation of the "law of nations." The "Texians," as Jackson frequently called them, must realize that annexation would take time and careful planning. Thus, when Stephen F. Austin sent him an impassioned letter requesting assistance, Jackson wrote the following endorsement: "[Austin] does not reflect that we have a treaty with Mexico, and our national faith is pledged to support it. The Texians before they took the step to declare themselves independent, which has aroused and united all mexico against them ought to have pondered well, it was a rash and premature act, our neutrality must be faithfully maintained.''

And there were other problems. Abolitionists, for one. These troublemakers would exploit any issue to attack slavery, said Jackson, even if it ruptured relations between the North and South. They intended to oppose the admission of Texas because it represented the continued expansion of slavery. Texas, therefore, posed a possible threat to the Union, which hobbled Jackson's efforts to negotiate a swift treaty of admission. His passion for Texas could never match his passion for the Union. ''Prudence,'' he later wrote, seemed to dictate that ''we should stand aloof'' and see how things would develop. No doubt he was also fearful of jeopardizing the election of his handpicked successor to the Presidency, Martin Van Buren.

At this juncture Sam Houston decided to send Santa Anna to Washington to meet Jackson in the hope that their talks together would help the cause of Texas annexation. Houston released the Mexican, presented him with a handsome horse, and headed him (under armed escort) to the capital. Santa Anna arrived on January 17, 1837.

At the moment, Old Hickory was recovering from a severe ''hemorrhage of the lungs'' that had almost ended his life. For months he remained in his room, not daring to expose himself to a relapse by needless movement around the White House. In fact, he left his room only four times during the final six months of his administration. Still, on state occasions, Jackson could muster great presence and exude the appearance of enormous strength. For his part, Santa Anna, despite his long trip, looked refreshed and relaxed. He was amused and rather pleased by the notoriety that his arrival in the capital had provoked. Many assumed he would look malevolent. They were surprised to find him a gracious and cultivate man of impeccable manners and dress.

On Thursday, January 19, 1837, the Mexican general was escorted into the presence of the American general at the White House. The two men greeted one another politely and with a degree of dignified reserve. Always the gentleman, Old Hickory assured his guest that he was most welcome in Washington and expressed pleasure in meeting him at long last. ''General Andrew Jackson greeted me warmly,'' Santa Anna later wrote, ''and honored me at a dinner attended by notables of all countries.'' Jackson treated him not as an enemy but as a head of state, even though Santa Anna had been succeeded in Mexico by Anastasio Bustamante.

The official greeting, reception, and dinner went extremely well, but the conversations involved nothing of substance. Not until the following day did the two men turn to the matter that had brought them together.

Santa Anna began by proposing the cession of Texas for a "fair consideration." The United States, responded Jackson, could do nothing about a cession until the "disposition of the Texians" was resolved. "Until Texas is acknowledged independent," said the President, this nation could make no official move. At some point in the conversation, Jackson outlined a proposal for the Mexican to take back to his country. Beginning with the supposition that Mexico would officially acknowledge the independence of Texas at some point early on, Jackson suggested that the boundary of the United States be extended to include Texas and northern California—in effect, this would run the "line of the U. States to the Rio grand—up the stream to latitude 38 north & then to the pacific including north California." In return the United States would compensate Mexico with $3,500,000. "But before we promise anything," Jackson continued, "Genl Santana must say that he will use his influence to suspend hostilities." The President assured his visitor that the principal objective of the United States was not territorial acquisition or the further embarrassment of the Mexican Republic, but rather to "secure peace & tranquility on our respective borders & lay the foundation of a permanent tranquility between the U.S. and Mexico."

The interview ended on a polite but indefinite note. President Jackson provided Santa Anna with a warship to carry him to Veracruz, and the Mexican had nothing but gratitude for his treatment.

A little later Jackson mentioned his conversation with Santa Anna to William Wharton, recently arrived in Washington to represent Texas. Wharton protested: Texan independence was an accomplished fact achieved through her own military power, and Mexico had no right to make a treaty that in any way bound her. What the United States must do, insisted Wharton, was to recognize Texan independence; then the nation could move on to the question of possible annexation.

Jackson grimaced. Perhaps, suggested the President to Wharton, as a way of quieting the sectional rivalry that recognition was sure to provoke, Texas might claim California in order to "paralyze" Northern opposition to annexation. Acquisition of California along with

Texas meant the continuation of representational balance in the Senate between free and slave states. The suggestion did not elicit much enthusiasm from Wharton. Texas could never legitimately claim California or undertake a war to assert its claim. California was simply not on the negotiating table.

Congress, however, responded to the wishes of the "Texians" without grappling with the sectional consequences and, during the final days of Jackson's administration, recognized the independence of the Texas Republic. The President quickly appointed Alcée Louis La Branche of Louisiana as chargé d' affaires to Texas, and the Senate confirmed the nomination only hours before the final adjournment of Congress. Around midnight, when word came that La Branche had been confirmed, Jackson met with Wharton and a few others to celebrate. They lifted their glasses in a single toast: Texas!

But Jackson returned home defeated in his one great effort to reach the Rio Grande. He rightly feared his failure might jeopardize the integrity and tranquility of the Union.

The more he thought about it, as he sat in his study at the Hermitage reading the reports that arrived daily from Washington, the more he convinced himself that the security of the United States demanded the acquisition of Texas. Never mind the machinations of abolitionists. They were nothing compared with the danger posed by foreign enemies: Great Britain, for example.

If Britain should decide to reenter the continent through Texas and attempt a linkup with Canada, then war would be inevitable. "The safety of the republic being the supreme law, and Texas having offered us the key to the safety of our country from all foreign intrigues and diplomacy," Jackson wrote, "I say accept the key . . . and bolt the door at once." If England concluded an alliance with the "Texians"—which seemed under way at that very moment—then she would most likely move "an army from canady, along our western frontier," march through Arkansas and Louisiana, seize New Orleans, "excite the negroes to insurrection," "arouse the Indians on our west to war," and "throw our whole west into flames that would cost oceans of blood & hundreds of millions of money to quench, & reclaim. . . ." As he wrote these words, Jackson worked himself into a passion. "Texas must be ours," he raged. "Our safety requires it." Later he repeated his demand with a little less passion but with the same determination. We must have Texas, "peaceably if we can, forcibly if we must."

Despite strong Northern pressure, the new President, John Tyler, obtained a treaty of annexation signed by representatives of Texas and the United States in April 1844 and submitted it to the Senate for ratification. It was accompanied by an extraordinary letter to the British minister to Washington, Richard Pakenham, written by the secretary of state, John C. Calhoun. In it Calhoun contended that the treaty had been signed for the express purpose of protecting American slavery from British attempts to bring about universal emancipation. The extension of the American slave interests into Texas, he said, would nullify that "reprehensible" goal.

Friends of annexation groaned when they read copies of Calhoun's provocative letter. The secretary had placed annexation "*exclusively* upon the ground of *protection* of *Slavery* in the *Southern States!*" and the senators from the non-slaveholding states who favored annexation were furious because "it would be death to them, politically, if they were to vote for the Treaty based on such principles."

Why had Calhoun done it? Why had he jeopardized the treaty by the gratuitous mention of slavery? Maj. William B. Lewis, one of Jackson's oldest friends, claimed to know. The secretary of state meant to kill the treaty, he wrote, in order to "drive off every Northern man from the reannexation" and thereby give him a "pretext to unite the whole South upon himself as the Champion of its cause." Put simply, he meant to divide the Union, create a Southern confederacy, and make himself the "great man of this fragment which he expects to tear from the embrace of our glorious Govt." Like abolitionists, Lewis added, Southern hotheads were determined to disrupt the Union to achieve their own selfish objectives. Unfortunately, Texas had become a pawn in the fatal game of personal ambition. As far as Jackson was concerned, between "that arch fiend, J. Q. Adams" and that "*Cateline,*" John C. Calhoun, they were tearing the Union apart.

So the treaty failed. And shortly thereafter the ostensible Whig and Democratic candidates for the Presidency in the next election, Henry Clay and Martin Van Buren, publicly announced their opposition to annexation. Clay (himself a slave owner) regarded annexation as dangerous to the country because it might provoke a war with Mexico, excite sectional passions over slavery, and prove financially disastrous, since the $10 million Texas debt would have to be assumed by the United States. Van Buren was especially concerned over the sectional rancor and possibility of war.

Jackson "shed tears of regret" when he read the letter of his old friend Martin Van Buren. "I would to god I had been at Mr. V. B. elbow when he closed his letter. I would have brought to his view *the proper conclusion*." The only course of action left was to dump Van Buren as a presidential candidate and nominate someone else, someone who "is an annexation man," he wrote, "and from the Southwest." Other Democrats agreed, and at the national nominating convention in Baltimore, they "arranged" to replace Van Buren with James K. Polk.

Clay and Polk ran a close race. Among other things, Polk promised to "reannex" Texas, claiming like Jackson that it was part of the Louisiana Purchase and had been shamefully surrendered by that "crazy old man, John Quincy Adams." In election, he won 170 electoral votes to Clay's 105. The popular vote was even closer: 1,337,243 to 1,299,062. Polk defeated Clay by a 1.4 percent margin. "A mere *Tom Tit*" growled John Quincy Adams, had triumphed over the "old Eagle. The partial associations of Native Americans, Irish Catholics, abolition societies, liberty party, the Pope of Rome, the Democracy of the sword, and the dotage of a ruffian [Andrew Jackson] are sealing the fate of this nation, which nothing less than the interposition of Omnipotence can save."

Between the time of his election and inauguration, Polk met several times with Jackson at the Hermitage. Old Hickory instructed his friend on the necessity of annexing Texas in order to "put to rest the vexing question of abolitionism, the dangerous rock to our Union, and put at defiance all combined Europe, if combined to invade us." But Polk needed no instruction. Upon his arrival in Washington, he was queried by many members of Congress about his plans and goals. "He is for Texas, Texas, Texas," reported Sen. Willie P. Mangum of North Carolina, "& talks of but little else."

The outgoing President, John Tyler, saw his opportunity to capitalize on Polk's victory, and he helped arrange a joint resolution of annexation for both houses of Congress. After considerable politicking the House and Senate gave their approval, and Tyler signed the resolution on March 1, 1845, just three days before he was to leave office. A messenger was immediately dispatched to Texas with the "glorious" news.

"Texas is ours," trumpeted the newspapers. "The Union is safe." A feeble old man who had only a few months to live added his voice to the general acclaim. Andrew Jackson thanked God that he had lived to see this happy day. "I . . . congratulate my beloved country [that] Texas is reannexed,'' he wrote, ''and the safety, prosperity, and the greatest interest of the whole Union is secured by this . . . great and important national act.''

But others expressed more disturbing views. They feared that the admission of Texas would lead inevitably to war with Mexico and possibly civil war. And their direst predictions proved correct. Texas ratified annexation on July 4 and was admitted into the Union as a slave state on December 29, 1845. The following spring—on May 11, 1846—the United States declared war against Mexico. Later the North and South submitted their dispute over slavery to a frightful test of arms. Within twenty years the Union cracked apart, and to weld it back together did indeed take ''oceans of blood & hundreds of millions of money.''

14

Southern Separation

David Potter

The South had long contemplated the possibility of separation from the rest of the Union, certainly since the nullification controversy of 1832. During the 1850s the distance between North and South widened to an unbridgeable chasm. David Potter brilliantly analyzes the various forces driving the South toward separation.

Ten days after the election of Lincoln, the Augusta, Georgia, *Daily Constitutionalist* published an editorial reflecting on what had happened to American nationalism:

The most inveterate and sanguine Unionist in Georgia, if he is an observant man, must read, in the signs of the times, the hopelessness of the Union cause, and the feebleness of the Union sentiment in this State. The differences between North and South have been growing more marked for years, and the mutual repulsion more radical, until not a single sympathy is left between the dominant influences in each section. Not even the banner of the stars and stripes excites the same thrill of patriotic emotion, alike in the heart of the northern Republican and the southern Secessionist. The former looks upon that flag as blurred by the stain of African slavery, for which he feels responsible as long as that flag waves over it, and that it is his duty to humanity and religion to obliterate the stigma. The latter looks upon it as the emblem of a gigantic power, soon to pass into the hands of that sworn enemy, and knows that African slavery, though panoplied by the Federal Constitution, is doomed to a war of extermination. All the powers of a Government which has so long sheltered it will be turned to its destruction. The only hope for its preservation, therefore, is out of the Union. A few more years of unquiet peace may be spared to it, because Black Republicans cannot yet get full possession of every department of the Government. But this affords to the South no reason for a moment's delay in seeking new guards for its future safety.[1]

When the *Constitutionalist* declared that not a single sympathy was left between the two sections, it exaggerated the degree to which Unionism had been eroded. The tenacity with which Maryland, Virginia, North Carolina, Kentucky, Tennessee, Missouri, and Arkansas clung to the Union during the next five months proved that Unionism retained much vigor. The great body of Americans, in both the North and the South, still cherished their images of a republic to which they could respond with patriotic devotion, and in this sense American nationalism remained very much alive—so much alive, in fact, that it was able to revitalize itself speedily after four years of devastating war. But though they cherished the image, the sectional conflict had neutralized their many affinities, causing antislavery men to depreciate the value of a Union which was flawed by slavery, and causing men in the slaveholding states to give the defense of the slave system such a high priority that they could no longer offer loyalty to a Union which seemed to threaten that system. As these forces of repulsion between North and South came into play, the southern states were, at the same time, drawn closer together by their common commitment to the slave system and their sense of need for mutual defense against a hostile antislavery majority. Southern separatism had been developing for several decades, and how it was about to end in the formation of the Confederate States of America. Historians have spoken of this separatism as "southern nationalism," and of the Confederacy as a "nation." Yet it is clear that much of the old devotion to the Union still survived among many citizens throughout the South and even dominated the action of some southern states until they found themselves forced to fight on one side or the other. Therefore, one must ask: What was the nature of southern separatism? What was the degree of cohesion within the South on the eve of the Civil War? Had the cultural homogeneity of the southern people, their awareness of shared values, and their regional loyalty reached the point of resembling the characteristics of nationalism? Were they drawn together by a sense of separate destiny which required separate nationhood, or were they rather impelled to united action by their common fears of forces that seemed to threaten the foundations of their society?[2]

The understanding of any so-called nationalism—indeed of any development involving sustained cohesive behavior on the part of a large group of people—is complicated by two kinds of dualism. One of these is the dualism of objective and subjective factors, or, one might say, of cultural realities and states of mind. Cohesion can scarcely exist among an aggregate of people unless they share some objective characteristics. Classic criteria are common descent (or ethnic affinities), common language, common religion, and most important and most intangible of all, common customs and beliefs. But these features alone will not produce cohesion unless those who share them also share a self-consciousness of what they have in common, unless they attach distinctive value to what is shared, and unless they feel identified with one another by the sharing. A second dualism lies in the interplay between forces of attraction and forces of repulsion. Wherever and whenever nationalism has developed in notably vigorous form, it has been in circumstances of conflict between the nationalizing group and some other group. In such a situation, the rejection of the out-group not only strengthens the cohesion of the in-group, but imparts to the members of the in-group a greater awareness of what they share. Indeed, it gives them new things to share—common danger, common efforts against the adversary, common sacrifice, and perhaps a common triumph. Sometimes it even impels them to invent fictitious affinities. Thus, conflict and war have been the great catalysts of nationalism, and forces of repulsion between antagonistic groups have probably done more than the forces of affinity within compatible groups to forge the kind of unity that translates into nationalism.

The problem of the South in 1860 was not a simple one of southern nationalism versus American nationalism, but rather one of two loyalties coexisting at the same time—loyalty to the South and loyalty to the Union. Because these loyalties were soon to be brought into conflict, they have often been categorized as "conflicting loyalties," with the implication that if a person has two political loyalties they are bound to conflict, that one of the two must be illegitimate, and that a right-minded person would no more maintain two loyalties then he would commit bigamy. But in fact, strong regional loyalties exist within many nations, and they existed in the United States in other areas besides the South. There was nothing inherently incompatible between regional loyalties and national loyalties as long as they could both be aligned in a pattern in which they remained congruent with one another instead of being at cross-purposes with one another. Any region which had enough power in the federal government could always prevent federal policy and regional policy from coming into any sort of major collision. But the South, by 1860, no longer had such power, or at least no longer had confidence of maintaining such power. Thus the loyalties of southerners became "conflicting loyalties," not necessarily because they loved the Union less but because they had lost the crucial power to keep them from conflicting.[3]

But what were the factors of affinity making for cohesion within the South in 1860, and what were the factors of repulsion between the South and the rest of the Union which gave negative reinforcement to southern unity?

The vast and varied region extended from the Mason-Dixon line to the Rio Grande and from the Ozarks to the Florida Keys certainly did not constitute a unity, either physiographic or cultural. But the whole area lay within what may be called the gravitational field of an agricultural economy specializing in staple crops for which plantations had proved to be effective units of production and for which Negro slaves had become the most important source of labor. This, of course, did not mean that all white southerners engaged in plantation agriculture and owned slaves—indeed only a small but very influential minority did so. It did not even mean that all of the states were heavy producers of staple crops, for the cotton states were only in the lower South. But it did mean that the economy of all of these states was tied, sometimes in secondary or tertiary ways, to a system of plantation agriculture.

Agricultural societies tend to be conservative and orthodox, with strong emphasis on kinship ties and on the observance of established customs. If land is held in great estates, such societies tend to be hierarchical and deferential. Thus, even without slavery, the southern states would have shared certain attributes to a high degree. But the presence of slavery had dictated conditions of its own, and these too were shared very widely throughout the South. Indeed they became the criteria for determining what constituted the South.

A slave system, since it means the involuntary subordination of a significant part of the population, requires a social apparatus distinctively adapted in all its parts to imposing and to maintaining such subordination. In the South, this subordination was also racial, involving not only the control of slaves by their masters but also the control of a population of 4 million blacks by 8 million whites. Such a system cannot be maintained simply by putting laws on the statute books and making formal records that one individual has acquired legal ownership of another. It is axiomatic that the enslaved will tend to resist their servitude and that the slaveowners must devise effective, practical means of control. The first requisite is that the system shall be able to deal with the contingency of insurrection. This alters the priorities, for though the system of subordination may have originated as a means to an end—to assure a permanent labor supply for the cultivation of the staple crops—the immediacy of the hazard of insurrection soon makes the subordination of the slaves an end in itself. This was what Thomas Jefferson meant when he said, "We have a wolf by the ears."

The question of the extent to which the South stood in real danger of slave insurrection is a most difficult one, complicated by the fact that the white South could never for a moment rid itself of the fear of insurrection, yet at the same time could never admit even to itself, much less to others, that its "civilized," "contented," and "loyal" slaves might some day massacre their masters.[4] The fear was probably out of proportion to the actual danger. But the point is that white southerners shared, subjectively, a fear of what the slaves might do, and, objectively, a social system designed to prevent them from doing it.

From the time of Spartacus, all slaveholding societies had lived with the danger of slave revolt. But for the South, no reminders from antiquity were needed. On the island of Santo Domingo, between 1791 and 1804, black insurrectionists under a series of leaders including Toussiant L'Ouverture and Jean Jacques Dessalines had risen in revolt, virtually exterminating the entire white population of the island and committing frightful atrocities, such as burying people alive and sawing them in two. Survivors had fled to New Orleans, Norfolk, and other places in the United States, and southerners could hear from their own lips the stories of their ordeal. Santo Domingo lived as a nightmare in the mind of the South.[5] Within the South itself, of course, there were also revolts or attempted revolts.[6] Gabriel Prosser led one at Richmond in 1800. Some sort of conspiracy under the leadership of Denmark Vesey apparently came near to hatching at Charleston in 1822. Nat Turner led his famous insurrection in Southampton County, Virgina, in 1831. All of these were negligible compared with Santo Domingo or even with revolts in Brazil,[7] but, each one hit an exposed nerve in the southern psyche. Also there were local disturbances. Altogether, one historian has collected more than two hundred instances of "revolts," and while there is reason to believe that some of these were wholly imaginary and that many others did not amount to much, still every one is a proof of the reality of southern apprehensions if not of the actual prevalence of the danger.[8] On isolated plantations, and in districts where blacks heavily outnumbered whites, the peril seemed a constant one. Every sign of restlessness in the slave quarters, every stranger seen along a lonely road, every withdrawn or cryptic look on a slave face, even the omission of some customary gesture of deference, might be the forewarning of nameless horrors lurking just beneath the placid surface of life.

This pervasive apprehension explains much, of course, about southern reaction to the antislavery movement. The southerners were not deeply concerned with what the abolitionists might persuade Congress or the northern public to do—indeed the whole elaborate territorial controversy had many of the aspects of a charade—but with what they might persuade the slaves to do. Southerners were acutely sensitized to direct abolitionist efforts at incitation, such as Henry H. Harnett's speech at a national Negro convention in 1843 in which he urged slaves to kill any master who refused to set them free.[9] It was seldom difficult to make an equation between abolitionist exhortation and slave violence. Thus southerners tried to link Nat Turner's revolt in August 1831 with the first appearance of the *Liberator* eight months previously, but in truth it appears likely that Turner was more influenced by an eclipse of the sun in February than by William Lloyd Garrison in January. Twenty-eight years later, however, John Brown made the equation explicit: a white abolitionist was caught trying to rouse the slaves to revolt. Brown's tying of the bond between abolition and slave revolt gave electrifying importance to what might otherwise have been dismissed as an act of suicidal folly.

This concern about antislavery propaganda as a potential cause of slave unrest also explains in part why white southerners seemed so oblivious to the great difference between the moderate attitude of an "ultimate extinctionist" like Lincoln and the flaming abolitionism of an "immediatist" like Garrison. When southerners thought of extinction it was in terms of Santo Domingo and not in terms of a gradualist reform to be completed, maybe, in the twentieth century. From their standpoint, the election to the presidency of a man who stated flatly that slavery was morally wrong might have a more inciting effect upon the slaves than denunciatory rhetoric from the editor of an abolitionist weekly in Boston.[10]

Since the determination to keep blacks in subordination took priority over other goals of southern society, the entire socioeconomic system had to be conducted in a way that would maximize the effectiveness of racial control. This went far beyond the adoption of slave codes and the establishment of night patrols in times of alarm.[11] It meant also that the entire structure of society must be congruent with the objective, and no institutional arrangements should be countenanced which would weaken control. The blacks should live on plantations not only because plantations were efficient units for cotton production, but because in an era prior to electronic and bureaucratic surveillance, the plantation was a notably effective unit of supervision and control. Also, it provided maximum isolation from potentially subversive strangers. Slaves should be illiterate, unskilled, rural workers not only because the cotton economy needed unskilled rural workers for tasks in which literacy would not increase their usefulness, but also because unskilled rural workers were limited in their access to unsupervised contacts with strangers, and because the illiterate could neither read seditious literature nor exchange surreptitious written communication. In fact, the conditions of employment in the cotton culture seemed to fit the needs of a slave system as neatly as the conditions of slavery fitted the needs of employment in the cotton culture, and if cotton fastened slavery upon the South, it is also true that slavery fastened cotton upon the South.

Even beyond these broad relationships, the system of subordination reached out still further to require a certain kind of society, one in which certain questions were not publicly discussed. It must give blacks no hope of cultivating dissension among the whites. It must commit the nonslaveholders to the unquestioning support of racial subordination, even though they might suffer certain disadvantages from a slave system in which they had no economic stake. This meant that books like *The Impending Crisis* must not circulate, and, indeed, universal education, extending literacy indiscriminately to all lower-class whites, need not be encouraged. In a mobile society it would be harder to keep slaves firmly fixed in their prescribed positions; therefore, the society must be relatively static, without the economic flexibility and dynamism of a money economy and a wage system. The more speculative a society became in its social thought, the more readily it might challenge the tenets of the established order. Therefore the South tended toward a religion which laid major emphasis on personal salvation and on a Bible-based orthodoxy; toward an educational system which stressed classical learning; and toward reforms of a pragmatic kind, such as better care for the blind, rather than reforms associated with ideology.[12] In short, the South became increasingly a closed society, distrustful of isms from outside and unsympathetic toward dissenters. Such were the pervasive consequences giving top priority to the maintenance of a system of racial subordination.[13]

By 1860, southern society had arrived at the full development of a plantation-oriented, slaveholding system with conservative values, hierarchical relationships, and authoritarian controls. No society is complete, of course, without an ethos appropriate to its social arrangements, and the South had developed one, beginning with a conviction of the superior virtues of rural life. At one level, this conviction embodied a Jeffersonian agrarianism which regarded landowning cultivators of the soil as the best kind of citizens, because their landownership and their production for use gave them self-sufficiency and independence, uncorrupted by commercial avarice—and also because their labor had dignity and diversity suitable to well-rounded men. But at another level, the commitment to rural values had led to a glorification of plantation life, in which even slavery was idealized by the argument that the dependence of the slave developed in the master a sense of responsibility for the welfare of the slaves and in the slaves a sense of loyalty and attachment to the master. This relationship, southerners argued, was far better than the impersonal, dehumanized irresponsibility of "wage slavery, which treated labor as a commodity.

From an idyllic image of slavery and plantation conditions, it was but a short step to the creation of a similar image of the planter as a man of distinctive qualities. Thus, the plantation virtues of magnanimity, hospitality, personal courage, and loyalty to men rather than to ideas held a social premium, and even the plantation vices of arrogance, quick temper, and self-indulgence were regarded with tolerance. From materials such as these, in an era of uninhibited romanticism and sentimentality, the southern upper class built a fully elaborated cult of chivalry, inspired by the novels of Sir Walter Scott and including tournaments, castellated architecture, a code of honor, and the enshrinement of women. Thus, with a mixture of self-deception and idealism, the South adopted an image of itself which some men used as a fiction to avoid confronting sordid reality, while others used it as a standard toward which to strive in order to develop, as far as they were able, the better aspects of human behavior that were latent even in a slaveholding society.[14]

One other belief shared by the men of the South in 1860 was especially important because they felt just uncertain and insecure enough about it to be almost obsessively insistent and aggressive in asserting it. This was the doctrine of the inherent superiority of whites over Negroes. The idea was not distinctively southern, but it did have a distinctive significance in the South, for it served to rationalize slavery and also to unite slaveholders and nonslaveholders in defense of the institution as a system, primarily, of racial subordination, in which all members of the dominant race had the same stake.

This racial prejudice against Negroes cannot, of course, be dismissed as nothing but a rationalization to justify their subordination of the blacks, for in fact it was in part just such prejudice which had originally made blacks and Indians subject to enslavement, while servants of other races were not. Initially, the prejudice may have stemmed from the superiority which technologically advanced societies feel over less advanced societies; it may have reflected something of the attitude of Christians toward the "heathen"; it may have reflected the universal antagonism of in-groups and out-groups or the universal distrust of the unfamiliar. In these aspects, prejudice may even be regarded as a relatively innocent form of ethnocentrism, uncorrupted by consideration of self-interest. But once it became firmly tied to slavery, prejudice began to have certain functional uses which added immeasurably both to the strength of slavery and also to its brutalizing quality. Racial prejudice and slavery together created a vicious circle in which the assumed inferiority of the blacks was used as justification for their enslavement, and then their subordination as slaves was used to justify the belief that they were inferior. The stigma of race increased the degradation of slavery, and servile status, in turn, reinforced the stigma of race.[15]

Doctrines of race not only served to minimize the potentially serious economic divisions between slaveholders and nonslaveholders, but also furnished southerners with a way to avoid confronting an intolerable paradox: that they were committed to human equality in principle but to human servitude in practice. The paradox was a genuine one, not a case of hypocrisy, for though southerners were more prone to accept social hierarchy than men of other regions, still they responded very positively to the ideal of equality as exemplified by Jefferson of Virginia and Jackson of Tennessee. In their politics, they had moved steadily toward democratic practices for whites, and in fact it was argued, with a certain plausibility, that the system of slavery made for a greater degree of democracy within that part of the society which was free, just as it had made for democracy among the freemen of ancient, slaveholding Athens.[16] Still, this only made the paradox more glaringly evident, and no doubt it was partly because of the psychological stress arising from their awareness of the paradox that southern leaders of the late eighteenth and early nineteenth centuries had played with the idea of some day eliminating slavery. That was, in part, why the South had acceded to the exclusion of slavery from the Northwest Territory in 1787 and to the abolition of the African slave trade in 1808. It was why a limited number of southerners had emancipated their slaves, especially during the half-century after the Declaration of Independence, and why a greater number had indulged themselves in a rhetoric which deplored slavery without exactly condemning it. Some had even joined antislavery societies, and southerners had taken the lead in emancipating slaves and colonizing them in Liberia. Thus, for a generation, the great paradox had been masked by the vague and pious notion that at some remote future, in the fullness of time and God's infinite wisdom, slavery would pass away.[17]

By the 1830s, however, this notion had begun to lose its plausibility, for even the most self-deceiving of wishful thinkers could not completely ignore the changes under way. In the lower South the great cotton boom was extending slavery westward across Georgia, Alabama, Mississippi, and Louisiana, and into Arkansas and Missouri. Texas had set up as an independent slaveholding republic. The traffic in slaves between these new states and the older centers of slavery was probably greater in magnitude than the traffic from Africa to the thirteen colonies had ever been.[18] Compared to the birth rate of new slaves, the rate of emancipation was as nothing. Meanwhile, the New England states, New York, Pennsylvania, and New Jersey had abolished slavery.[19] Concurrently, northern anti-slavery men had begun to abandon their tone of gentle, persuasive reproachfulness in discussing slavery and had fallen not only to denouncing slavery as a monstrous sin, but also to castigating slaveholders, as hideous sinners.[20] One should not accept the apologia that the South would itself have got rid of slavery if this indiscriminate onslaught had not compromised the position of the southern emancipationists,[21] but it does seem valid to say that, in the face of such bitter condemnation, white southerners lost their willingness to concede that slavery was an evil—even an inherited one, for which Yankee slave sellers and the southern slave buyers of the eighteenth century shared responsibility. Instead they responded by defending slavery as a positive good.[22] But this made all the more stark the contradiction between equality in theory and servitude in practice, and their only escape was to deny that the blacks were qualified for equality on the same basis as other men. Some theoreticians of race even denied that blacks were the descendants of Adam, which was a long step toward their exclusion not only from equality but also from the brotherhood of man.[23]

With the theory of race thus firmly linked to the theory of slavery, the belief in Negro inferiority was as functional and advantageous psychologically as slavery itself was economically. The belief could be used to justify a certain amount of ill treatment of the blacks and even hostility toward them, since, lacking full humanity, they did not deserve fully human treatment and might justifiably be despised for their inherent deficiencies. By maintaining slavery, the South had violated its own ideal of equality, but by adopting racist doctrine it had both perverted and rejected the ideal, as the only way, other than emancipation, to escape from their dilemma.

All these shared institutions, practices, attitudes, values, and beliefs gave to southern society a degree of homogeneity and to southerners a sense of kinship.[24] But a sense of kinship is one thing, and an impulse toward political unity is another. If one searches for explicit evidence of efforts to unify the South politically because of cultural homogeneity, common values, and other positive influences, rather than as a common negative response to the North, one finds relatively little of it.

Yet any separatist movement in the middle of the nineteenth century could scarcely fail to absorb some of the romantic nationalism that pervaded the Western world. At the Nashville convention in 1850, Langdon Cheves of South Carolina had appealed to all the slaveholding states, "Unite, and you shall form one of the most splendid empires in which the sun ever shone, one of the most homogeneous populations, all of the same blood and lineage [note that to Cheves the black population was invisible], a soil the most fruitful and a climate the most lovely."[25] At about the same time, another South Carolinian had declared that as long as the South was in the Union, it occupied a false and dangerous position as "a nation within a nation."[26]

During the fifties, the spirit of southernism continued to grow. For example, in 1852, the governor of South Carolina spoke of "our place as a Southern Confederacy amongst the nations of the earth."[27] Near the end of the decade a Virginia Unionist complained that Alabamians denounced "anyone who professes the smallest love of the Union as a traitor to his country, namely the South."[28] When secession came, many southerners who favored it held back from separate state action because they wanted the South to act as a unit. Thus the principal opponent of immediate secession in Alabama wrote to a friend in Tennessee, "I resisted the secession of Alabama to the last moment, not because I doubted that it must come sooner or later, but because I preferred to wait until you in Tennessee were ready to go with us."[29] Even more, some southerners who chose to remain with the Union at the same time prepared to defend other southerners who might choose to go out of it. A Missouri newspaper declared that the border states, "while they are devoted to the Union, . . . will not stand idly by and see their sister States—bone of their bone and flesh of their flesh-trampled in the dust. They will not do it."[30]

Even when men in the southern states saw their political destiny as being outside the American union, they did not necessarily visualize a southern republic as the alternative. In 1832, John Pendleton Kennedy declared, "Virginia has the sentiments and opinions of an independent nation," but he meant independence of the Gulf Coast states as well as the Yankees.[31] Twenty-eight years later, Kennedy denounced South Carolina's secession as "a great act of supreme folly and injustice passed by a set of men who have inflamed the passions of the people."[32]

State loyalty no doubt gave ground to regional loyalty between the 1830s and the 1860s, but localism by no means ceased to compete with southernism. It is significant that Robert E. Lee, who was opposed to secession, had no thought of resigning his commission in the United States army until Virginia seceded, but then he "went with his state." It is perhaps also significant that the vice-president of the Confederacy, who had repeatedly hampered its power by his localistic objections, when imprisoned at Fort Warren after the war wrote, "My native land, my country, the only one that is country to me, is Georgia."[33]

The "set of men" whom Kennedy denounced as inflaming the passions of the people might have included at least four well-known southern figures. Two of these, Edmund Ruffin of Virginia and William Lowndes Yancey, might well be labeled southern nationalists, for they both had the vision of a South united by shared distinctive qualities, and both seemed to care more for the South as a whole than for their own states. The other two, Robert Barnwell Rhett of South Carolina and James D. B. De Bow of Louisiana, were also major actors in the secession movement, but for them a united South was primarily an alliance against the North. If nationalism means something more than bitterness against another country, it would be difficult to show that Rhett and De Bow were southern nationalists.

Ruffin, as early as 1845, had declared, "We shall have to defend our rights by the strong hand against Northern abolitionists and perhaps against the tariffites," and he had formed an intense aversion to all Yankees. He later boasted that he was "the first and for some years the only man in Virginia who was both bold and disinterested enough to advocate the dissolution of the Union." After working steadily for more than a decade to publicize the cause of southern rights, Ruffin came forward early in 1858 with a proposal for a League of United Southerners, of which he besought Yancey to assume the leadership. The League was to consist of citizens who would pledge themselves to defend and secure the constitutional rights and interests of the southern states. Members might form local clubs or chapters, which could sent delegates to a general council. "By discussion, publication, and public speeches," the League would have its impact upon the public mind of the South and would offset the excessive individualism with which many southerners approached public questions. In 1860, after Lincoln's election, Ruffin wrote, "If Virginia remains in the Union under the domination of this infamous, low, vulgar tyranny of Black Republicanism, and there is one other state in the Union that has bravely thrown off the yoke, I will seek my domicile in that state and abandon Virginia forever." True to his word, Ruffin went to South Carolina to encourage secession there in December, and to Georgia and to Florida during the weeks that followed, for the same purpose. In April, this sixty-seven-year-old champion of secession was given the distinction of firing one of the first shells in the bombardment of Fort Sumter. In the spring of 1865, utterly broken and unwilling to survive the Confederacy, he took his own life by shooting himself.[34]

Ruffin's friend and associate Yancey was another southerner who had proven extremely jealous in the assertion of southern rights, both in Congress in 1845–1847 and in his refusal to support the Democratic party in 1848 because it would not affirm the rights of slavery in the territories. But his public advocacy of southern separatism came much later and was somewhat inhibited until 1861 by the general stigma attached to the idea of disunion. By 1858, however, he seems to have become fully committed to the idea of a southern republic. In that year, he followed up Ruffin's proposal by organizing at Montgomery the first chapter of the League of United Southerners. In the same year, at a meeting in Montgomery of one of the annual commercial conventions, he sought to stress the southern rather than the purely states' rights theme by addressing his auditors as "My Countrymen of the South," and by suggesting that their gathering was "a foreshadow of a far more important body" which must "ere long assemble upon Southern soil" if injustice and wrong should "continue to rule the hour and the councils of the dominant section of this country." It was at this time also that Yancey put the rhetorical question: "Are you ready, countrymen? Is your courage up to the highest point? Have you prepared to enter upon the great field of self-denial as your fathers did, and undergo, if necessary, another seven years of war in order that you and your posterity may enjoy the blessings of liberty?" But perhaps his most straightforward statement was in a letter to a fellow Alabamian, also in 1858: "No national party can save us; no sectional party can do it. But if we could do as our fathers did, organize Committees of Safety all over the cotton states, (and it is only in them that we can hope for any effective movement), we shall fire the Southern heart—instruct the Southern mind—give courage to each other, and at the proper moment, by one, organized, concerted action, we can precipitate the cotton states into a Revolution."[35]

James D. B. De Bow made his contribution to the southern cause primarily by serving as editor, from 1846, of *De Bow's Review,* the most vigorous and effective of antebellum southern periodicals. With an enlightened feeling for breadth of coverage, he made the *Review* a vehicle for distributing information about the South as a whole and, especially, the southern economy. In the late fifties, he became one of the foremost advocates of secession. No southern nationalist exceeded him in zeal, but under analysis, his southernism seems to be about one part concern for the unity and cultural integrity of the South and nine parts hostility toward abolition and the economic hegemony of the North. If there had been no abolitionists, it appears that De Bow might have remained, as he began, an exultant spokesman of expansionist American nationalism.[36]

Robert Barnwell Rhett, affiliated with the Charleston *Mercury* since 1830, had been demanding separation from the North intermittently for a generation. His speech at Grahamville, South Carolina, on July 4, 1859, was a prelude to the final push by the fire-eaters, for Rhett declared that the South should either prevent the election of a Republican president in 1860 or secede. In his peroration he began with the incredible statement that he had spent twenty years trying to preserve the Union, and then, he said, "I turned at last to the salvation of my native land—the South—and in my latter years did all I could to dissolve her connection with the North, and to establish for her a Southern Confederacy." A toast was drunk that day to "The election of a Black Republican President—the signal for the dissolution of the Federal Union and the establishment of a Southern Confederacy."[37]

For all the electrifying rhetoric on this and other occasions there were no committees of correspondence, and the League of United Southerners apparently never expanded beyond three towns in Alabama. There was, however, one widespread southern organization, though it never did anything effective for the cause of southern nationalism. In 1859, at Louisville, Kentucky, a somewhat itinerant promoter and self-styled general, George F. Bickley, launched a fraternal enterprise which he called the Knights of the Golden Circle. Whether Bickley really had gorgeous dreams of a tropical empire or was merely selling such dreams to earn a living is not clear, but during 1860 he spent much of his time perambulating the South recruiting knights. The KGC, taking shrewd advantage of the spirit of filibusterism both in the South and in other parts of the country, and also of the rising tide of southernism, proposed that Mexico be acquired for the United States through negotiation with Benito Juárez. This annexation would solve the difficulties of the South as a minority section by bringing twenty-five new slave states into the Union. But if the North should spurn this glorious opportunity, or if sectional antagonisms should lead to disruption of the Union, the South could make the annexation alone and create a great tropical empire extending in a golden circle from the tip of Florida, around the shores of the Gulf of Mexico, to the Yucatán Peninsula. The southern press lavished an astonishing amount of favorable attention upon this hare-brained scheme, and General Bickley, a man not given to understatement, claimed a membership of 65,000 Knights in September 1860, and 115,000 in November. Probably one figure was as reliable as the other. In any case, the Knights played no significant part in 1861 in either forming or upholding the southern Confederacy.[38]

The southern commercial conventions provided perhaps the best opportunities to coordinate the impulses of southern nationalism. At first, they had carefully disavowed any spirit of sectional antagonism, even toasting the North and proclaiming a purpose to emulate the enterprise of their northern brothers. But at Charleston in 1854, Albert Pike of Arkansas advocated a program of southern joint action in the form of a corporation, chartered and financed by the fifteen slave states collectively, to build a Pacific railroad by the southern route. Pike also introduced overtly, perhaps for the first time at any of these conventions, the theme of disunion. The South, he said, should seek equality with the North within the Union, but if the South "were forced into an inferior status, she would be better out of the Union than in it." The following year at New Orleans, one delegate proposed the reopening of the African slave trade, another complained that the monopoly of northern textbooks in southern schools made for an education that was "unsouthern," and the St. Louis *Democrat* denounced the conventions as disunionist. At Richmond in 1856, a toast was offered which for the first time defined the boundaries of a prospective southern republic: "on the North by the Mason-Dixon line, and on the South by the Isthmus of Tehuantepec, including Cuba and all other lands on our Southern shore which threaten Africanization."

In the last four conventions, held at Savannah, Knoxville, Montgomery, and Vicksburg from 1856 to 1859, politicians and fire-eaters had largely replaced businessmen as the dominant delegates, and the meetings had become to a great extent rallies in support of disunion and a southern nation. At Savannah, the chairman spoke of "the beloved Southern section" and addressed his auditors as "free citizens of the South." The *New York Times* concluded that the primary object of the conventions was "to separate in the public mind of the South, Southern interests from national interests," while the Louisville *Journal* denounced most of the members of the convention as "brazen-faced disunionists . . . as thoroughly treasonable as the vilest conclave that ever polluted the soil of South Carolina."[39]

The convention at Montgomery in 1858 marked a high tide of militant southernism. With Ruffin, Yancey, and Rhett all in attendance, disunion had a field day, but the discussions also revealed the lack of a united South and the dilemma which secessionists would face: if they forced the issue, they might destroy the southern unity they were seeking to create; if they waited for such unity to become complete, they might never act. Yancey spoke eloquently of "a unity of climate, a unity of soil, a unity of production, and a unity of social relations." The business committee harmoniously endorsed the League of United Southerners. But when Yancey called for reopening the African slave trade, Roger Pryor of Virginia charged that his real purpose was dissolution of the Union. He, Pryor, would not dissolve it on this ground. Questioned as to the ground on which he would be willing to dissolve it, he replied, "Give me a case of oppression and tyranny sufficient to justify a dissolution of the Union, and give me a united South, and then I am willing to go out of the Union." A delegate retorted that if Pryor had to wait for an undivided South, he would never secede, but Pryor, not at all abashed, told him to remember that, in case of war, "the first onset would have to be met by Virginia, and one must not expect of her the same inordinate enthusiasm felt by others not as vulnerably situated as she." The impasse was partially broken by a more conservative Alabamian, Henry Hilliard, who suggested that the election of a Black Republican to the presidency would result in the subversion of the government and the dissolution of the Union—with the implication that the former would justify the latter. Pryor agreed that the election of a Republican president would probably be sufficient grounds for secession, adding that in such an event Virginia would be as ready to act as Alabama.[40]

Since nationalism is frequently as much a negative phenomenon as a positive one, it does not disprove the reality of southern nationalism to say that the southern movement arose primarily from antagonism to the North. Yet one is left with a feeling that the South did not want a separate destiny so much as it wanted recognition of the merits of southern society and security for the slave system, and that all the cultural ingredients of southern nationalism would have had very little weight if that recognition and that security had been forthcoming. Southern nationalism was born of resentment and not of a sense of separate cultural identity. But the cultural dissimilarities of North and South were significant enough to turn a campaign for the protection of southern interests into a movement with a strong color of nationalism. This does not mean that there was *never* a deeply felt southern nationalism. There was. But it resulted from the shared sacrifices, the shared efforts, and the shared defeat (which is often more unifying than victory) of the Civil War. The Civil War did far more to produce a southern nationalism which flourished in the cult of the Lost Cause than southern nationalism did to produce the war.

Even the manifestoes of the self-appointed custodians of southernism do not reflect the impulse to fulfill the unique potentialities of a unique society. Their complaint was not that the Union inhibited a robust but repressed culture struggling to be born, but rather that their cultural dependence upon the Yankees was humiliating. Why must southern children study textbooks written and published in the North, and incompatible with southern values? Why must southern readers subscribe to northern magazines instead of supporting southern journals which published southern authors? The frequency and the plaintiveness of this question is evidence of the rather self-conscious literary irredentism of a very small number of southern writers, but it also affords striking proof of the lack of cultural self-consciousness on the part of a large number of southern readers who ignored these pleas and continued to get their reading matter from the North. What the South's struggling authors wanted was not separation from the North but recognition by the North. Why must northern critics insist, they wanted to know, on lauding the doggerel of John Greenleaf Whittier while ignoring the genius of William Gilmore Simms? It was intolerable to have the *Atlantic Monthly* characterizing the South as a coarse and sordid oligarchy unhallowed by antiquity and unadorned by culture. But instead of separation, what they wanted was to escape the condescension of the metropolis toward the provinces, to attain some literary triumph which would force the North to acknowledge southern merit. Meanwhile, they retorted in kind, disparaging northern society as mercenary, materialistic, hypocritical, Godless, ill-mannered, and lacking in any class of gentlemen.[41] In 1858 a prominent Tennessee historian declared, "The high-toned New England spirit has degenerated into a clannish feeling of profound Yankeeism. . . . The masses of the North are venal, corrupt, covetous, mean, and selfish." But "the proud Cavalier spirit of the South," he added, not only remained but had become "intensified."[42] Early in 1860, Robert Toombs remarked in the Senate, "The feeling of a common interest and a common destiny, upon which foundations alone society can securely and permanently rest, is . . . rapidly passing away."[43] Later in the same year, conditions reminded Francis Lieber of what Thucydides had said of Greece at the time of the Peloponnesian War: "The Greeks did not understand each other any longer, though they spoke the same language."[44] As the secession movement got under way, the antitheses were drawn sharper and the stereotypes became caricatures. The "Yankee-Union" was "vile, rotten, infidelic, puritanic, and negro-worshipping."[45] The people of the South were descended from Cavaliers, the people of the North from Roundheads; the people of the South from the conquering Normans of 1066; the people of the North from the subjugated race of Saxons.[46] With such dualisms as these, it was an easy step to the view that the day for brotherhood was "past, irrevocably past," or that the North and the South must separate, not because of Lincoln's election, but because of "the incompatibility growing out of two systems of labor, crystallizing about them two forms of civilization."[47]

In December 1860, when South Carolina seceded, she gave formal affirmation to all these ideas in an Address of the People of South Carolina. "The Constitution of the United States," it declared, "was an experiment. The experiment consisted, in uniting under one Government, peoples living in different climates, and having different pursuits and institutions." In short, the experiment failed. Instead of growing closer together, the sections grew farther apart. By 1860, "their institutions and industrial pursuits, have made them, totally different peoples. . . . All fraternity of feeling between the North and the South is lost, or had been converted into hate; and we, of the South, are at last, driven together, by the stern destiny which controls the existence of nations."[48]

During the secession winter, the South produced a ceaseless flow of statements such as these—all affirmed with such intensity that they suggest the rise of southern nationalism to a fully matured, triumphant, and unchallenged fulfillment.[49] If antipathy toward the Yankees and antipathy toward the American Union could be equated, this inference might be valid. But feelings of anger and fear which part of a society may feel toward another part are not the same as the cultural differences between two distinct civilizations. Nor did hostility toward other elements in the Union necessarily imply hostility toward the Union itself. There was still a vigorous Union nationalism remaining in the South, and in spite of all the emotional fury, there was probably more cultural homogeneity in American society on the eve of secession than there had been when the Union was formed, or than there would be a century later. Most northerners and most southerners were farmer folk who cultivated their own land and cherished a fierce devotion to the principles of personal independence and social equalitarianism. They shared a great pride in the Revolutionary heritage, the Constitution and "republican institutions," and an ignorance about Europe, which they regarded as decadent and infinitely inferior to the United States. They also shared a somewhat intolerant, orthodox Protestantism, a faith in rural virtues, and a commitment to the gospel of hard work, acquisition, and success. Southern aristocrats might disdain these latter attributes, but the cotton economy was itself prime evidence of southern possession of them. The development of steamboats and railroads and the telegraph had generated an internal trade which bound the sections increasingly closer economically and had generated a nationwide faith in American progress and in the greatness of America's destiny. The South participated in all of these experiences, and the crisis of 1860 resulted from a transfer of power, far more than from what some writers have called the divergence of two civilizations.[50]

The degree to which southern nationalism still fell short of a culmination was evident from the continued devotion to the Union of a large part of the population of the South. In the election of 1860, southern voters had had a choice between two stout defenders of the Union—Douglas and Bell—and one candidate who denied that he favored disunion. The Unionist candidates carried 49 percent of the vote in the seven states of the original Confederacy.[51] Even after Lincoln's election, Unionism survived in those states and maintained dominance in the upper South. A high proportion of former Whigs, who had supported Bell in the election, boldly reaffirmed their Unionism. The

Vicksburg *Whig* declared, "It is treason to secede." It also predicted the consequences of secession: "strife, discord, bloodshed, war, if not anarchy." Disunion would be a "blind and suicidal course."[52] The Unionists also castigated the secessionists for their irresponsibility. The governor of Louisiana said regretfully that the dissolution of the Union was spoken of, "if not with absolute levity, yet with positive indifference"; and Alexander H. Stephens complained that the secessionists really did not want redress for their grievances; they were "for breaking up" merely because they were "tired of the govnt."[53] In the upper South, the Unionists reminded one another of the importance of their material ties with the North. Senator Crittenden of Kentucky had pointed out in 1858 that "the very diversity of . . . resources" of the two sections led to interdependence and was "a cause of natural union between us." In 1860 a Tennessee newspaper declared: "We can't do without their [the North's] productions, and they can't do without our Rice, Sugar, and Cotton."[54]

Besides, the Union itself remained a priceless asset, an "empire of freemen," in the words of one southern president, with "the most stable and permanent Government on earth."[55] "As a nation," said a North Carolina newspaper, "We possess all the elements of greatness and power. Peace smiles upon us from all quarters of the globe; a material prosperity, unparalleled in the annals of the world, surrounds us; our territory embraces almost the entire continent; we enjoy widespread intelligence and universal plenty; we are happy; WE ARE FREE."[56]

Southern nationalism had arrived, but Union nationalism had by no means departed. Sometimes, indeed, a man might declare his allegiance to both, in the same breath. Thus, Alexander H. Stephens as early as 1845 had said, "I have a patriotism that embraces, I trust, all parts of the Union, . . . yet I must confess that my feelings of attachment are most ardent towards that with which all my interests and associations are identified. . . . The South is my home—my fatherland."[57]

To one who thinks of nationalism as a unique and exclusive form of loyalty, the divisions of the South between Union nationalism and southern nationalism, and the movement of individuals from one camp to the other, will look like some sort of political schizophrenia. But if one thinks of nationalism instead as but one form of group loyalty, it becomes easier to see that the choice between Union nationalism and southern nationalism was basically a question of means—a question of whether the slaveholding society would be safer in the

Union or in a southern Confederacy. The South had fared extremely well in the Union of 1787, with its bisectional balance, its lack of centralized power, and most of all, its indulgent attitude toward slavery. As these advantages dwindled, men began to speak of the Union of 1787 as the "Old Union," and the South cherished its memory with nostalgia and reverence, as "the Union of our Fathers." In 1861 the New Orleans *Picayune* opposed secession and called instead for "the reconstruction of the old Union."[58]

Not only did southerners think fondly of a nation within which the southern social system had been secure. They also said quite directly that the security of their system was the criterion by which they should choose between the existing nation and the incipient one. Many recognized that even if a southern confederacy were successfully formed, its existence would not prevent slaves from fleeing north to freedom, would not silence abolitionist attacks on slavery, and would probably mean an abandonment of the rights which slavery, under the Dred Scott decision, enjoyed in the territories. The South would have to resist antislavery in any case, and so perhaps it could fight more effectively inside the Union than outside. Abolitionists might be more dangerous as foreign neighbors than as fellow citizens. The Union, said Benjamin F. Perry of South Carolina, "should be saved as a bulwark against abolition."[59] Secession would endanger slavery more than Lincoln would. Alexander H. Stephens warned that nothing was more dangerous for the South than "unnecessary changes and revolutions in government." He considered "slavery much more secure in the Union than out of it" and thought that Lincoln would make "as good a President as Fillmore did."[60] Hershel V. Johnson, a secessionist in 1850 but converted to Unionism by 1860, offered a simple and pragmatic explanation for his change: "I had become satisfied that Slavery was safer in than out of the Union."[61] The *North Carolina State Journal* denied that the essential problem was a conflict of loyalties. "The question," it said, "is not union or disunion, but what shall she [North Carolina] do to protect herself."[62]

As long as the North and the South had remained fairly equal in economic and political power, and as long as slavery had been immune to serious attack, the two sections had coexisted in a reasonably harmonious way. They could differ and even quarrel fiercely over various political questions without placing the Union in great danger. But as time passed, the sections ceased to be evenly balanced, and slavery lost its immunity. These simultaneous developments had an overpowering effect in the South. They generated a feeling of being on the defensive, the psychology of a garrison under siege.[63]

At the beginning of the century, the population of the slave states had been equal to that of the North, and the South had had 40 percent of the total white population. But by 1860, northerners outnumbered southerners in a ratio of 6:4 in total population and 7:3 in white population. At the beginning of the century, Virginia and Kentucky might talk about the power of individual states to prevent enforcement of the Alien and Sedition Acts, but they really did not need to resort to such minority devices, for they still had enough political muscle to put a Virginian into the White House in 1801 and to keep the presidency in the hands of southerners for forty-two of the next fifty years. But by 1860, a man might win the presidency without even being on the ticket in most of the southern states. The increasing discrepancies in wealth, productive capacity, and technological advancement were equally apparent. William L. Yancey told a New York audience in 1860, "You have power in all the branches of the government to pass such laws as you like. If you are actuated by power, or prejudice, or by the desire of self-aggrandizement, it is within your power . . . to outnumber us and commit aggression upon us." The South was not only in a minority but, more ominously, in a permanent and dwindling minority.[64]

Its power was dwindling, moreover, at the very time when the South found itself exposed to increasingly sharp attack by antislavery spokesmen. During the first forty years of the republic, slavery had certainly been criticized, but it had virtually never been threatened. Antislavery men had been gradualists, who proposed no sudden action; emancipationists, who relied on reasoned appeals to the slaveholders to practice voluntary manumission; colonizationists, whose program looked to the removal of the blacks along with the removal of slavery. Slavery had been respectable, and eight of the first twelve men who reached the presidency were slaveholders. Until 1856, no major political party had ever, at the national level, made a public pronouncement against slavery, and in northern cities, mobs that included "gentlemen of property and standing" had hounded and harassed the abolitionists.[65] But in the 1830s, the abolitionists had captured the antislavery movement, demanding immediate, involuntary emancipation enforced by law, denouncing all slaveholders with unmeasured invective, and even sometimes proclaiming the equality of the blacks.[66] Antislavery parties had appeared for the first time in the 1840s, and a major antislavery party in the mid-fifties. In 1856 the

Republicans had branded slavery as a relic of barbarism, and in 1860 they had elected to the presidency a man who said that slavery must be put on a course toward ultimate extinction. In 1859 many northerners had mourned the hanging of a would-be leader of slave insurrection. Meanwhile, slavery had been disappearing from the Western world and remained significant only in Brazil, Cuba, and the southern United States.

If the government of the United States should pass into the control of opponents of slavery, as it seemed about to do in 1860, the South had realistic reason to fear the consequences, not so much because of legislation which the dominant party might adopt, but because the monolithic, closed system of social and intellectual arrangements upon which the South relied for the perpetuation of slavery might be disrupted. Once Lincoln was in office, he could appoint Republican judges, marshals, customs collectors, and postmasters in the South. This would strike a heavy blow at the mystique of planter control which had been vital to the maintenance of the southern system. With their political domination challenged, the planter class might lose some of their social ascendancy also. More explicitly, Lincoln might appoint abolitionists or even free Negroes to public office in the South. And even if he did not do this, the new Republican postmasters would refuse to censor the mails or to burn abolitionist papers.[67] The temptation of postmasterships might attract some nonslaveholding southerners and make them the nucleus of an antislavery force in the South. For a slave system vitally dependent upon the solidarity of the whites, this loomed as a frightful menace. It was irrelevant to say that the Republicans did not constitute a threat because they still lacked the majorities which would enable them to enact legislation in Congress. They did not need to enact legislation.[68]

By 1860, southerners were acutely conscious of their minority status and their vulnerability to abolitionist agitation. After Harpers Ferry, a wave of fear swept through the South, subsiding somewhat in the spring and then rising again during the presidential campaign. There were reports and more reports of dark conspiracies for slave revolts, engineered by abolitionist incendiaries infiltrating the South in guises such as peddlers and itinerant piano tuners. Though seldom verified, the rumors were usually rich in details of plots uncovered; murder, rape, and arson prevented; and malefactors punished. For a time, the atmosphere was such that any fire of unknown origin or any white southerner's death of obscure causes might set off a report of arson or poisoning. And editors, no more immune than their readers, transformed into "news items" the fantasies of a society obsessed with fears of slave insurrection and with apocalyptic visions of terrible retaliation.[69]

When Lincoln's election came at last, the people of the slaveholding states were not united in any commitment to southern nationalism, nor to a southern republic, nor even to political separatism. But they *were* united by a sense of terrible danger. They were united, also, in a determination to defend slavery, to resist abolitionism, and to force the Yankees to recognize not only their rights but also their status as perfectly decent, respectable human beings. "I am a Southern man," a Missouri delegate had asserted in the Baltimore convention, "born and raised beneath the sunny sky of the South. Not a drop of blood in my veins ever flowed in veins north of Mason's and Dixon's line. My ancestors for 300 years sleep beneath the turf that shelters the bones of Washington, and I thank God that they rest in the graves of honest slaveholders."[70]

Motivated by this deeply defensive feeling, the people of the South also tended to accept an interpretation of the Constitution maximizing the autonomy of the separate states. According to this view, each state, when ratifying the Constitution, had retained its full sovereignty. The states had authorized the federal government, as their agent, to administer for them collectively certain of the functions which derive from sovereignty, but they had never transferred the sovereignty itself, and they could resume the exercise of all sovereign functions at any time by an act of secession, adopted in the same kind of state convention that had ratified the Constitution. However arid, and antiquarian it may now seem, the acceptance of this doctrine by a majority of the citizens of the Old South gave to it a historical importance independent of its validity as a consitutional theory. It is impossible to understand the rift between North and South without recognizing that one factor in this rift was a fundamental disagreement between the sections as to whether the American republic was a unitary nation in which the states had fused their sovereign identities or a pluralistic league of sovereign political units, federated for certain joint but limited purposes. Perhaps the United States is the only nation in history which for seven decades acted politically and culturally as a nation, and grew steadily stronger in its nationhood, before decisively answering the question of whether it was a nation at all. The framers of the Constitution had purposely left this question in a state of benign ambiguity. They did so for the best possible reason, namely that the states in 1787 were in hopeless disagreement about it, and some would have refused to ratify an explicitly national Constitution. Thus, the phrase "*E pluribus unum*" was a riddle as well as a motto. The utmost which the nationalists of 1787 could accomplish was to create the framework within which a nation might grow, and to hope it would grow there. But the legal question of the nature of the Union had been left in doubt and became a subject of controversy. The leading spokesmen on both sides were lawyers who confined themselves largely to drawing refined inferences from the exact wording of the Constitution and following every clue as to the intentions of the framers. In this kind of deductive reasoning, as it turned out, the defenders of state sovereignty had quite a strong case, made up essentially of five arguments:

First, at the time of the Articles of Confederation, proposed in 1777 and ratified in 1781, the states had explicitly included a statement that "each state retains its sovereignty, freedom and independence," and the treaty by which Britain recognized independence in 1783 named each of the thirteen states individually and acknowledged them to be "free, sovereign and independent states."[71]

Second, when the Constitution was framed in 1787, it was ratified by each state, acting separately and for itself only, so that the ratification of the requisite number of states (nine) would not have made any other state a member of the "more perfect union" under the Constitution unless that other state ratified.[72] It was true that the preamble said, "We the people of the United States . . . do ordain and establish this Constitution," and Daniel Webster, the Great Expounder of the Constitution and the great oracle of nationalism, had rung the changes on "We the people" as a proof that the citizens of all the states were merged into a consolidated Union.[73] But the term "people" was not used to indicate that one people instead of thirteen peoples were ratifying, but rather to distinguish between action by state governments and action by citizens exercising their ultimate power. Under the Articles, the central government had derived its power from the state governments and they in turn had derived their power from the people. Hence the central government could act only upon the state governments and not upon any citizens directly. But under the state constitutions *and* the Constitution of 1787, the people of each state (or the peoples of the thirteen states), by two separate acts, established for themselves two separate governments—a state government, operating locally for that state only, and a central government, operating collectively for the states together. Neither government had created the other; neither was subordinate to the other; they were coordinate governments, both sanctioned directly by the action of citizens, both operating directly on citizens without having to mediate through the machinery of the other government, and both subject to the ultimate authority, not of one or the other,[74] but of the constituencies which had established them. It was a truly dualistic system. This was the real implication of the term "We the people," and in the Convention the framers had originally planned a phrasing which would have avoided the confusion that later arose. They had agreed to list by name, one after another, "the people" of each of the thirteens states, severally, as the ordained and establishing parties. But recognizing the awkwardness that would result if the Constitution should name as a member of the Union a state whose people later refused to ratify, they substituted the term "We the people of the United States," using it as a plural and not as a singular term.[75]

Third, the proceedings of the Convention showed clearly that its members had deliberately taken up the question of whether the federal government could coerce a state government, and had positively refused to confer any such power.[76]

Fourth, at the time of ratification, three states had specifically reserved their right to resume the powers which they were granting by their acts of ratification.[77]

Fifth, the continued integrity of the states was reflected in the structural features of the new government which provided that the states should be represented equally in the Senate, that the states alone could cast electoral votes for president, that the states alone could ratify amendments to the Constitution, and that, under the Tenth Amendment in the Bill of Rights, "The powers not delegated to the United States by the Constitution nor prohibited by it to the States are reserved to the states respectively, or to the people."[78]

From these arguments, the political theorists of the South had developed the doctrine of state sovereignty and, from it, of the right of secession. The Virginia and Kentucky Resolutions of 1798, written by Jefferson and Madison, had asserted state sovereignty and had declared each state to be "the judge . . . of the mode and measure of redress" in cases in which the federal government might violate the Constitution. In 1803, St. George Tucker of Virginia, in a treatise on the Constitution, had asserted that each state, "still sovereign, still independent . . . is capable . . . to resume the exercise of its functions to the most unlimited extent." Later, Spencer Roane and John Taylor of Virginia and Robert Y. Hayne of South Carolina, in his famous debates with Webster, all added cogent affirmations of state sovereignty. In 1832, Calhoun's state papers on Nullification gave classic formulation to the same doctrine. Calhoun did not want to secede, and did not emphasize a doctrine of secession, but he made explicit his view that a state's ultimate recourse was to withdraw from the Union. In 1840, Abel P. Upshur of Virginia published a treatise which a modern critic has called "perhaps the strongest historical analysis for the support of state sovereignty . . . ever . . . written." Three years later, Henry St. George Tucker, a law professor like his father, compiled the existing arguments and added some of his own. Before his death in 1850, Calhoun again discussed the nature of the Union in his *Discourse on the Constitution*. By this time, the doctrine of secession had become, for a majority of politically minded southerners, a fundamental tenet of southern orthodoxy.[79]

There were, to be sure, a good many southerners who preferred to claim instead a right of revolution, as asserted in the Declaration of Independence. But the southern majority had committed itself to the right of secession during the crisis of 1846–1850, and James M. Mason, in 1860, was able to say, "Fortunately for the occasion and its consequences, this is not an open question in Virginia. Our honored state has ever maintained that our Federal system was a confederation of sovereign powers, not a consolidation of states into one people. . . . Whenever a state considered the compact broken, and in a manner to endanger her safety, such state stood remitted, as in sovereign right, to determine for herself . . . both the mode and measure of redress."[80]

Against the defenders of this doctrine, the defenders of nationalism did not come off as well as they might have, partly because they accepted the assumption that the nature of the Union should be determined by legal means, somewhat as if it were a case in the law of contracts. Yet in fact, the nature of the Union had been changing constantly, as the states increased in number until those which had created the Union were outnumbered by those which the Union had created. Between 1804 and 1865, the Constitution was not once amended, the longest such interval in American history. But while the text of the charter remained the same, the republic itself was transformed.

A thousand forms of economic and cultural interdependence had developed. Such changes do not occur without corresponding changes in the attitude of the people, and in a century of rampant nationalism throughout the Western world, there were probably no people who carried national patriotism and self-congratulation to greater lengths than the Americans, and this included the South. Regardless of arrangements made in 1787, nationalism changed the nature of the

Union and began to answer the riddle of *pluribus* or *unum*. But nationalism grew at different rates and in different ways in North and South, and by 1860, the sections found themselves separated by a common nationalism. Each was devoted to its own image of the Union, and each section was indistinctly aware that its image was not shared by the other. The South had no idea how ruthlessly its northern Democratic allies were prepared to deal with anyone who tried to tamper with the Union. The North had no idea how fiercely southern Unionists who valued the Union for themselves would defend the right of other southerners to reject it for *them*selves and to break it up without being molested.

The dual focus of southern loyalties, even as late as 1860, has led one author to say very aptly that the South by then had become a kingdom, but that it did not become a nation until thrust into the crucible of the Civil War.[81] Within this kingdom there was sharp disagreement between the advocates of a southern Confederacy and those who favored remaining in the Union. Yet underneath the disagreement was consensus on two important points. Most southern Unionists shared with secessionists the conviction that no state should be forced to remain in the Union, and most of them also believed in secession as a theoretical right. Whether it was justified or opportune could still be debated. But for southerners generally, the *right* of a state to secede, if it chose to do so, had become an article of faith.

Notes

1. Dwight Lowell Dumond (ed.), *Southern Editorials on Secession* (New York, 1931), p. 242.
2. "The only question is . . . can the Union and slavery exist together." William Henry Trescot to William Porcher Miles, Feb. 8, 1859, quoted in Steven A. Channing, *Crisis of Fear: Secession in South Carolina* (New York, 1970), p. 69.
3. David M. Potter, "The Historian's Use of Nationalism and Vice Versa," in his *The South and the Sectional Crisis* (Baton Rouge, 1968), pp. 34–83.
4. On southern fears of slave insurrection, see especially Clement Eaton, *Freedom of Thought in the Old South* (Durham, N.C., 1940), pp. 89–117; Eaton, *The Growth of Southern Civilization, 1790–1860* (New York, 1961), pp. 72–97; John S. Kendall, "Shadow over the City" [New Orleans], *LHQ*, XXII (1939), 142–165; Harvey Wish, "The Slave Insurrection Panic of 1856," *JSH*, V (1939), 206–222; Ollinger Crenshaw, *The Slave States in the Presidential Election of 1860* (Baltimore, 1945), pp. 89–111; Channing, *Crisis of Fear*, pp. 17–62, 92–93, 264–273; Kenneth M. Stampp, *The Peculiar Institution: Slavery in the Ante-Bellum South* (New York, 1956), pp. 132–140; also, citations in note 6, below.
5. Winthrop D. Jordan, *White Over Black: American Attitudes toward the Negro, 1550–1812* (Chapel Hill, 1968), pp. 375–386.
6. Joseph Cephas Carroll, *Slave Insurrections in the United States, 1800–1865* (Boston, 1938); Herbert Aptheker, *American Negro Slave Revolts* (New York, 1943); Marion D. deB. Kilson, "Towards Freedom: An Analysis of Slave Revolts in the United States," *Phylon*, XXV (1964), 175–187; Harvey Wish, "American Slave Insurrections before 1861," *JNH*, XXII (1937), 299–320; Nicholas Halasz, *The Rattling Chains: Slave Unrest*

and Revolt in the Antebellum South (New York, 1966); R. H. Taylor, "Slave Conspiracies in North Carolina," *NCHR,* V (1928), 20–34; Davidson Burns McKibben, "Negro Slave Insurrections in Mississippi, 1800–1865," *JNH,* XXXIV (1949), 73–90; William W. White, "The Texas Slave Insurrection of 1860," *SWHQ* LII (1949), 259–285; Wendell G. Addington, "Slave Insurrections in Texas," *JNH,* XXXV (1950), 408–434; Edwin A. Miles, "The Mississippi Slave Insurrection Scare of 1835," *JNH,* XLII (1957), 48–60.

7. For these insurrections see Aptheker and Carroll, cited in note 6. Also, John M. Lofton, *Insurrection in South Carolina: The Turbulent World of Denmark Vesey* (Yellow Springs, Ohio, 1964); Richard C. Wade, "The Vesey Plot: A Reconsideration," *JSH,* XXX (1964), 143–161; Carl N. Degler, *Neither White nor Black: Slavery and Race Relations in Brazil and the United States* (New York, 1971), pp. 47–51; John W. Cromwell, "The Aftermath of Nat Turner's Insurrection," *JNH,* V (1920), 208–234; F. Roy Johnson, *The Nat Turner Slave Insurrection* (Murfreesboro, N.C., 1966); Herbert Aptheker, *Nat Turner's Slave Rebellion* (New York, 1966); Kenneth Wiggins Porter, "Florida Slaves and Free Negroes in the Seminole War, 1835–1842," *JNH,* XXVIII (1943), 390–421; Porter, "Negroes and the Seminole War, 1817–1818," *JNH,* XXXVI (1951), 249–280.
8. Aptheker, *American Negro Slave Revolts.*
9. Benjamin Quarles, *Black Abolitionists* (New York, 1969), pp. 225–235; Howard H. Bell, "National Negro Conventions of the Middle 1840's: Moral Suasion versus Political Action," *JNH,* XLII (1957), 247–260; Bell, "Expressions of Negro Militancy in the North, 1840–1860," *JNH,* XLV (1960), 11–20.
10. When John Slidell made a farewell address before leaving the Senate after Louisiana's secession, he declared that Lincoln's inauguration would have been regarded by the slaves as "the day of their emancipation." *Congressional Globe,* 36 Cong, 2 sess., pp. 720–721. Also, on Dec. 12, 1860, John Bell wrote a public letter in which he said the "simple announcement to the public that a great party at the North, opposed to slavery, has succeeded in electing its candidate to the Presidency, disguise it as we may, is well calculated to raise expectations among slaves, and might lead to servile insurrection in the Southern States." Quoted in Mary Emily Robertson Campbell, *The Attitude of Tennesseans toward the Union 1847–1861* (New York, 1961), pp. 147–148.
11. H. M. Henry, *The Police Control of the State in South Carolina* (Emory, Va., 1914); Ulrich Bonnell Phillips, *American Negro Slavery* (New York, 1918), pp. 489–502, on slave codes and the policing of slaves.
12. Clement Eaton, "The Resistance of the South to Northern Radicalism," *NEQ* VIII (1935), 215–231.
13. "The whole social institutions of the people in the slave-holding states rested as they then supposed upon the stability of the right, which was involved with the ownership of slaves. It was reputed to be the cornerstone of that society, which for ages had rested upon it, and which it was supposed would be overthrown at its removal. All of the transactions of life were based upon it; all of the arrangements for the progress of society were made with reference to it; . . . It was thus that the remarkable unanimity was produced in all of these states. No other cause would have produced it." A. G. Magrath, Nov. 20, 1865, quoted in Charles Edward Cauthen, *South Carolina Goes to War* (Chapel Hill, 1950), p. 72. See also Eaton, *Freedom of Thought,* pp. 280–332.
14. Ulrich Bonnell Phillips, *Life and Labor in the Old South* (Boston, 1929); William E. Dodd, *The Cotton Kingdom* (New Haven, 1919); Avery O. Craven, *The Coming of the Civil War* (New York, 1942), pp. 17–38; J. G. Randall and David Donald, *The Civil War and Reconstruction* (2nd ed.; Boston, 1969), pp. 29–49; Eaton, *Growth of Southern Civilization,* pp. 295–324; Eugene Genovese, "Marxian Interpretations of the Slave South," in Barton J. Bernstein (ed.), *Toward a New Past: Dissenting Essays in American History* (New York, 1968), pp. 90–125; Genovese, "The Slave South: An Interpretation," in his *The Political Economy of Slavery* (New York, 1965), pp. 13–39; William H. Dodd, "The Social Philosophy of the Old South," *American Journal of Sociology,* XXIII (1918), 735–746; Wilbur J. Cash, *The Mind of the South* (New York, 1941), Book 1 Rollin G. Osterweis,

Romanticism and Nationalism in the Old South (New Haven, 1949) Louis Hartz, *The Liberal Tradition in America* (New York, 1955), part IV, "The Feudal Dream of the South"; John Hope Franklin, *The Militant South, 1800–1861* (Cambridge, Mass., 1956); William R. Taylor, *Cavalier and Yankee: The Old South and the American National Character* (New York, 1961); Clement Eaton, *The Mind of the Old South* (Baton Rouge, 1964); David Donald, "The Proslavery Argument Reconsidered," *JSH*, XXXVII (1971), 3–18; Jay B. Hubbell, "Cavalier and Indentured Servant in Virginia Fiction," *SAQ*, XXVI (1927), 23–39; Esther J. Crooks and Ruth W. Crooks, *The Ring Tournament in the United States* (Richmond, 1936); William O. Stevens, *Pistols at Ten Paces: The Story of the Code of Honor in America* (Boston, 1940); Guy A. Cardwell, "The Duel in the Old South: Crux of a Concept," *SAQ*, LXVI (1967), 50–69; David Donald, "The Southerner as Fighting Man," in Charles G. Sellers (ed.), *The Southerner as American* (New York, 1966), pp. 72–88; Grace Warren Landrum, "Sir Walter Scott and His Literary Rivals in the South," *American Literature*, II (1930), 256–276; George Harrison Orians, *The Influence of Walter Scott upon America and American Literature before 1860* (Urbana, Ill., 1929); Orians, "Walter Scott, Mark Twain and the Civil War," *SAQ*, XL (1941), 342–359.

15. Two major studies, neither of which is wholly responsible for the interpretation above, but which dominate the extensive literature dealing with the origins and nature of racial prejudice and racial subordination in the Negro-white context, are Jordan, *White Over Black*, and David Brion Davis, *The Problem of Slavery in Western Culture* (Ithaca, N.Y., 1966).
16. Eaton, *Growth of Southern Civilization*, pp. 152, 158, 307–309; Fletcher M. Green, "Democracy in the Old South," *JSH*, XII (1946), 3–23; Frank L. and Harriet C. Owsley, "The Economic Basis of Society in the Late Ante-Bellum South," *JSH*, VI (1940), 24–45; Blanche H. Clarke, *The Tennessee Yeoman, 1840–1860* (Nashville, 1942); Herbert Weaver, *Mississippi Farmers, 1850–1860* (Nashville, 1945); Frank L. Owsley, *Plain Folk of the Old South* (Baton Rouge, 1949); Fabian Linden, "Economic Democracy in the Slave South: An Appraisal of Some Recent Views," *JNH*, XXXI (1946), 140–189; James C. Bonner, "Profile of a Late Ante-Bellum Community," *AHR*, XLIX (1944), 663–680.
17. On antislavery in the early South, see citations in chap. 2, note 26. Also, John Spencer Bassett, *Anti-Slavery Leaders of North Carolina* (Baltimore, 1898); Ruth Scarborough, *The Opposition to Slavery in Georgia Prior to 1860* (Nashville, 1933); H. M. Wagstaff (ed.), *North Carolina Manumission Society, 1816–1834* (Chapel Hill, 1934); Early Lee Fox, *The American Colonization Society, 1817–1840* (Baltimore, 1919); P. J. Staudenraus, *The African Colonization Movement, 1816–1865* (New York, 1961); Beverley B. Munford, *Virginia's Attitude toward Slavery and Secession* (New York, 1909); Asa Earl Martin, *The Anti-Slavery Movement in Kentucky Prior to 1850* (Louisville, 1918); Merton L. Dillon, *Benjamin Lundy and the Struggle for Negro Freedom* (Urbana, Ill., 1966); Matthew T. Mellon, *Early American Views on Negro Slavery* (Boston, 1934); Richard Beale Davis, *Intellectual Life of Jefferson's Virginia, 1790–1830* (Chapel Hill, 1964).
18. Frederic Bancroft, *Slave-Trading in the Old South* (Baltimore, 1931), pp. 269–364, 382–406.
19. Athur Zilversmit, *The First Emancipation: The Abolition of Slavery in the North* (Chicago, 1967).
20. For changes in the tone of abolitionist literature, see note 66, below.
21. Hilary A. Herbert, *The Abolition Crusade and Its Consequences* (New York, 1912).
22. William Sumner Jenkins, *Pro-Slavery Thought in the Old South* (Chapel Hill, 1935); William B. Hesseltine, "Some New Aspects of the Proslavery Argument," *JNH*, XXI (1936), 1–14; Eric L. McKitrick (ed.), *Slavery Defended: The Views of the Old South* (Englewood Cliffs, N.J., 1963); Harvey Wish, *George Fitzhugh, Propagandist of the Old South* (Baton Rouge, 1943); Eugene D. Genovese, *The World the Slaveholders Made* (New York, 1969), part II: "The Logical Outcome of the Slaveholders' Philosophy," pp. 115–244; Wilfred Carsel, "The Slaveholders' Indictment of Northern Wage Slavery," *JSH*, VI (1940), 504–520; Robert Gardner, "A Tenth Hour Apology for Slavery," *JSH*, XXVI (1960), 352–367; Ralph E. Morrow, "The Proslavery Argument Revisited," *MVHR*, XLVIII (1961), 79–94;

Alan Dowty, "Urban Slavery in Pro-Southern Fiction of the 1850's," *JSH*, XXXII (1966), 25–41; Lewis M. Purifoy, "The Southern Methodist Church and the Pro-Slavery Argument," *JSH*, XXXII (1966), 325–341; Jeannette Reid Tandy, "Pro-Slavery Propaganda in American Fiction of the Fifties," *SAQ*, XXI (1922), 41–50, 170–178.

23. William R. Stanton, *The Leopard's Spots: Scientific Attitudes toward Race in America, 1815–1859* (Chicago, 1960), pp. 110–112, 155–160.
24. "There is a community of interest and feeling between the fifteen Southern States, fully as great, perhaps greater, than existed between the original thirteen," Augusta, Georgia, *Daily Chronicle and Sentinel*, Nov. 13, 1860, quoted in Dumond, *Southern Editorials*, p. 232.
25. Quoted in Nathaniel W. Stephenson, "Southern Nationalism in South Carolina in 1851," *AHR*, XXXVI (1931), 314–335.
26. William H. Trescot, *The Position and Course of the South* (Charleston, 1850), pp. 6–18.
27. Message of Governor John H. Means in 1852, quoted in Cauthen, *South Carolina Goes to War*, p. 6.
28. Eugene Blackford to Mary L. Minor, Nov. 9, 1860 quoted in Crenshaw, *Slave States in the Election of 1860*, p. 251.
29. Jeremiah Clemens to Solon Borland, quoted in Durward Long, "Unanimity and Disloyalty in Secessionist Alabama," *CWH*, XI (1965), 259.
30. St. Louis *Missouri Republican*, Nov. 21, 1860, in Dumond, *Southern Editorials*, p. 259.
31. Jay B. Hubbell, "Literary Nationalism in the Old South," in David Kelley Jackson (ed.), *American Studies in Honor of William Kenneth Boyd* (Durham, N.C., 1940), p. 177.
32. Hubbell, *The South in American Literature* (Durham, N.C., 1954), p. 487; also, William P. Trent, *English Culture in Virginia* (Baltimore, 1889).
33. Myrta Lockett Avary (ed.), *Recollections of Alexander H. Stephens* (New York, 1910), p. 253.
34. Avery Craven, *Edmund Ruffin, Southerner: A Study in Secession* (New York, 1932), quotations from pp. 107, 162, 198. The text of the constitution of the League of United Southerners is in John Witherspoon Du Bose, *The Life and Times of William Lowndes Yancey* (2 vols.; Birmingham, Ala., 1892), I, 377–378.
35. Du Bose, *Life of Yancey*, I, 358–360, 376; Joseph Hodgson, *The Cradle of the Confederacy; or the Times of Troup, Quitman, and Yancey* (Mobile, 1876); Austin L. Venable, "William L. Yancey's Transition from Unionism to State Rights," *JSH*, X (1944), 331–342; Venable, "The Public Career of William Lowndes Yancey," *AR*, XVI (1963), 200–212; Eaton, *The Mind of the Old South*, pp. 202–221; Alto L. Garner and Nathan Stott, "William Lowndes Yancey: Statesman of Secession," *AR*, XV (1962), 190–202; Malcolm C. McMillan, "William L. Yancey and the Historians: One Hundred Years," *AR*, XX (1967), 163–186, *De Bow's Review*, XXIV (1858), 578–588.
36. Ottis Clark Skipper, "J. D. B. De Bow, the Man," *JSH*, X (1944), 404–423; Skipper, *J. D. B. De Bow, Magazinist of the Old South* (Athens, Ga. 1958); Robert F. Durden, "J. D. B. De Bow: Convolutions of a Slavery Expansionist," *JSH*, XVII (1951), 441–461.
37. Laura A. White, *Robert Barnwell Rhett, Father of Secession* (New York, 1931), is standard and excellent. A more recent study is H. Hardy Perritt, "Robert Barnwell Rhett, South Carolina Secession Spokesman" (Ph.D. dissertation, University of Florida, 1954). Perritt, "Robert Barnwell Rhett's Speech, July 4, 1859," in J. Jeffery Auer (ed.), *Anti-Slavery and Disunion, 1858–1861: Studies in the Rhetoric of Compromise and Conflict* (New York, 1963), pp. 98–107, is especially pertinent to the paragraph above.
38. Ollinger Crenshaw, "The Knights of the Golden Circle: The Career of George Bickley," *AHR*, XLVII (1941), 23–50; C. A. Bridges, "The Knights of the Golden Circle: A Filibustering Fantasy," *SWHQ*, XLIV (1941), 287–302; Jimmie Hicks, "Some Letters Concerning the Knights of the Golden Circle in Texas, 1860–1861," *SWHQ*, LXV (1961), 80–86; Roy Sylvan Dunn, "The KCC in Texas, 1860–1861," *SWHQ*, LXX (1967), 543–573.
39. Herbert Wender, *Southern Commercial Conventions, 1837–1859* (Baltimore, 1930), pp. 123–129, 155–156, 162–228.

40. *Ibid.*, pp. 208–209, 214–217, 220–222. Robert R. Russel, *Economic Aspects of Southern Sectionalism, 1840–1861* (Urbana, Ill., 1924), pp. 123–150; John G. Van Deusen, *The Ante-Bellum Southern Commercial Conventions* (Durham, N.C., 1926); Weymouth T. Jordan, *Rebels in the Making: Planters' Conventions and Southern Propaganda* (Tuscaloosa, Ala., 1958).
41. On literary and cultural nationalism in the South, see titles by Hubbell, above in notes 31, 32; by Osterweis and Eaton, cited in note 14; and also: Merle Curti, *The Growth of American Thought* (New York, 1943), pp. 427–453; John S. Ezell, "A Southern Education for Southrons," *JSH,* XVII (1951), 303–327; Howard R. Floan, *The South in Northern Eyes, 1831–1861* (Austin, 1958).
42. J. G. Ramsey to L. W. Spratt, quoted in James Welch Patton, *Unionism and Reconstruction in Tennessee* (Chapel Hill, 1934), p. 3.
43. *Congressional Globe,* 36 Cong. I sess., appendix, pp. 88–93.
44. Thomas Sergeant Perry (ed.), *The Life and Letters of Francis Lieber* (Boston, 1882), p. 314.
45. Joseph Carlyle Sitterson, *The Secession Movement in North Carolina* (Chapel Hill, 1939), p. 238. See also William Howard Russell, *Pictures of Southern Life* (New York, 1861), pp. 5–8.
46. Osterweis, *Romanticism and Nationalism,* pp. 110, 148.
47. Clarence Phillips Denman, *The Secession Movement in Alabama* (Montgomery, Ala., 1933), p. 89; Cauthen, *South Carolina Goes to War,* p. 40. See also Henry T. Shanks, *The Secession Movement in Virginia, 1847–1861* (Richmond, 1934), p. 166.
48. Edward McPherson (ed.), *Political History of the United States during the Great Rebellion* (Washington, 1876), pp. 12–15.
49. "We separated because of incompatibility of temper; we are divorced, North from South, because we have hated each other so." Mary Boykin Chesnut, *A Diary from Dixie* (Boston, 1949), p. 20.
50. For a classic statement of the homogeneity of American culture in all parts of the country in the generation before the Civil War, see Allan Nevins, *Ordeal of the Union* (2 vols.; New York, 1947), I, 34–112. Also, J. G. Randall and David Donald, *The Civil War and Reconstruction* (2nd ed.; Lexington, Mass., 1969), pp. 1–28 and esp. p. 29; Randall, *Lincoln: The Liberal Statesman* (New York, 1947), pp. 41–43, 49–54; Carl Bode, *The Anatomy of American Popular Culture, 1840–1861* (Berkeley, 1959).
51. Thomas B. Alexander, "Persistent Whiggery in the Confederate South, 1860–1877," *JSH,* XXVII (1961), 307.
52. Quoted in Percy Lee Rainwater, *Mississippi: Storm Center of Secession, 1856–1861* (Baton Rouge, 1938), p. 164.
53. Jefferson Davis Bragg, *Louisiana in the Confederacy* (Baton Rouge, 1941), p. 2; Ulrich Bonnell Philips (ed.), *The Correspondence of Robert Toombs, Alexander H. Stephens, and Howell Cobb,* AHA *Annual Report,* 1911, II, 526.
54. *Congressional Globe,* 35 Cong., I sess., pp. 1153–1159; Campbell, *Attitude of Tennesseans,* p. 140.
55. Zachary Taylor's first annual message, Dec. 4, 1849, James D. Richardson (ed.), *A Compilation of the Messages and Papers of the Presidents* (11 vols.; New York, 1907), V, 9.
56. Dumond, *Southern Editorials,* p. 227. James L. Orr of South Carolina said, "When this government is destroyed, neither you, nor I, your children nor my children will ever live to see so good a government reconstructed." Quoted in Laura A. White, "The National Democrats in South Carolina, 1850 to 1860," *SAQ,* XXVIII (1929), 381.
57. *Congressional Globe,* 28 Cong., 2 sess., appendix, p. 314.
58. Howell Cobb to Absalom H. Chappell, Feb. 7, 1851, in Phillips (ed.), *Toombs, Stephens, Cobb Correspondence,* p. 221; New Orleans *Picayune,* quoted in Willie Malvin Caskey, *Secession and Restoration of Louisiana* (University, La., 1938), p. 36. See also Campbell, *Attitude of Tennesseans,* p. 171; Richard Harrison Shryock, *Georgia and the Union in 1850* (Durham, N.C., 1926), pp. 293–294.

59. Benjamin Franklin Perry, *Biographical Sketches of Eminent American Statesmen* (Philadelphia, 1887), pp. 171–180.
60. Stephens to J. Henly Smith, July 10, 1860, in Phillips (ed.), *Toombs, Stephens, Cobb Correspondence*, pp. 486–487.
61. Percy Scott Flippin, *Herschel V. Johnson of Georgia: State-Rights Unionist* (Richmond, 1931), p. 93.
62. Sitterson, *Secession Movement in North Carolina*, p. 213.
63. Rich in relevant data and quotations is Jesse T. Carpenter, *The South as a Conscious Minority, 1789–1861* (New York, 1930).
64. Emerson David Fite, *The Presidential Campaign of 1860* (New York, 1911), pp. 301–329.
65. Leonard L. Richards, *Gentlemen of Property and Standing: Anti-Abolition Mobs in Jacksonian America* (New York, 1970).
66. For the mild tone of earlier abolitionist literature, see Locke and Adams, as cited in chap. 2, note 26. For the increasingly militant tone after 1831, see titles in chap. 2, note 28; also, Herbert Aptheker, "Militant Abolitionism," *JNH*, XXVI (1941), 438–484; Bell, "Expressions of Negro Militancy," pp. 11–22; Bell, "National Negro Conventions," pp. 247–260; Quarles, *Black Abolitionists;* John Demos, "The Antislavery Movement and the Problem of Violent Means," *NEQ*, XXXVII (1964), 501–526; Martin Duberman (ed.), *The Antislavery Vanguard: New Essays on the Abolitionists* (Princeton, 1965), pp. 71–101, 270–298, 417–451; James B. Stewart, *Joshua R. Giddings and the Tactics of Radical Politics* (Cleveland, 1970); Stewart, "The Aims and Impact of Garrisonian Abolitionism, 1840–1860," *CWH*, XV (1969), 197–209; Lewis Curtis Perry, "Antislavery and Anarchy: A Study of the Ideas of Abolitionism before the Civil War" (Ph.D. dissertation, Cornell University, 1967). For the impact of this militancy on the South, Arthur Y. Lloyd, *The Slavery Controversy, 1831–1860* (Chapel Hill, 1931); Henry H. Simms, "A Critical Analysis of Abolitionist Literature," *JSH*, VI (1940), 368–382; Simms, *A Decade of Sectional Controversy, 1851–1861* (Chapel Hill, 1942), pp. 146–168; Simms, *Emotion at High Tide: Abolition as a Controversial Factor* (n.p., 1960).
67. For the importance of postal censorship to the South see Clement Eaton, "Censorship of the Southern Mails," *AHR*, XLVIII (1943), 266–280; William Sherman Savage, *The Controversy over the Distribution of Abolition Literature, 1830–1860* (Washington, 1938).
68. Roy F. Nichols, *The Disruption of American Democracy* (New York, 1948), pp. 352–353. For southern anxiety about the nonslaveholding whites, see Hesseltine, "Some New Aspects of the Proslavery Argument"; Channing, *Crisis of Fear*, pp. 254–256.
69. Crenshaw, *Slave States in the Election of 1860*, pp. 89–111; Nichols, *Disruption*, pp. 351, 367.
70. N.C. Claiborne, June 22, 1860, in Murat Halstead, *Caucuses of 1860* (Columbus, 1860), p. 239.
71. Henry Steele Commager (ed.), *Documents of American History* (7th ed., 2 vols.; New York, 1963), I, 111, 117.
72. North Carolina did not ratify the Constitution until Nov. 21, 1789, nor Rhode Island until May 29, 1790, and neither was a member of the Union when Washington became president.
73. E.g., speech of Webster in Senate, Jan. 27, 1830, in *Register of Debates in Congress*, 21 Cong., 1 sess., cols. 74, 77. Webster argued that the powers conferred on the new government were perfectly well understood to be conferred, (1) not by any state, or (2) the people of any state, but (3) by the people of the United States. Since the only thing that made the Constitution applicable in any state was ratification by a convention of that state, it is very difficult to see any rational basis for Webster's rejection of (2).
74. It has been argued, of course, that this coordinate status is eliminated and federal ascendancy is established by Article VI of the Constitution, which declares that the Constitution and "the Laws of the United States which shall be made in pursuance thereof . . . shall be the Supreme Law of the Land." But under the theory of a dualistic system federal supremacy would not follow. Instead the argument would run that each state, having made two constitutions—one by itself, for local matters controlling only the state government, and

the other jointly with other states, for general matters, controlling both state governments and the federal government—does not diminish its autonomy by providing that in cases of conflict between the two, the latter shall take priority. The "supreme law" clause gives a federal statute force only if it is "in pursuance of" the Constitution. Since both constitutions emanated from the same authority, the people of the states, acting severally in one case and jointly in another, the ultimate question was not which constitution should control in cases of conflict, but which government—federal or state—should act as arbiter for the people of the state in construing the constitution in question. Should each state act as its own arbiter, as Jefferson and Madison had argued in the Virginia and Kentucky resolutions of 1798; or should the federal judiciary act as arbiter, as in the cases of Fletcher *v.* Peck (1810) and Cohens *v.* Virginia (1821), when the Supreme Court asserted the power to declare the act of a state legislature void if contrary to the federal Constitution, and to reverse the decision of the highest court of a state?

75. Clinton Rossiter, *1787: The Grand Convention* (New York, 1966), p. 229; for the preamble as reported by the committee on detail, Aug. 6, 1787, and as reported back by the committee on style, see Charles C. Tansill (ed.), *Documents Illustrative of the Formation of the Union of the American States* (Washington, 1927), pp. 471, 989.
76. On May 29, 1787, Edmund Randolph introduced resolutions in the constitutional convention, including a provision that "the National Legislature ought to be empowered . . . to call forth the force of the Union against any member of the Union failing to fulfill its duty under the articles thereof." This was taken up on May 31. Madison was apparently the only speaker. He opposed it on the ground that "the use of force against a state would look more like a declaration of war than an infliction of punishment, and would probably be considered by the party attacked as a dissolution of all previous compacts by which it might be bound." He moved to postpone, and the motion was adopted unanimously. Tansill, *Documents,* pp. 117, 131. Andrew C. McLaughlin, *A Constitutional History of the United States* (New York, 1935), p. 598, offers an argument that the action on this resolution did not mean what it appears to mean.
77. Virginia's ratification, June 27, 1788, specified that "the powers granted under the Constitution being derived from the people of the United States may be resumed by them whensoever the same shall be perverted to their injury or oppression." New York's ratification, July 26, specified, "We the Delegates declare and make known that the Powers of Government may be resumed by the People, whensoever it shall become necessary to their happiness"; Rhode Island, May 29, 1790, adopted the same provision as New York. Tansill, *Documents,* pp. 1027, 1034, 1052.
78. It became a truism that the government under the Constitution was neither wholly federal nor wholly national, but mixed. The best analysis of the nature of this mixture is by Madison in *The Federalist,* number 39. William Paterson declared that "as in some respects, the States all to be considered in their political capacity, and in others as districts of individual citizens the two ideas—instead of being opposed to each other, ought to be combined; that in *one* branch the people ought to be represented; in the other, the states." Tansill, *Documents,* p. 297.
79. The historical literature on the development of the doctrine of secession is scanty. A brief but very able account is Carpenter, *The South as a Conscious Minority,* pp. 171–220. Also see Ulrich Bonnell Phillips, "The Literary Movement for Secession," in *Studies in Southern History and Politics Inscribed to William Archibald Dunning* (New York, 1914), pp. 33–60; William E. Dodd, "John Taylor: Prophet of Secession," in *John P. Branch Historical Papers,* 1908 (Ashland, Va., 1908), pp. 214–252; articles and correspondence of Spencer Roane, *ibid.,* 1905, pp. 51–142, and 1906, pp. 78–183.
80. Carpenter, *South as a Conscious Minority,* pp. 194–200, discusses the preference of some southerners for claiming a right of revolution rather than a right of secession. The quotation from Mason, taken from Richmond *Enquirer,* Nov. 23, 1860, is at p. 200.
81. Henry Savage, Jr., *Seeds of Time: The Background of Southern Thinking* (New York, 1959), pp. 49–136.

15

The Making of a President

Benjamin Thomas

Abraham Lincoln's rise to the presidency has often been chronicled. All too often the brilliant convention work which led to his nomination over William Seward is overlooked. In his book on Abraham Lincoln, Benjamin Thomas clearly revealed the factors and results of his men securing the nomination.

I have been on expenses so long without earning anything that I am absolutely without money now for even household purposes,'' Lincoln lamented to Norman Judd in reply to a plea for help in making up the campaign deficit. Yet, since he had held the place of honor on the ticket, he felt obliged to give what he could spare, and contributed \$250 more, bringing his total outlay to well over \$500. Then, weary in mind and body, he returned once again to his law practice.

Scarcely had the outcome of the campaign become known when small-town newspapers in Illinois, and even a few Republican journals in other states, began to mention Lincoln as a worthy presidential candidate. At dusk one day, when Lincoln left the courthouse at Bloomington, Jesse Fell took him by the arm and guided him to his brother's law office. Founder of the *Bloomington Pantagraph,* a large landowner, a canny politician, and a man of wide-ranging intellect, Fell had just returned from the East, where, time and again, persons had asked him: ''Who is this man Lincoln, who is opposing Douglas?'' Lincoln was acquiring a national reputation, Fell would have him know, and if his background and opinions were sufficiently brought before the people, Fell believed he could become a formidable presidential candidate.

Lincoln was not impressed. What was the use of talking about him for the Presidency, he replied, when such men as Seward, Chase, and others of almost equal prominence were in the running? Everyone knew them. Scarcely anyone outside of Illinois knew Lincoln. Besides, such men were more deserving of the honor; they had fought for Republican principles from the beginning on the national level in the face of opposition and abuse.

Fell conceded the truth of Lincoln's argument. But personal service and merit did not always signify a winning candidate. Both Seward and Chase had made enemies and uttered radical statements. Perhaps they could not be elected, even if nominated. The Republican candidate in 1860 must be a man of the people, conservatively antislavery, with no tincture of radicalism about him. Lincoln was such a man. Fell wanted Lincoln to write a short autobiographical sketch suitable for publicity purposes.

But Lincoln did not warm to the idea. Fell paid him a great compliment, he said, and he confessed he would like to be President. But he would try to keep his ambition within attainable limits. What he wanted was Douglas's Senate seat in 1864.

Three months later, when Thomas J. Pickett, editor of the *Rock Island Register,* proposed to come out publicly for him, Lincoln begged him not to do it. "I must, in candor, say I do not think I am fit for the Presidency," he wrote. And when Pickett insisted that he planned to consult other Illinois Republican editors with a view to a simultaneous endorsement of Lincoln, the latter again protested his unfitness and assured Pickett: "I really think it best for our cause that no concerted effort, such as you suggest, should be made."

Wittingly or unwittingly, and whatever Lincoln's secret feelings may have been, he acted wisely in declining the overtures of those who wished to push him forward. Premature announcement of his candidacy would immediately have brought him under rival fire. A presidential candidate is often in a stronger position when he seems not to seek the office.

Lincoln's correspondence shows that his influence in party affairs now extended beyond the borders of his state. He proffered advice regarding the Republican platform in Kansas. He counseled Chase that the plank in the Ohio platform calling for repeal of the Fugitive Slave Law endangered the party's fortunes in more conservative regions and must by all means be kept out of the national convention. Lincoln advised Schuyler Colfax, an Indiana party leader, that every local convocation of Republicans must be careful to do nothing calculated to alienate voters elsewhere. "In a word," he cautioned, "in every locality we should look beyond our noses, and at least say *noth-*

ing on points where it is probable we shall disagree.'' Aware of the importance of the cohesive and increasing German vote, in late May 1859 Lincoln through his friend John Bunn purchased from Theodore Canisius the type and other equipment of the *Illinois Staats Anzeiger*, a German-language newspaper published in Springfield, and granted Canisius full control of it so long as it should support the Republican Party. The consideration was $400, which Bunn may have advanced. After the election Lincoln resold the paper to Canisius for the same price he paid for it.

If Lincoln refused to allow himself to be projected into the presidential arena, he overlooked no opportunity to influence his party's policies. On a business and pleasure trip to Iowa in August, he accepted an invitation to speak at Council Bluffs. There and at St. Joseph, Missouri, he consulted Republican leaders. Throughout the summer, invitations to speak had come to him from places as far distant as New Hampshire, New York, Minnesota and Pennsylvania. Most of these he was obliged to decline. But in September he made a swing through Ohio, where Douglas had recently spoken in aid of the Democratic candidates in the fall elections. After speeches at Columbus, Dayton, Hamilton, and Cincinnati, Lincoln delivered an address at Indianapolis on his route back home. Eight days later he was off for Milwaukee, where he had agreed to give the annual oration at the Wisconsin State Fair.

A political speech was not appropriate to the occasion; but, after discoursing on the possibility of improving farm machinery and augmenting crop yields, Lincoln expounded on the opportunities for advancement offered by a system of free labor and subtly pointed out that a compliant attitude of mind toward slavery might eventually lead to the enslavement of all workingmen, white as well as black.

In a later day Lincoln himself would be regarded as the pre-eminent example of the self-made man so much admired by Americans, and already he saw himself as living proof of the chance for personal improvement offered by a system of free enterprise. If the factory system already tended to shackle the laboring man, Lincoln did not seem to be aware of it. The Northern laborer was surely better off than the Southern ''mudsill'' whose advancement was obstructed by slavery and the planter class. The period in which Lincoln grew up offered opportunities for self-betterment seldom equaled in American history, and among all places such opportunities were greatest in the Northwest. All about him, at home and on the circuit, Lincoln saw men who, starting life as farmhands, clerks, mechanics, or flatboat men, had become lawyers, merchants, doctors, landed farmers, and successful politicians. "There is no permanent class of hired laborers among us," he had declared in his speech at Cincinnati. "Twenty-five years ago, I was a hired laborer. The hired laborer of yesterday, labors on his own account to-day, and will hire others to labor for him to-morrow. Advancement—improvement in condition—is the order of things in society of equals."

Lincoln believed that labor is superior to capital, "and deserves much the higher consideration. Capital has its rights, which are as worthy of protection as any other rights. Nor is it denied that there is, and probably always will be, a relation between capital and labor producing mutual benefits. The error is in assuming that the whole labor of a community exists within that relation. . . . A large majority belong to neither class."

The basic tenet of Lincoln's economic thinking was equal opportunity for all. Living part of his life in an age of craftsmanship and part of it in an age of burgeoning industrialism, with cheap land always available, he saw perseverance, thrift, and enterprise rewarded. Under a system of individualistic enterprise it seemed of first importance to him—indeed, it seemed sufficient—merely to keep the road to high attainment clear of inequitable obstructions, with government aid to projects of general benefit.

After a second speech in Milwaukee, which was unequivocally political in character, Lincoln accepted invitations to speak at Beloit and Janesville en route to Chicago, where he stopped off a few days for political consultations.

All through the hot summer days of 1859, while he wrote letters and made occasional speeches, but for the most part put in long hours with the law to build up his depleted bank balance, the Illinois Republican organization was hard at work, raising money, instructing county leaders, building local organizations to peak strength. Jesse Fell, as corresponding secretary, traveled widely throughout the state, interviewing political leaders and ordinary citizens, calculating their reactions to possible candidates. As a rule he found the people anxious to have "Abe" Lincoln as a presidential candidate; but the local party leaders, stonily unemotional, hungry for loaves and fishes, coldly calculating in their desire for a candidate most likely to bring victory, were not so sure about their native son.

*

One day in October, while Lincoln was attending court at Urbana, news flashed across the country that old John Brown, abolitionist fanatic and veteran of the Kansas troubles, with some eighteen deluded followers, had seized the Federal arsenal at Harpers Ferry, Virginia, with the purpose of instigating a slave revolt. The South was horrified; the North was shocked. The whole country hung breathless on the news as Brown and his handful of brave, foolhardy men held off Virginia militiamen and a detachment of United States Marines commanded by Colonel Robert E. Lee until all but two of the band were dead or wounded.

Extreme abolitionist applauded Brown's reckless exploit and began to make a martyr of the patriarch. Responsible Republican leaders regretted and repudiated it. In the minds of Southerners, however, it raised the ever haunting specter of a slave revolt; this was the fruit of antislavery agitation. With the November elections impending, Democrats charged that Republicans were implicated in Brown's plot and that Brown drew his inspiration from Republican doctrine. In a parallel column with the news from Harpers Ferry, the *New York Herald* printed a year-old speech of Seward's forecasting an "irrepressible conflict." The event played into the hands of Southern radicals who were urging secession as the only recourse for the South in the event of Republican victory. Henceforward many persons both North and South would be guided by their emotions rather than their sober judgment.

*

On a raw day in late November, Lincoln started out at the behest of friends in Kansas to make several speeches in that territory. Having been won for freedom at long last, Kansas had adopted a constitution, elected a legislature, and was about to choose territorial officers and a delegate to Congress. As wintry winds lashed the forlorn frontier settlements and drove plainsmen to the shelter of their shanties and sod houses, Lincoln traveled from Elwood, where the largest auditorium was the hotel diningroom, to Troy, Doniphan, Atchison, and Leavenworth. On December 2, as he spoke at Atchison, John Brown went to the gallows in Charles Town, Virginia, seated imperturbably on his coffin and remarking as he gazed at the blue haze softening the outline of the mountains: "This *is* a beautiful country."

Lincoln had the old man on his mind and referred to him more than once in his Kansas speeches. Brown had shown surpassing courage and rare unselfishness. But his lawlessness was indefensible.

Slavery should be dealt with at the ballot box, said Lincoln; the North could offer no objection to Brown's punishment. Opposition to slavery could never justify violence, bloodshed, and treason. Then to his proslavery auditors Lincoln declared that the South, too, must learn the lesson of John Brown. For if the South should undertake to destroy the Union, "it will be our duty to deal with you as old John Brown has been dealt with."

*

During the autumn Lincoln was frequently mentioned as a presidential dark horse. Two presidential hopefuls, Chase and Simon Cameron, Republican boss of Pennsylvania, indicated a desire to have him as a vice-presidential running mate. Local leaders in Illinois were coming over to him in increasing numbers; more of the Illinois hierarchy were convinced he could win. On November 1, in a letter to W. E. Frazer, of Pennsylvania, Lincoln gave the first inkling that he thought he might have a chance when he wrote: "For my single self, I have enlisted for the permanent success of the Republican cause; and, for this object, I shall labor faithfully in the ranks, unless, as I think not probable, the judgment of the party shall assign me a different position."

On December 20 Lincoln sent Jesse Fell the autobiographical sketch he had requested a year before. "There is not much of it," he explained, "for the reason, I suppose, that there is not much of me. If any thing be made out of it, I wish it to be modest, and not to go beyond the material." Fell sent it to a newspaper friend, editor of a small-town Pennsylvania journal, who made it the basis of an article used extensively by other papers. At almost the same time Lincoln was preparing this sketch, however, he wrote to Lyman Trumbull that he would rather be senator than President.

Near the end of 1859 Norman Judd made an astute move. When the Republican National Committee met in New York to select a site for the party convention, several cities favored by one or another of the prospective candidates came up for consideration. Rivalry was keen, and Judd, sharply alert but seemingly casual, suggested Chicago as a neutral place, since Illinois had no candidate of her own. The committee immediately fell in with the idea; the presidential sweepstakes would be run in Lincoln's own state.

This being the case, Lincoln, still looking primarily to another try for the Senate in 1864, concluded that his chances would be impaired unless his home-state delegates gave him a complimentary first-ballot endorsement. "I am not in a position where it would hurt much for me to not be nominated on the national ticket,'' he wrote to Judd, ''but I am where it would hurt some for me to not get the Illinois delegates.'' Thus Lincoln became avowedly a candidate—not with any real hope of success, but as a means of promoting his senatorial prospects. His friends were pleased. They were more optimistic than he.

For several weeks the influential *Chicago Tribune* had been keeping Lincoln's name before its readers with extracts from his speeches and accounts of his activities. A reprint from a Milwaukee newspaper argued that Lincoln was more ''available'' than Seward or Chase. A long communication from ''A Union Lover'' protested Seward's radicalism. Joseph Medill, the *Tribune's* editor, himself journeyed to Washington to convince Republican Congressmen of Lincoln's superior chances to carry the doubtful states. On February 16, 1860 the *Tribune* came out emphatically for Lincoln.

*

Back in October, Lincoln had been invited to lecture at the Reverend Henry Ward Beecher's celebrated Plymouth Church in Brooklyn. It was a high compliment. But Lincoln had tried lecturing before, without success. In several towns in Illinois he had delivered a prepared address on ''Discoveries and Inventions,'' but it had not gone over well, and once the crowd was so small that the meeting had been called off. Lincoln realized that his forte was politics and asked the committee on arrangements if a political lecture would be acceptable. When they consented, he went to work in earnest.

He and Douglas had differed sharply on the attitude of the Founding Fathers about the extension of slavery, but neither man had adduced evidence to clinch his argument. Proposing now to do so, Lincoln embarked upon sustained historical research, poring over Elliot's *Debates on the Federal Constitution,* putting in hour after hour at the State Library, where he examined the *Annals of Congress* and the *Congressional Globe* and turned interminable pages of old, dusty newspapers as he sat hunched over a table, running his long fingers through his coarse black hair.

Arriving in New York after a tiring two-day trip, Lincoln learned that the Young Men's Central Republican Union of New York City had taken over the sponsorship of his address, which would be given at Cooper Union, in New York, instead of at Beecher's church. Ostensibly the purpose of the Young Men's Union was to promote a series of political lectures for the enlightenment of busy citizens, but actual leadership of the organization was vested in a group of veteran Republican politicians intent on thwarting Seward's aspiration to the Presidency.

All day on February 27, 1860 Lincoln was entertained at the Astor house as a visiting celebrity. That night, despite a snowstorm, fifteen hundred persons filed into Cooper Union, the largest assemblage "of the intellect and culture of our city" since the days of Clay and Webster, according to Horace Greeley. The famous editor, once an ally of Seward and Weed but now their avowed enemy, sat conspicuously on the platform, to which Lincoln was conducted by the prominent New York lawyer David Dudley Field and the celebrated literary figure William Cullen Bryant, editor of the New York *Evening Post.* Cheers rang out as the towering Midwesterner, know to his audience as Douglas's most formidable antagonist, was escorted down the aisle.

Lincoln felt nervous when he was introduced. He feared that his Western mannerisms and quaint rural accent might be amusing to sophisticated Easterners. He felt uncomfortably conscious of his new broadcloth suit, which did not seem to hang right and looked rumpled from his long trip. But his audience were with him from the start, and he soon thought only of convincing them.

Bringing to bear the facts he had gleaned from days of research, Lincoln proved that of the thirty-nine signers of the Constitution twenty-one, a clear majority, together with the seventy-six members of the Congress that passed the first ten amendments, "certainly understood that no proper division of local from federal authority, nor any part of the Constitution, forbade the Federal Government to control slavery in the federal territories," while all the rest of the signers of the Constitution probably shared that opinion. Consequently, he argued, quoting Douglas's own words against his rival, let all who believe that the fathers of the Republic "understood this question just as well, and even better than we do now, speak as they spoke, and act as they acted upon it."

Appealing directly to the Southern people, Lincoln took up one after another the accusations that some Democratic leaders were bringing against the Republicans. His party was not sectional, he said, except as the South made it so. It was not radical or revolutionary; it was conservative. It was the South that had rejected the old policies and in so doing caused the agitation of the slavery question. The Republicans had not instigated John Brown's raid, he said. Nor did Republican doctrines sanction such violent actions. The threat of secession in the event of Republican victory he likened to a highwayman holding a pistol to his victim's head.

Then Lincoln addressed himself to the Republicans. There must be peace. Republicans must do their part to cherish it. They must placate the South whenever possible in order to convince their Southern brethren that they did not seek to disturb them. But would they be convinced? Lincoln feared not, because nothing short of an admission of the rightfulness of slavery would satisfy them. "All they ask, we could readily grant, if we thought slavery right," Lincoln conceded; "all we ask, they could as readily grant, if they thought it wrong. Their thinking it right, and our thinking it wrong, is the precise fact upon which depends the whole controversy. Thinking it right, as they do, they are not to blame for desiring its full recognition, as being right; but thinking it wrong, as we do, can we yield to them? Can we cast our votes with their view, and against our own? In view of our moral, social, and political responsibilities, can we do this?

"If our sense of duty forbids this, then let us stand by our duty fearlessly and effectively. . . . Neither let us be slandered from our duty by false accusations against us, nor frightened from it by menaces of destruction to the Government nor of dungeons to ourselves. *Let us have faith that right makes might, and in that faith let us, to the end, dare to do our duty as we understand it.*"

As the intense figure on the rostrum uttered this stirring peroration, men and women rose to their feet, shouting, waving hats and handkerchiefs, in a long-sustained ovation. Men rushed to the platform to grasp the speaker's hand. Charged with deep emotion, the crowd was slow to disperse. Seldom had a visitor made such a profound impression on a New York audience. The next morning four New York papers printed the speech in full. Editors were lavish with praise. The *Chicago Tribune* brought out the speech in pamphlet form. Lincoln had materially enhanced his reputation in the East.

*

One reason for Lincoln's agreeing to go East was that the trip would enable him to visit his son Robert, who, after failing fifteen of the sixteen entrance examinations at Harvard, was spending a year at Phillips Exeter Academy in New Hampshire in order to try again. As Lincoln's purpose to visit New Hampshire became known, delegations from cities along his route invited him to speak. The Governor of Rhode Island sat on the platform when he spoke at Providence. Large crowds turned out at Concord, Dover, and Exeter. At Manchester Lincoln was introduced as the next President.

At Hartford, where the shoemakers were on strike, Lincoln declared: "I am glad to see that system of labor prevails in New England under which laborers *can* strike when they want to, where they are not obliged to work under all circumstances, and are not tied down and obliged to labor whether you pay them or not! I like the system which lets a man quit when he wants to, and wish it might prevail everywhere. . . . I don't believe in a law to prevent a man from getting rich; it would do more harm than good. So while we do not propose any war upon capital, we do wish to allow the humblest man an equal chance to get rich with everybody else. When one starts poor, as most do in the race of life, free society is such that he knows he can better his condition; he knows that there is no fixed condition of labor, for his whole life."

A brass band conducted Lincoln to his lodgings after a successful speech at New Haven. Meriden put on a torchlight demonstration. Woonsocket, Norwich, and Bridgeport offered gratifying crowds. His tour became a triumph as Republican admirers thronged his trains to accompany him from one town to another. With little advance notice of his coming, the demonstrations were largely spontaneous.

*

When Lincoln returned to Springfield after this dazzling Eastern trip, Milton Hay, addressing him on behalf of the local Republican Club, declared that "No inconsiderable portion of your fellow citizens in various portions of the county have expressed their preference for you as the candidate of the Republican party for the next Presidency. . . . There are those around you sir who have watched with manly interest and pride your upward march from obscurity to distinction. There are those here who know something of the obstacles which have lain in your pathway. Our history is prolific in examples of what may be achieved by ability, perseverance [*sic*] and integrity . . . but in the long list of those who have thus from humblest beginnings won their way worthily to proud distinction there is not one can take precedence of the name of Abraham Lincoln. . . .

"When in 1854 sectional strife and controversy were invited into the councils of the nation, a betrayed people began to see in your eloquent denunciations of that wanton act, and in your able vindication of the principles and policies thereby infracted, more high qualities and that true statesmanship which demonstrated their possessor to be well worthy of the highest offices and honor within their gift—well worthy the Presidency itself. We feel well assured that we shall look in vain amongst all the high names of the Republic for the man combining in himself, in his record, and in his history more of those elements which fit the man for the time, the occasion and the place than yourself."

These assurances, added to the unmistakable evidences of popularity that had been manifested on his Eastern trip, gave Lincoln a new confidence. He no longer made light of his chances. "The taste *is* in my mouth a little," he confessed to Trumbull when the Senator asked if he was a candidate. By means of adroit letters Lincoln sought to line up delegates wherever possible without being too obvious about it.

By the time the Illinois Republican convention met at Decatur on May 9 and 10, Lincoln's self-appointed managers had their strategy well planned. Lincoln came in late and received a tumultuous ovation as he was invited to a seat on the platform. Soon afterward Dick Oglesby, one of Lincoln's firm supporters and later Governor of Illinois, announced that an old Macon County Democrat wished to offer a contribution. "Receive it," roared the delegates, by this time worked up to a high pitch of excitement. With that, Lincoln's country cousin, weather-beaten old John Hanks, assisted by a friend,

ABRAHAM LINCOLN
The Rail Candidate for President
in 1860

Two Rails from a Lot of 3,000 Made in 1830 by Thos. Hanks and Abe Lincoln—Whose Father was the First Pioneer of Macon County.[1]

marched proudly down the aisle with a curious banner, supported between two fence rails bedecked with flags and streamers, which proclaimed:

The crowd broke loose in pandemonium. Men cheered, screamed, tossed hats and newspapers high in the air, and pommeled one another until part of the awning forming the roof of the hastily erected structure came down upon their heads. When the wreckage had been cleared away, the crowd called for Lincoln to speak. Rising slowly and pointing to the banner, he said: "I suppose I am expected to reply to that." He could not say whether he had made those rails or not, but he surely had mauled better ones. With that he sat down and the cheering broke out afresh. Thus Lincoln gained the cognomen of "Rail-Splitter," a good vote-getting nickname in that it symbolized his humble origin and kinship with the workingman.

The next day, with other business disposed of, John M. Palmer, a former Democrat, offered a resolution "That Abraham Lincoln is the choice of the Republican party of Illinois for the Presidency, and the delegates from this state are instructed to use all honorable means to secure his nomination by the Chicago Convention, and to vote as a unit for him."

Lincoln had been apprehensive lest the strong Seward sentiment in northern Illinois and the popularity in southern Illinois of Edward Bates, of Missouri, and old-line Whig, might, as he put it, squeeze him out in the middle with only slight support. But his managers had handled matters deftly. The Seward and Bates backers saw the futility of putting up a fight, and, as Palmer's resolution was unanimously adopted, Lincoln was not only certain to be put in nomination at Chicago, but could count on twenty-two votes. This was not an impressive number, but they would come from a pivotal state, whose wishes would command consideration.

*

Almost before the Decatur convention adjourned, the Republican host began converging on Chicago, now a city of 110,000. A robust center of trade and manufacturing, already rivaling Cincinnati as the chief location of the packing industry, Chicago still displayed a frontier lustiness. Served by fifteen railroads, its skyline stippled with the spires of fifty-six churches and the looming bulk of numerous grain elevators, it also flaunted more than a thousand saloons, grogships, and weinstubes, together with eighty ballrooms. Its plank sidewalks, following the natural undulations of the land, rose and fell like the waves of Lake Michigan.

Proud to be host to the Republican convention, Chicago had prepared against its coming by erecting a rambling frame structure, known as the Wigwam, designed to hold ten thousand people. But even this would be too small, for besides the usual galaxy of delegates, professional politicians, newspaper reporters, and hangers-on, thousands of other persons planned to attend the convention. New York sent more than two thousand men to cheer for Seward. Pennsylvania was represented by fifteen hundred. Hundreds more came from New England. And from all over Illinois the Lincoln men poured in, taking advantage of the cheap railroad fares that Norman Judd had wangled.

Bands blared. Processions marched and countermarched on the flag-bedecked streets. Men clustered in little groups with their arms about one another, whispering supposed secrets most of which were common knowledge, circulating rumors, speculating, arguing, haranguing anyone who deigned to listen. Bars and hotel lobbies were crammed. Feet were stepped on, ribs were jabbed, occasionally a nose was punched.

Lincoln's managers set up headquarters in the Tremont House. Their chief strategist was David Davis, of Bloomington. An enormous man, weighing more than three hundred pounds, rich, sagacious, indomitable, he was judge of the Eighth Circuit, which he had traveled with Lincoln for many years, sharing his room, roaring at his stories, sometimes chiding him for impoverishing the bar with his low fees, coming to appreciate his qualities of mind and character. On hand to assist Davis was a coterie of Lincoln's friends, many of them his associates on the circuit—Norman Judd, Stephen T. Logan, Leonard Swett, Joseph Medill, Jesse Fell, Republican gubernatorial nominee Richard Yates, Orville Browning, and a score of others.

No novices in the game of politics, they knew they faced a formidable but by no means hopeless task, for Lincoln's strength lay in his rivals' weaknesses. The acknowledged leader of the party was Seward, experienced, calculating, and somewhat cynical, a former Governor of New York, a United States Senator since 1848, and a forthright opponent of slavery extension. Backed solidly by the New York delegation, led by the smart manipulator Thurlow Weed, Seward was immensely popular. But he also had enemies, notably Horace Greeley, who, banned from the New York delegation, had contrived to be chosen a delegate from Oregon. Actually more of a compromiser than Lincoln, Seward by reason of his "higher law" and "irrepressible conflict" utterances was reputed to be a radical. Out to defeat him, besides Greeley, were Henry S. Lane, of Indiana, and Andrew G. Curtin, of Pennsylvania, both candidates for governor, who maintained that with Seward as the standard-bearer the Republicans would lose their states. The Illinois men also played upon this theme. The campaign of 1856 had demonstrated that Republican victory would hinge on Pennsylvania, Indiana, Illinois, and New Jersey; and

Seward, so his antagonists alleged, could not carry a single one of them.

Salmon P. Chase, of Ohio, twice Governor and once a United States Senator, not only was more radical than Seward and far less popular, but could not even command the full support of his own state. Conservative Edward Bates, of Missouri, had antagonized the German voters by consorting with the Know-Nothings. Simon Cameron, of Pennsylvania, had an unsavory reputation and, like Chase, was opposed in his own state delegation. Colorless John McLean, of the United States Supreme Court, was seventy-five years old.

Lincoln, on the other hand, did not enjoy sufficient prominence to have been marked either as a conservative or as a radical. He had no public record he must defend. His lowly birth and self-made attributes found favor with the masses. Six weeks before the convention Lincoln correctly appraised his situation when he wrote to a friend in Ohio: "My name is new in the field; and I suppose I am not the *first* choice of a very great many. Our policy, then, is to give no offence to others—leave them in a mood to come to us, if they shall be impelled to give up their first love."

Seating himself behind a big table in the unobtrusive Lincoln headquarters, Davis sent emissaries to visit the various delegations. Samuel C. Parks, a native of Vermont, established a liaison with the Green Mountain boys. Leonard Swett, of Maine, dropped in to talk with men from the Pine Tree State. Other New England delegations were similarly cultivated. The day before the official opening of the convention, Lincoln, waiting anxiously in Springfield, received a telegram from Nathan M. Knapp, a delegate from Winchester: "Things are working; keep a good nerve—be not surprised at any result—but I tell you that your chances are not the worst. . . . We are dealing tenderly with delegates, taking them in detail, and making no fuss. Be not too expectant, but rely upon our discretion. Again I say brace your nerves for any result."

On the eve of the convention it appeared that Indiana might be persuaded to give Lincoln her twenty-six votes on the first ballot, and that a goodly number of Pennsylvania votes might be obtained on the second ballot if Lincoln's chances appeared good. Davis was dickering with all the finesse he could command, when a telegram came from Lincoln: "I authorize no bargains and will be bound by none." Lincoln's friends were confounded. From an experienced politician such an admonition was unthinkable. Did Lincoln mean to shackle them, they wondered, or was he writing for the record? "Lincoln ain't here," the perspiring Davis grunted, "and don't know what we have to meet." Davis proceeded to clinch the Indiana delegation with a promise of the Secretaryship of the Interior to Caleb B. Smith and the Commissionership of Indian Affairs to William P. Dole.

*

Into the vast pine-board Wigwam on the morning of Wednesday, May 16, trooped ten thousand people, while twice as many swarmed hopefully outside. Ticket-holders took seats in the galleries, whence they looked down upon the huge platform where delegates and party leaders milled about, and in front of which, on a series of wide landings rising gradually to the rear of the building, non-ticket-holding spectators were privileged to stand, jammed in so tightly they could scarcely move. Pillars were wreathed with flags and bunting. Busts of notables stood in the corners. Portraits of statesmen and allegorical paintings of Justice, Liberty, and the like adorned the barren walls.

The first two days were devoted to routine business and the adoption of the platform. During recesses delegations met in caucus. The suspense became harrowing. The Seward men wished to ballot for President on Thursday afternoon, but the opposition effected a postponement. "There were hundreds of Pennsylvanians, Indianians and Illinoisans, who never closed their eyes that night," one participant observed. "I saw Henry S. Lane at one o'clock, pale and haggard, with cane under his arm, walking as if for a wager, from one caucus room to another, at the Tremont House." Curtin, of Pennsylvania, appeared equally agitated. Some time after midnight the Pennsylvania delegation, despite promises from Weed of tempting sums of money for campaign purposes if they would swing their strength to Seward, agreed to go for Cameron on the first ballot, McLean on the second, and Lincoln on the third. Since their first two votes were recognized as being merely complimentary, this action amounted to a commitment to Lincoln if he was still in the running when the third ballot came. In another midnight caucus the Illinoisans persuaded the New Jersey delegates to support Lincoln after a complimentary vote for William L. Dayton, their native son.

The Pennsylvanians were not won without a recompense. Davis promised Cameron a cabinet post. Recounting the history of the convention, one Pennsylvanian declared that Pennsylvania had decided for Lincoln before this promise was made, and that immediately following the decision one of Cameron's lieutenants cornered Swett and Davis and persuaded them that Cameron should be rewarded.

Conscious of the decisive part that crowd psychology might play in the morrow's session, one member of the Illinois delegation wished that the host of Seward shouters could be kept out of the Wigwam. Why not? asked somebody with a flash of inspiration. Ward Hill Lamon and Jesse Fell ordered a large supply of extra tickets printed and got them judiciously distributed to Lincoln men, all of whom were instructed to present them early. A Chicagoan reputedly able to shout across Lake Michigan was enlisted to take a strategic position in the hall and bellow lustily whenever Judd took out his handkerchief. Another man from Ottawa, equally endowed with vocal strength, was instructed to exercise his talent from another section of the Wigwam. Having done everything within their power, the weary Illinoisans snatched what sleep they could.

The convention reassembled at ten o'clock Friday morning. The hall was packed as usual. Outside, however, some extremely angry ticket-holders could not get in. For, while the Sewardites paraded, Lincoln's supporters had used their bogus tickets to advantage.

Nominations began at once, and as the name of Seward was presented, a tremendous shout went up—not all his friends remained outside by any means. But the racket merely served to inspire the Illinoisans. When Judd nominated Lincoln, their wild yell, according to one witness, "made soft vesper breathings of all that had preceded. No language can describe it. A thousand steam whistles, ten acres of hotel gongs, a tribe of Comanches, headed by a choice vanguard from pandemonium, might have mingled in the scene unnoticed."

Dayton of New Jersey, Cameron, and Chase were speedily put in nomination without the long-winded speeches of our present-day conventions. Then, before the nominations were finished, Caleb Smith of Indiana broke in with a second for Lincoln. It had been planned the night before. Again the Illinoisans shrieked and howled. But they were clearly bested when Seward's nomination was seconded, for so fiercely did the outnumbered New Yorkers respond that many persons stopped their ears.

But another second for Lincoln came from an Ohio delegate, and this time the Lincoln men, calling on the last full measure of their lung power, fairly made the building quiver. Many faces in the New York delegation blanched as "the Lincoln *yawp*" swelled through the building.

Bates, McLean, Cameron, and others were nominated, and the balloting commenced. After the long roll call the chairman announced the result: Seward 173 1/2, Lincoln 102, Cameron 50 1/2, Chase 49,

Bates 48, with the remainder scattering. It looked henceforward like a two-way fight.

Seward gained only 11 votes on the second ballot, while Lincoln picked up 79 as Pennsylvania, unmindful of McLean, swung a thumping 48 additional votes to Lincoln and he gained others elsewhere. Chase and Bates trailed with 42 1/2 and 35 respectively.

The tension became almost unbearable as a clerk called the roll again. Hundreds of pencils kept tally. Lincoln steadily picked up. His vote reached 231 1/2; 233 would nominate him. Joseph Medill, who had seated himself quietly among the Ohio delegation, leaned over to whisper to David Cartter, chairman of the Ohioans: "If you can throw the Ohio delegation to Lincoln, Chase can have anything he wants." Cartter, a stammerer, bounded up, exclaiming excitedly: "I-I a-a-rise Mr. Chairman, to a-a-nnounce the c-ch-change of f-four votes, from Mr. Chase to Mr. Lincoln."

There was a moment's silence. Then the wildest yell of all was loosed. Men danced and jumped. Hats, handkerchiefs, banners, canes were tossed aloft. The noise lulled, only to swell again. A cannon on the roof let go with a salute. Boat whistles answered from the river. The city's bells joined in the din. Across the nation thousands of telegraph instruments commenced to chatter.

*

Back in Springfield, Lincoln had gone to his office in the morning. He was talking with two young law students when Edward L. Baker, coeditor of the *Journal*, burst in with the result of the first ballot. Unable to stay calmly in his office, Lincoln started for the *Journal* building with Baker. On the way they stopped at the telegraph office, but no further news had come. The crowd that waited there shouted encouragement. At the *Journal* office Lincoln slumped into a chair. Another message came—the second ballot. At last a wire notified Lincoln: "Vote just announced—whole no 466—necessary to choice 234—Lincoln 354 votes—on motion of Mr. Evarts of NY the nomination made unanimous amid intense excitement."

Lincoln learned that Hannibal Hamlin, of Maine, had been chosen as his running mate. Messages of congratulation began ticking in. "We did it. Glory to God," wired Delegate Knapp.

Lincoln, beaming, shook hands all around. Then he started home to tell his wife. That night Springfield went wild. Friends and neighbors thronged the Lincoln home.

*

The day after the adjournment of the Chicago convention a group of distinguished Republican politicians got off the train at Springfield to notify Lincoln officially of his nomination. He received them in the modest parlor of his home. Only a few of them had ever seen him; several were bitterly disappointed by his victory, and some had misgivings about his ability to fulfill the duties of the nation's highest office. All of them scrutinized Lincoln closely as George Ashmun of Massachusetts, their chairman, presenting him with a letter of notification and a copy of the platform, made a short congratulatory speech.

Standing quietly before them in his ill-fitting clothes, head sunk, shoulders drooping, his huge hands clasped in front of him, and a sad, impenetrable expression on his scraggy face, Lincoln seemed embarrassed and irresolute. Ashmun finished, and the bent head lifted. The drooping body straightened to its full height. The dull eyes lighted with an intelligence that animated the whole countenance. The irresolute figure took on a calm, sure dignity.

Lincoln's words were brief—thanks for the honor done him, a recognition of the responsibility of his position, a promise to respond formally in writing when he had studied the platform. He wished to take each visitor by the hand, he said, and with that he passed from man to man, greeting each one cordially, talking easily and sometimes humorously. Governor Edwin D. Morgan of New York was somewhat startled when Lincoln, appraising his lofty stature, asked how tall he was. Refreshments were served, and the committee left.

"Why, sir, they told me he was a rough diamond," said George Boutwell, Governor of Massachusetts, to one of Lincoln's townsmen at a reception for the committee at the Chenery House. "Nothing could have been in better taste than that speech." And Judge W. D. Kelley, of Pennsylvania, turning to Carl Schurz as the committeemen walked down Eighth Street, observed: "Well, we might have done a more brilliant thing, but we could certainly not have done a better thing."

*

Ever the practical politician, Lincoln reckoned his chances of election. They seemed good, even if he was accounted a sectional candidate. Studying the platform, he noted that it had been carefully framed to appeal to diversified groups. A tariff plank, designed to attract the protectionists of Pennsylvania, New Jersey, and New England without alienating the antislavery Democrats who had joined the Republican

Party, conformed to Lincoln's own somewhat equivocal inclination toward "a moderate, carefully adjusted, protective tariff" which would not be "a perpetual subject of political strife, squabbles, changes, and uncertainties." A homestead plank, similar to a bill passed by the lower house of Congress but blocked in the Democratic Senate, courted those who wanted free land. River and harbor improvements appealed to the Northwest. A Pacific railroad and a daily overland mail furnished other examples of the positive economic program offered by the Republicans as opposed to Democratic traditions of laissez-faire. A pronouncement against restrictions on immigration and the granting of citizenship offered an enticement to the Germans and other foreign groups.

The platform extolled the Union, censured the Democrats for corruption and extravagance, branded the proposed reopening of the slave trade as a crime, denounced popular sovereignty, and demanded the admission of Kansas as a free state. On the general issue of slavery in the territories, however, the Republicans spoke less forthrightly than in 1856. In that year they had asserted the "imperative duty" of Congress to keep slavery out of the territories, whereas now, anxious to attract conservative votes, they simply denied the authority of Congress or a territorial legislature to give legal sanction to slavery in a territory.

Avoiding any strong pronouncement against slavery, and acknowledging the right of each state to order its own domestic institutions, the Republicans played down the moral question wherever it might lose them votes, shifting their emphasis to whatever economic issue seemed best calculated to appeal to a particular group or region.

Republican organization was thorough. The party's techniques were skilled. Speakers and campaign literature made the most of Lincoln's boyhood poverty, his pioneer background, his native genius, his rise from obscurity to fame. His nicknames, "Honest Abe" and "the Rail-Splitter," were exploited to the full. The party went into the campaign united, for Seward, suppressing the black disappointment the news from Chicago brought him, took the stump for Lincoln. Chase, Bates, and all the lesser aspirants supported him no less loyally. Pole-raisings, rallies, barbecues, songs, and speeches generated wild enthusiasm. All over the North the Republican Wide-Awakes—young men in glazed hats and capes, bearing flaming torches or lamps attached to fence rails—marched in zigzag formation simulating a rail fence.

*

With the Republicans presenting a united front, the Democratic ranks were sorely split. The Buchanan-Douglas feud showed no abatement, and the slavery issue threatened to disrupt the Democrats as it had previously undone the Whigs. Far and away the outstanding party figure in the North, Douglas had powerful enemies among the "Buchaneers." "I do not," proclaimed Senator Jesse D. Bright of Indiana, a strong administration man, "nor shall I ever regard a set of men in this country who call themselves 'anti-Lecompton Democrats' in any other light than Abolitionists, and most of them rotten in every sense of the term. I court and defy the opposition of every one of them, from their lying, hypocritical, demagogical master Douglas, down to the sorriest puppy in the kennel."

In the South, Douglas had wide popular support, but the extremist leaders were determined to defeat him at all costs, for to them the exclusion of slavery from the territories by "unfriendly legislation" was as hateful as the Republican doctrine of Congressional prohibition. Among this group were men resolved to rule or ruin. Their last hope of keeping control of the government was to control the Democratic Party. If they failed in that, they proposed to take the South out of the Union.

One such intransigent was spade-bearded Robert Barnwell Rhett, of South Carolina, who, almost from the beginning of his political career, had preached Southern independence as preferable to Northern dominance. Another was pugnacious William Lodnees Yancey, of Alabama, all through the fifties a promoter of sectional consciousness and Southern self-sufficiency. Of like mind were Edmund Ruffin, a Virginia agriculturalist; James D. B. DeBow, New Orleans editor; and John Slidell, Louisiana politician.

On the eve of the Democratic national convention Yancey contrived to have the Alabama delegates instructed to leave the national meeting unless the platform called specifically for the free entry of slavery into all territories and its protection there by positive Federal legislation. South Carolina endorsed this "Alabama platform," as did Mississippi, Florida, Louisiana, Arkansas, and Texas. Douglas could not stand on such a platform, though he was willing again to leave the territorial question to the decision of the Supreme Court. But the fire-eaters were adamant. Douglas's policy of "unfriendly legislation" had given them a means of defeating the exponent of the strong nationalistic sentiment of the Northwest and of rallying the South behind their cause. And in their efforts to encompass the defeat of Douglas, Buchanan's train-bearers in the North would back them up.

As the national convention convened in the fervidly Southern atmosphere of Charleston, South Carolina, on April 23, three weeks before the Republicans met in Chicago, Douglas controlled enough delegates to dictate the platform but too few to obtain the presidential nomination under the Democrats' two-thirds rule. The convention considered the platform first, and Yancey, introducing the Alabama formula, blamed Douglas's type of popular sovereignty for weakening the party in the North. Advocates of Douglas's pet policy, he declared, had virtually acknowledged that slavery existed neither by the law of nature nor by that of God, but solely by popular enactment. "That was your position and it was wrong," he chided. "If you had taken the position directly that slavery was right, and therefore ought to be . . . you could have triumphed, and anti-slavery would now be dead in your midst."

Here was the moral issue, so clearly recognized by Lincoln, voiced by a Southern radical, an issue on which men of moral sensitivities both North and South could not give way. And Douglas, refusing to take a forthright moral stand, would soon find himself between the sectional millstones.

For on the issue of the platform the convention split—unnecessary outcome because slavery's fate had been decided in almost all the national domain. What the radical forces wanted, however, was acknowledgment of the rightfulness of slavery. Defeated, they marched out of the hall, Yancey's Alabamians in the lead, followed by the entire delegations of Mississippi, Louisiana, South Carolina, Texas, and Florida, with scattering support from Arkansas, Missouri, Georgia, Virginia, and Delaware.

Under the chairman's ruling that the party's presidential candidate must have the votes of two thirds of the delegates chosen, rather than two thirds of those who remained, Douglas could not be nominated. Neither could anyone else. So Douglas's managers, hoping that Union-loving people would replace the seceders with men of more moderate opinions, recessed the convention for six weeks to meet again on June 18 in Baltimore. Thereupon the seceders, who had adjourned to a neighboring hall, likewise recessed to meet in Richmond on June 11.

Convening in the Virginia capital, the Southern extremists marked time while a number of delegates went on to Baltimore to seek readmission to the regular convention. Some were granted seats, but withdrawals began again, until of the original 303 party representatives only 192 1/2 votes remained. This time the chairman ruled that two thirds of those present could select the nominee, and on the second ballot Douglas became the party's choice.

Meanwhile the Southern seceders had met in Market Hall in Baltimore, where a few die-hard Buchananites from Oregon, California, Pennsylvania, New York, and Minnesota joined them. Adopting the platform of positive protection of slavery that had been rejected at Charleston, they nominated John C. Breckinridge of Kentucky. The Richmond convention then reconvened and endorsed their action.

The situation became more complicated when a group composed mostly of elderly old-line Whigs and former Know-Nothings also met in Baltimore and formed the Constitutional Union Party. Hoping to avert disunion, they declared for "the Constitution of the country, the Union of the states, and the enforcement of the laws," and nominated John Bell, of Tennessee, and Edward Everett, of Massachusetts, as their standard-bearers. The Republicans called them "do-nothings."

Thus, with three opposition tickets in the field, the prospects favored Lincoln. In the North the contest was primarily between Lincoln and Douglas; in the South it was Douglas versus Breckinridge, with Bell also a factor in the border states.

*

In keeping with the tradition that enjoined a candidate from campaigning in his own behalf, Lincoln remained quietly in Springfield. At the insistence of John Locke Scripps of the *Chicago Tribune* he wrote another autobiographical sketch, which became the basis of Scripps's campaign biography as well as others. But he issued no statement of policy, since, as he said, he had already fully defined his position and any new expression would be twisted by his enemies. His only speeches were informal greetings to paraders and well-wishers.

Lincoln's new distinction brought no change in his simple manner of life. He remained as modest, as genial, and as easily accessible as he had always been. But so many people wished to see him that neither his home nor his office would accommodate them, and the Governor's room on the second floor of the statehouse was put at his disposal. Serious, systematic John George Nicolay, a German-born Pike County editor, recently in the employ of the Illinois secretary of state, became Lincoln's private secretary, with dapper, sapient John Hay as his assistant. Both of these young men, Nicolay twenty-eight and Hay twenty-two, were destined to serve Lincoln for the rest of his career.

Lincoln's office had no anteroom, but the door to the hall was seldom shut. All day visitors trooped in and out—friends, politicians, favor-seekers, reporters, profferers and seekers of advice, the merely curious—while Nicolay at his desk in a corner tried to breast the tidal wave of mail, and sometimes in another corner a portrait-painter worked on Lincoln's likeness. Lincoln never seemed hurried, never lost his patience, was always master of the situation. Questioners never drew him out against his will. He imparted only what he wished to. Orville H. Browning recorded in his diary that "Lincoln bears his honors meekly. As soon as other company had retired after I went in he fell into his old habit of telling amusing stories, and we had a free and easy talk of an hour or two." Midway of the campaign nine-year-old Willie Lincoln came down with a bad case of scarlet fever. A sore throat and a headache led Lincoln to believe he had a touch of it himself.

In October a letter from "a number of very earnest Republicans" in New York suggested that Lincoln's dignity might be enhanced with a beard, and soon afterward the same advice was proffered by eleven-year-old Grace Bedell, of Westfield, New York, who believed that since "all the ladies like whiskers" they would "tease their husbands to vote for you." Lincoln doubtless chuckled, and replied in his own handwriting: "As to the whiskers, having never worn any, do you not think people would call it a piece of silly affect[at]ion if I were to begin it now?" Soon afterward, however, he allowed his beard to grow.

If Lincoln took no public part in the campaign, his seeming inactivity was merely superficial. He followed events closely and kept a sensitive finger on the public pulse. He wrote numerous letters. Whenever a breach threatened in the Republican dike, he was quick with advice or warning. Douglas would make a supreme effort in New York, he cautioned Weed. He admonished Hannibal Hamlin, his running mate, that any show of weakness in the early-voting state of Maine might "put us on the down-hill track," and lose the state elections in Pennsylvania and Indiana and perhaps the national contest in November. While keeping close touch with the situation country-wide, Lincoln carefully stayed clear of local party squabbles and rivalries.

*

As Lincoln measured the progress of events from Springfield, ominous news came from the South, where the extremist politicians, having disrupted the Democratic Party, now warned of the consequences of Republican victory. The protective tariff, the homestead law, and government expenditures for internal improvements were all means of plundering the South for Yankee benefit, they claimed. Slavery and the Southern way of life would be destroyed if Lincoln won.

Lincoln did not treat such bluster seriously, though he watched the situation carefully. The Southern people, he wrote to a correspondent in August, had too much common sense and good temper to break up the government rather than see it administered in the manner of those who formed it. In some respects his confidence seemed justified, for in every Southern state Unionist groups contended with the fire-eaters. Furthermore, even if the Republicans elected a President and won a majority in the House, the Democrats were sure to retain control of the Senate. How could the Republicans enact legislation destructive of Southern rights? All the presidential candidates—even Breckinridge—were committed to the Union. How could the secession peril become acute? Lincoln had often heard this threat before. It had been used effectively against Frémont. Its purpose now was to accomplish his defeat, he thought.

*

In contrast to Lincoln, Douglas threw tradition to the winds and campaigned strenuously. As the only anti-Republican candidate with a chance to carry the free states, he put everything into the fight. And despite the odds against him he still thought he might win. Knowing the Southern temper better than Lincoln, he gave more credence to Southern threats. His own election would assure peace. He must get his message to the people.

So Douglas stumped the nation, an unheard-of thing for a presidential candidate. He had been ill; his throat was bad; but he worked with superhuman energy, traveling through New England, North Carolina, and the middle states, then to the West.

In August, local elections in Vermont and Maine produced large Republican majorities. In a desperate effort to head off defeat, the anti-Republican parties attempted fusion in some Northern states. During the second week in October, however, state elections in Pennsylvania and Ohio confirmed the early trend, and Douglas, learning by telegraph of these Republican victories, remarked gravely to his secretary: "Mr. Lincoln is the next President. We must try to save the Union. I will go South."

His speeches there were fiercely Unionist. The election of a Republican offered no justification for secession, he insisted. Abolitionists and seceders alike deserved to dangle at a rope's end. Douglas appealed to the whole nation, but it was his misfortune to be accounted proslavery in the North and antislavery in the South.

*

Despite every effort of Douglas and the Southern Unionists, fear overspread the South. Wild rumors circulated. Abolitionists were said to be working secretly among the Negroes. Wells had been poisoned in Texas. Drought added to the despair as it threatened the cotton crop. Heavy debts to Northern banks and importers oppressed farmers and planters. The South was restless, frustrated, alarmed.

The economic loss that threatened if the Republicans should free the slaves was not the South's chief concern; only a relatively small proportion of Southerners owned slaves. What haunted everyone was the specter of savage black men roaming the country uncontrolled, or of Negroes claiming social and economic equality with the whites, attending their schools and churches, competing for their jobs, outvoting them at the polls. All classes shared these fears, because, while the planters might be badly hurt by emancipation, they could survive, whereas the poor white man faced not only destitution but degradation. For slavery gave even the meanest white man a measure of respectability; there was always the black man below him in the social scale.

What if Lincoln were elected, people asked. He had said he would not free the slaves. But how about his abolitionist cohorts? Could he hold out against them, granting that he really wished to do so? Many persons believed him to be an abolitionist regardless of his denials. And even if Lincoln made no overt move, the Republican policy of containment meant slow death to slavery. At best, the evil day would merely be deferred.

Lincoln would control the patronage. Whom would he appoint to office in the South? Mudsills? Free Negroes? Abolitionists? Republican postmasters would not censor the mails; incendiary literature would flood the country. Men wondered if some sinister purpose inspired the organization of those well-drilled Wide-Awakes. Some planters saw the election of a scion of poor whites of Kentucky as incitement to submerged Southern whites to flout planter ascendancy.

In the little crossroads stores, on the village streets, in the parlors of isolated mansions and the kitchens of lonely backwoods farmhouses, men meeting quietly gave sober utterance to their forebodings.

Cherishing an archaic institution, the South had developed a provincial philosophy. The Southern people believed they had developed a superior civilization founded on a rightful institution. It was unmarred by those sordid conflicts between capital and labor which frequently plagued the North. It provided its workers with a social security unequaled anywhere. Yet the swindling, penny-pinching Yankees, who ground the faces of their own workers in the dust and threw them on their own resources when their working days were over, these self-righteous Yankees vilified the Southern way of life, and pronounced the slaveowner evil. For too long now the North had exploited the South and held it back. More and more, especially after John Brown's raid, Southerners yielded to the belief that the old union of hearts and souls was broken, and the South should go her own way. Providing the intellectual basis for state rights and Southern independence was the political philosophy of John C. Calhoun, so universally accepted in the South that, while many persons questioned the wisdom of secession, scarcely anyone denied the right.

This feeling of "Southernism" flourished most intensely in South Carolina, where members of the ruling oligarchy were resolved to retain power. Secession appeared to be their only hope; they would sunder the old affiliations and set up a government of their own. The Gulf states were in a mood to join them. How could the money-grubbing Yankees stop the movement when they would never fight? One Southerner sneered that if a Yankee ever pointed a gun at him he would simply ask how much he would take for it. Before election day six Southern governors and virtually every Senator and Congressman from the seven states of the lower South were on record as favoring secession if Lincoln should be elected.

*

Lincoln spent most of election day, November 6, at his office in the statehouse. About three o'clock he walked quietly to the polls at the courthouse, where, after cutting the names of his own electors from the top of the ballot, he voted a straight ticket. A dense crowd cheered him, following him through the hall and up the stairs, then down again.

That night Lincoln sat in the telegraph office while the returns came in. The outcome did not long remain in doubt. When the tabulation was completed, Lincoln had 1,866,452 votes, Douglas

1,376,957, Breckinridge 849,781, and Bell 588,879. Douglas and Bell together had 100,000 more votes than Lincoln; his three opponents out polled him by almost a million. Only Bell carried his home county—Sangamon went for Douglas by a narrow margin. Except for a few ballots in the border states and the Virginia panhandle, Lincoln polled not one vote in the South.

The electoral vote would shape up differently. Lincoln, carrying all the Northern states except New Jersey, whose vote he split with Douglas, would have 173 votes, Breckinridge 72, Bell 39, and Douglas 12. Yet such is the peculiarity of our electoral system that, if all the opposition votes had been united upon a single candidate, Lincoln would still have won. He would be a minority President, but there were no constitutional grounds on which to contest his election.

Notes

1. The sign should have read *John* Hanks; and Lincoln's father was by no means the first settler in the county.

16

Radical Rule in the South

Kenneth M. Stampp

The period of reconstruction of the South following the Civil War remains one of the most controversial in American History. The successes and failures of the various groups that vied for power is confusing and difficult to assess. In this article Kenneth Stampp gives a clear and penetrating appraisal of this time.

When Lord Bryce, in the 1880's, wrote *The American Commonwealth,* he commented at length on the southern state governments created under the radical plan of reconstruction. What he had to say about them was not remarkable for its originality, but a few passages are worth quoting to give the flavor of the approaching historical consensus. "Such a Saturnalia of robbery and jobbery has seldom been seen in any civilized country. . . . The position of these [radical] adventurers was like that of a Roman provincial governor in the latter days of the Republic. . . . [All] voting power lay with those who were wholly unfit for citizenship, and had no interest as taxpayers, in good government. . . . [Since] the legislatures were reckless and corrupt, the judges for the most part subservient, the Federal military officers bound to support what purported to be the consitutional authorities of the State, Congress distant and little inclined to listen to the complaints of those whom it distrusted as rebels, greed was unchecked and roguery unabashed."[1] In drawing this unpleasant picture Lord Bryce anticipated the generalizations of the Dunningites, as did many others.

Each of the eleven states of the former Confederacy, during all or part of the decade between 1867 and 1877, fell under the control of the radical Republicans. Tennessee was the first to be captured by them—indeed, it never had a Johnson government—but it was also the first to be lost. Tennessee was "redeemed," as southern white Democrats liked to call their return to power, as early as 1869. The last three states to be redeemed were South Carolina, Florida, and Louisiana, where the radical regimes lasted until the spring of 1877.

What, according to the conservatives, were the sins of the radical governments? The new governments they said, expelled from power the South's experienced statemen and natural leaders and replaced them with untrained men who were almost uniformly incompetent and corrupt. Among the radical leaders, the Yankee carpetbaggers, crafty adventurers who invaded the postwar South for political and economic plunder, were the most notorious. The scalawags, who assisted the carpetbaggers, were mostly degraded and depraved poor whites, betrayers of their race and section who sought a share of the radical spoils. The Negroes, ignorant and illiterate, played an essentially passive political role, casting their votes as radical agents of the Union League and Freedmen's Bureau told them to. Since the members of the radical coalition owned little or no property themselves, they increased state and local taxes until they came near to ruining the whole class of white property holders. Their extravagant appropriations, their waste, fraud, and corruption, caused shocking increases in southern state debts and brought some states to the edge of bankruptcy. Finally, said the conservatives, the radical governments threatened to destroy the white civilization of the South and to reduce it to African barbarism.

We must first consider the charge that the radicals expelled from power the South's natural leaders. One of the characters in Margaret Michell's popular novel, *Gone With the Wind,* complains that everybody who was anybody in the good old days was nobody in the radical regimes. A conservative Tennessean reported that the radicals in his state were "the party paying no taxes, riding poor horses, wearing dirty shirts, and having no use for soap." According to a Nashville newspaper, most of the so-called loyal men of the South were "the merest trash that could be collected in a civilized community, of no personal credit or social responsibility." Thus, concludes a historian of reconstruction in Tennessee, "the power, wealth, culture, and natural leadership" of the state had been evicted from political control.[2] An upper-class Virginian sent Thad Stevens a bitter protest against being subjected to "our former slaves and the mean white surfs [*sic*] of the earth. . . . We are the children of the Lees, Clays, Henrys, Jeffersons and Jacksons. Tell me if we are to be ruled by these people." This would seem to suggest that to some extent and in some places southern class divisions were sharpened during the era of reconstruction. But southern conservatives exaggerated the degree to which the division between them and the radicals was along class lines.

In any case, those who have referred to the South's antebellum political rulers as its natural leaders are seldom explicit about what they mean. Remembering what had happened to the South under the guidance of her prewar politicians, it would be hard to argue that they had won the right to lead because they had governed so wisely or so well. If it is valid to judge statesmen by their understanding of the problems of their age, and by their efforts to find constructive solutions, the old southern leaders would have to be pronounced failures on both counts; and many of them were, moreover, singularly irresponsible. Their strength was rooted in their economic power derived from large property holdings, and in their experience in the techniques of political manipulation. The conservatives' repeated complaint that the radicals paid no taxes and owned little property is highly suggestive, for their whole conception of natural political leadership ultimately boils down to this. When the radicals won control in the South, they did not displace a responsible political élite which had traditionally taken a large view of things; nor did they discharge a trained body of civil servants. This being the case, the change in leadership was far less disastrous than it has often been made to appear.

But the customary charges against the new southern leadership are extremely severe and need to be weighed carefully. It is essential, therefore, to examine in some detail each of the three elements in the radical coalition—the carpetbaggers, scalawags, and Negroes—to test the validity of the generalizations conservatives used to characterize them. The term "carpetbagger" was applied to recent northern settlers in the South who actively supported the radical Republicans.[3] Since the term has an invidious connotation, it is used here only for lack of another that is equally familiar but morally neutral. The so-called carpetbaggers were not all poor men who carried their meager possessions with them in carpetbags; they were not all ignorant; they were not all corrupt. Rather, they were a heterogeneous lot who moved to the South for a variety of reasons.

Among the carpetbaggers were some who fitted the stereotype: disreputable opportunists and corruptionist who went south in search of political plunder or public office. Because these carpetbaggers were so conspicuous and gained such notoriety, conservative southern Democrats succeeded in portraying them as typical, though actually they constituted a small minority.

Few of the carpetbaggers came to the South originally for the purpose of entering politics; many of them arrived before 1867 when political careers were not even open to them. They migrated to the South in the same manner and for the same reasons that other Americans migrated to the West. They hoped to buy cotton lands or to enter legitimate business enterprises: to develop natural resources, build factories, promote railroads, represent insurance companies, or engage in trade. A large proportion of the carpetbaggers were veterans of the Union Army who were pleased with the southern climate and believed that they had discovered a land of opportunity. Others came as teachers, clergymen, officers of the Freedmen's Bureau, or agents of the various northern benevolent societies organized to give aid to the Negroes. These people went south to set up schools for Negroes and poor whites, to establish churches, and to distribute clothing and medical supplies. They were of all types—some well trained for their jobs, others not. Seldom, however, can they be dismissed as meddlesome fools, or can the genuineness of their humanitarian impulses be doubted. But whether honest or dishonest, northern settlers who became active in radical politics incurred the wrath of most white southern conservatives. For their supreme offense was not corruption but attempting to organize the Negroes for political action.

A scalawag is by definition a scamp, and white Southerners who collaborated with the radicals were thus stigmatized by the pejorative term that identified them. In southern society, according to one critic, scalawags constituted the "tory and deserter element, with a few from the obstructionists of the war time and malcontents of the present who wanted office."[4] But here, as in the case of the carpetbaggers, the facts were more complex than this. All scalawags were not degraded poor whites, depraved corruptionist, or cynical opportunists who betrayed the South for the spoils of office.

The cases of three distinguished scalawags will illustrate the inadequacy of any simple generalization about the character or origin of this class of radicals. The first is that of Lieutenant General James A. Longstreet of the Confederate Army, a graduate of West Point and one of Lee's ablest corps commanders. After the war Longstreet moved to New Orleans and became a partner in a cotton factorage business and head of an insurance firm. In 1867, arguing that the vanquished must accept the terms of the victors, he joined the Republican party and endorsed radical reconstruction. In 1868 he supported Grant for President, and in subsequent years Republican administrations gave him a variety of offices in the federal civil service. The second case is that of James L. Orr of South Carolina, a secessionist who had sat in the Confederate Senate. After serving as the Johnsonian governor of his state, Orr switched to the radicals and in 1868 was rewarded with a circuit judgeship. In a private letter he explained why he now supported the Republicans: It is "important for our prominent men to identify themselves with the radicals for the purpose of controlling their action and preventing mischief to the state." The third case is that of R. W. Flournoy, a large slaveholder in ante-bellum Mississippi. Flournoy joined the radicals not for personal gain but because of a humanitarian interest in the welfare of the freedmen. In a letter to Stevens he once explained that he supported the Republicans as the party to whom the Negro "can alone look . . . for protection." Flournoy's support of racial equality made him one of the most hated scalawags in the state. None of these men fitted the scalawag stereotype.

Others unfortunately did. Among those who gave the scalawags their reputation for corruption was Franklin J. Moses, Jr., of South Carolina. The son of a distinguished father, Moses entered politics before the war and was known as an ardent secessionist. In 1867, after a brief period as a Johnsonian, he joined the radicals. Both as a legislator and, from 1872 to 1874, as governor he looted the public treasury and repeatedly accepted bribes for using his influence to secure the passage of legislation. Other scalawags appeared to be pure opportunists who simply joined the winning side. Joseph E. Brown, Georgia's Civil War governor, provides a classic example. After the war, claiming that he had sense enough to know when he was defeated, Brown quit the Democrats and urged Southerners to accept the radicals' terms. During the years of reconstruction, in addition to his political activities, he found the time (and the opportunity) to become a wealthy capitalist: president of a railroad, a steamship company, a coal company, and an iron company. When the radicals were overthrown in Georgia, Brown, as always, landed on his feet and returned to the Democratic party. Now he helped to organize a powerful Democratic machine that dominated the state for many years and eventually sent him to the United States Senate.

Always a minority of the southern white population, more numerous in some states than others,[5] the scalawags usually belonged to one or more of four distinct groups. The first and largest of these groups was the Unionists. Having been exposed to severe persecution from their Confederate neighbors during the war, southern Unionists were often the most vindicative of the radicals; they were quite willing to support those who would now retaliate against the secessionists, and they hoped that congressional reconstruction would give them political control in their states. Early in 1866 a North Carolinian wrote Stevens that Union men were disillusioned with Johnson but still hoped "that traitors will be punished for the treatment that union men received at their hands."

However, a very large proportion of this Unionist-scalawag element had little enthusiasm for one aspect of the radical program: the granting of equal civil and political rights to the Negroes. They favored the disenfranchisement of the Confederates to enable them to dominate the new state governments, but they were reluctant to accept Negro suffrage. "There is some small amount of squirming about the privileges extended to the recent slaves," a Virginia Unionist informed Stevens, "but time will overcome all this as there is no union man who does not infinitely more fear and dread the domination of the recent Rebels than that of the recent slaves." In 1866, General Clinton B. Fisk, an officer of the Freedmen's Bureau, told the congressional Committee on Reconstruction that in Tennessee "among the bitterest opponents of the negro . . . are the intensely radical loyalists of the [eastern] mountain districts. . . . The great opposition to the measure in the Tennessee legislature, giving the negro the right to testify and an equality before the law, has come from that section, chiefly. In Middle Tennessee and in West Tennessee the largest and the wealthiest planters . . . have more cordially cooperated with me in my duties than the people of East Tennessee." The planters believed that they could control the Negro vote, and the scalawags feared that they would.

Insofar as there was any relationship between scalawags and the class structure of the South, it resulted from the fact that a minority of the poor whites and yeoman farmers were attracted to the radical cause.[6] There had always been, as we have seen, an undercurrent of tension between them and the planter class, and some of them deserted President Johnson when it appeared that his program would return the planters to power. Lower-class whites who joined the radicals sometimes hoped for a seizure of the planters' lands. In South Carolina, according to a Union officer, the idea of confiscation "was received with more favor by this caste than by the Negroes." He recalled numerous occasions when "dirty, ragged, stupid creatures slyly inquired of me, 'When is our folks a-gwine to git the lan'?' "

But it was never easy for the yeomen or poor whites to become scalawags, for support of the radicals meant collaboration with Negroes, or at least acquiescence in Negro suffrage. As a result, this class of scalawags was most numerous in areas with a small Negro population. Elsewhere a few lower-class whites managed to submerge their race prejudice, but the great majority preferred the old conservative leadership to a party that seemed to preach equality of the races.

A third source of scalawag strength came from Southerners engaged in business enterprise and from those living in regions, such as East Tennessee, western Virginia and North Carolina, and northern Alabama, which were rich in natural resources and had an industrial potential. Among such men there was considerable support of the economic policies of the Republican party—for the national banking system, the protective tariff, and federal appropriations of internal improvements. In general, the radical governments invited northern capitalists to invest in the South, granted loans or subsidies to the railroads, and gave charters and franchises to new corporations. Some of the scalawags were thus identified with the concept of a New South whose economy would be more diversified than that of the Old.

Finally, the radicals drew a little of their scalawag support and some of their leaders from upper-class Southerners who had been affiliated with the Whig party before the Civil War. The Whig party had been particularly attractive to the more affluent and socially secure members of southern society, and after the war many Whigs were reluctant to join their old foes, the Democrats. A few of them now looked upon the Republican party as the heir to the Whig tradition and wondered whether it might be possible not only to join but also to control its organization in the South. Upper-class Whig scalawags found it relatively easy to accept equal civil and political rights for Negroes, first, because among them race hatred was less often the prime motivating force of political action and, second, because they were optimistic about their chances of controlling the Negro vote. In Mississippi, for example, James L. Alcorn, elected governor on the Republican ticket in 1869, had been a prominent Whig planter before the war, as had been numerous other leading scalawags. Thus it would appear that the scalawags were in part an absurd coalition of class-conscious poor whites and yeoman farmers who hated the planters, and class-conscious Whig planters and businessmen who disliked the egalitarian Democrats. But politics has a logic of its own, and the history of American political parties is full of contradictions such as this.

Joining the carpetbaggers and scalawags in the radical coalition was the mass of southern Negroes, most of them illiterate, many easily intimidated. Because of their political inexperience and economic helplessness, they were sometimes misled and victimized not only by Republicans but also by southern white Democrats. But it would be far from the truth to say that their political behavior during reconstruction was altogether passive or irresponsible. This was untrue, if for no other reason, because the issues of reconstruction, so far as the Negroes were concerned, were relatively simple and clear-cut. Given their condition and the limited political choices open to them, most Negroes responded to the appeals of rival politicians in a manner that had an obvious logic to it.

To begin with, suffrage was not something thrust upon an indifferent mass of Negroes. Their leaders had demanded it from the start; and when the Johnson governments limited the ballot to the whites, many meetings of southern Negroes sent protests to Congress. In Tennessee, for example, Negroes first petitioned the legislature for the ballot, then asked Congress not to seat Tennesseeans until their petition was granted. On May 7, 1866, a meeting of freedmen in New Bern, North Carolina, resolved "That so long as the Federal Government refuses to grant us the right to protect ourselves by means of the ballot . . . we will hold it responsible before God for our protection."

Moreover, most Negroes fully appreciated the importance of achieving literacy, and they took advantage of the limited educational opportunities offered them with almost pathetic eagerness. They also understood that in the rural South land was the key to economic independence and that they needed government aid to get it. In 1865 they heard rumors that Congress would provide each of them with forty acres and a mule at Christmas time; the next year they heard the same rumors again; once more in 1867 they hoped to get land when the radicals formulated their reconstruction program. But each time the Negroes were disappointed, and by 1868 they knew that the Republicans in Congress were not going to assist them.

Nevertheless, an overwhelming majority of Negro voters continued to support the Republican party, and in 1868 they helped to elevate General Grant to the presidency. In the political campaigns of the reconstruction era, Democratic candidates occasionally tried to bid for the Negro vote, but the record of the Johnson governments and the commitment of the Democratic party to white supremacy caused the mass of Negroes to remain loyal Republicans. "The blacks know that many conservatives hope to reduce them again to some form of peonage,'' a Tennessee carpetbagger wrote Stevens. ''Under the impulse of this fear they will roll up their whole strength . . . and will go entirely for the Republican candidate whoever he may be.'' As long as southern Democrats opposed Negro suffrage and insisted that white supremacy was the central political issue, this condition could hardly have changed. It was this that made it easy for the agents of the Republican Union League to mobilize and ''control'' the Negro vote. Yet white Democrats often cited this solid Negro support of the Republicans to illustrate the political irresponsibility of the freedmen. It was a curious argument, however, for the practical choice offered the Negro voters was between a party that gave them civil and political rights and a party whose stock-in-trade was racist demagoguery.

Perhaps the most important generalizations to be made about the role of the Negroes in reconstruction are the following. First, while they had influence in all of the southern radical governments—more in some than in others—they did not control any of them. They served in all of the state legislatures, but only in South Carolina, one of the two southern states in which they outnumbered the whites, were they in the majority.[7] In Mississippi, the other state in which the Negroes had a numerical majority, the carpetbaggers controlled politics; while in Tennessee, where the scalawags dominated the radical government, there were practically no Negro officeholders at all. Few Negroes were elected to higher offices; none became the governor of a state. At various times South Carolina had a Negro lieutenant governor, secretary of state, treasurer, speaker of the house, and associate justice of the state supreme court; Mississippi had a Negro lieutenant governor, secretary of state, superintendent of education, and speaker of the house; Louisiana had a Negro lieutenant governor, secretary of state, treasurer, and superintendent of public education; Florida had a Negro secretary of state, and superintendent of public instruction. Nearly all of them were men of ability and integrity. Fourteen Negroes were elected to the United States House of Representatives, six of them from South Carolina. Two Mississippi Negroes served in the United States Senate: Hiram R. Revels for a one-year unexpired term, and Blanche K. Bruce for a full term. (Revels and Bruce, incidentally, are the only Negroes who have ever been elected to the Senate from any state, North or South.*) In general, however, white men dominated the higher offices of the southern radical governments. The Negroes, though filling many city and county offices, ordinarily were unable to advance beyond the state legislatures.

Editor's note: In 1966 Edward Brook of Massachusetts was the first black since reconstruction to be elected to the Senate.

Second, the Negroes soon developed their own leadership and were not always the mere tools of white Republicans. In 1868 a Florida carpetbagger reported to Stevens that white radicals were having trouble getting the Negroes to support ratification of the new state constitution. "The colored preachers," he wrote, "are *the great power* in controlling and uniting the colored vote, and they are looked to, as political leaders, with more confidence . . . than to any other source of instruction and control." Some of the Negro leaders were corruptible, some incorruptible; some had great ability, some little. Most of them were conservatives on all issues except civil and political rights.

Finally, the Negroes were seldom vindictive in their use of political power or in their attitude toward native whites. To be sure, there were plenty of cases of friction between Negroes and whites, and Negro militiamen were sometimes inordinately aggressive. But in no southern state did any responsible Negro leader, or any substantial Negro group, attempt to get complete political control into the hands of the freedmen.[8] All they asked for was equal political rights and equality before the law. Thus, is 1866, a group of North Carolina Negroes in thanking Congress for the Civil Rights Act promised that "whenever the Elective Franchise is also guaranteed to us we will ask no further special protection from the Federal Government, for then united with our white friends in the South we will be able to secure for ourselves every desired or desirable means of prosperity." Negroes did not desire to have political parties divided along racial lines; rather, unlike most white Democrats, they were eager to drop the race issue and work with the whites within the existing party framework.

Many Negroes at this time were even willing to postpone action on social segregation, especially in the schools, preferring to avoid conflict over this issue while they concentrated on civil and political rights. A South Carolina Negro legislator declared: "I venture to say to my white fellow-citizens that we, the colored people, are not in quest of social equality. I for one do not ask to be introduced in your family circle if you are not disposed to receive me there." And yet a northern white conservative affirmed that in South Carolina radical reconstruction "is barbarism overwhelming civilization by physical force. It is the slave rioting in the halls of his master, and putting that master under his feet." Such a description should be taken for what it was: the hyperbole of partisan politics.

The first step in the organization of new southern state governments, as required by the reconstruction acts, was the election of delegates to conventions to frame new state constitutions. Since these conventions were controlled by the radicals, since they were the first political bodies in the South to contain Negroes,[9] white conservatives subjected them to violent denunciation. They contemptously called them "black and tan conventions"; they described the delegates as "baboons, monkeys, mules," or "ragamuffins and jailbirds." The South Carolina convention, according to a local newspaper, was the "maddest, most infamous revolution in history."

Yet, the invectives notwithstanding, there was nothing mad and little revolutionary about the work of these conventions.[10] In fact, one of the most significant observations to be made about them is that the delegates showed little interest in experimentation. For the most part the radicals wrote orthodox state constitutions, borrowing heavily from the previous constitutions, and from those of other states. To find fault with the way these southern constitutions were drawn is to find fault with the way most new state constitutions have been drawn; to criticize their basic political structure is to criticize the basic political structure of all the states. They were neither original nor unique. There was no inclination to test, say, the unicameral legislature, or novel executive or judicial systems.

Nor did the conventions attempt radical experiments in the field of social or economic policy. Since land reform had been defeated in Congress, a few delegates tried to achieve it through state action. The South Carolina convention provided for the creation of a commission to purchase land for sale to Negroes. In Louisiana, some Negro delegates proposed that when planters sold their estates purchases of more than 150 acres be prohibited. One white scalawag suggested a double tax on uncultivated land. A few delegates in other states advocated various policies designed to force the breakup of large estates. But these and all other attacks upon landed property were easily defeated.

As for the freedmen, the new constitutions proclaimed the equality of all men by quoting or paraphrasing the Declaration of Independence. Negroes were given the same civil and political rights as white men. "The equality of all persons before the law," proclaimed the Arkansas constitution, "is recognized and shall ever remain inviolate; nor shall any citizen ever be deprived of any right, privilege, or immunity, nor exempted from any burden or duty, on account of race, color, or previous condition." But on the subject of the social relations of Negroes and whites, most of the radical constitutions were evasive. South Carolina provided that its public schools were to be open to all "without regard to race or color," but only the state university actually made an attempt at integration. The Louisiana constitution declared: "There shall be no separate schools or institutions of learning established exclusively for any race by the State of Louisiana." In New Orleans from 1871 to 1877 about one third of the public schools were integrated, and white resistance was remarkably mild; but elsewhere in Louisiana segregation was the rule. Outside of South Carolina and Louisiana the radicals made no explicit constitutional provision for social integration. The Mississippi convention first defeated a proposal that segregated schools be required, then defeated a proposal that they be prohibited; the result was that the new constitution ignored the issue altogether. The only reference to segregation in it was a vague statement that "the rights of all citizens to travel upon public conveyances shall not be infringed upon, nor in any manner abridged in this state." But whether or not this clause prohibited segregation in public transportation is far from clear.

Yet, though the new constitutions were essentially conservative documents, they did accomplish some modest reforms, most of which were long overdue. In general, they eliminated certain undemocratic features of the old constitutions, for example, the inequitable systems of legislative apportionment that had discriminated against the interior regions of Virginia, North Carolina, and South Carolina. In the states of the Southeast, many offices that had previously been appointive were now made elective, and county government was taken out of the hands of local oligarchies. The rights of women were enlarged, tax systems were made more equitable, penal codes were reformed, and the number of crimes punishable by death was reduced. Most of the constitutions provided for substantial improvements in the state systems of public education and in the facilities for the care of the physically and mentally handicapped and of the poor.[11]

In South Carolina, according to the historians of reconstruction in that state, the radical convention was an orderly body which accomplished its work with reasonable dispatch. It produced a constitution "as good as any other constitution that state has ever had"—good enough to remain in force for nearly two decades after the white Democrats regained control. This was, in fact, the state's first really democratic constitution; for, in addition to removing distinctions based on race, it provided for manhood suffrage, abolished property qualifications for officeholding, gave the voters the power for the first time to select the governor and other state officers, and transferred the election of presidential electors from the legislature to the voters. Another important provision related to public education: unlike the previous constitution, "the fundamental law of the state carried the obligation of universal education" and aimed at "the creation of a school system like that of Northern states." Other reforms included an extension of women's rights, adoption of the state's first divorce law, strengthening of the state's fiscal power, revision of the tax system, and modernization of the judiciary and of county government.[12]

The responsible behavior of South Carolina's radical constitutional convention was in striking contrast to the angry and irresponsible criticism of the Democrats. Chiefly because of its provisions for racial equality, they ridiculed the new constitution as "the work of sixty-odd negroes, many of them ignorant and depraved, together with fifty white men, outcasts of Northern society, and Southern renegades, betrayers of their race and country." Specifically, the Democrats charged that manhood suffrage was designed to further the ambitions of "mean whites"; that Negro suffrage would bring ruin to the state; that the judicial reforms were "repugnant to our customs and habits of thought"; and that the public school requirements were "a fruitful source of petulant corruption." In spite of this fanciful criticism by a party whose chief appeal was to racial bigotry, the work of the radical convention was ratified by a majority of nearly three to one.

At the time that the new constitutions were ratified, elections were held for state officers and legislators. After the elections, when Congress approved of the constitutions, political power was transferred from the military to the new civil governments. Thus began the era of radical government in the South—an era which, according to tradition, produced some of the worst state administrations in American history. Some of the southern radical regimes earned their evil reputations, others did not; but viewed collectively, there was much in the record they made to justify severe criticism. To say that they were not always models of efficiency and integrity would be something of an understatement. "The great impediment of the Republican party in this state," wrote a Tennessee radical, "is the incompetence of its leaders. . . . After the war the loyal people in many counties had no competent men to be judges, lawyers or political leaders." Indeed, all of the radical governments suffered more or less from the incompetence of some, the dishonesty of a few, and above all the inexperience of most of the officeholders. Unquestionably the poorest records were made in South Carolina during the administrations of the carpetbagger Robert K. Scott and the scalawag Franklin J. Moses, Jr., and in Louisiana during the administrations of the carpetbaggers Henry C. Warmoth and William P. Kellogg.

The sins of various radical governments included fraudulent bond issues; graft in land sales or purchases and in the letting of contracts for public works; and waste and extravagance in the use of state funds. Governor Warmoth was reputed to have pocketed $100,000 during his first year in office, though his salary was $8,000; another governor was accused of stealing and selling the supplies of the Freedmen's Bureau. A scalawag governor admitted taking bribes of more than $40,000; another fraudulently endorsed state bonds over to a group of railroad promoters. In Louisiana under both Warmoth and Kellogg there was corruption in the granting of charters and franchises, in the negotiation of construction contracts, in the use of school funds, in the collection of state taxes, and in the awarding of printing contracts. Some of the radical legislators, especially in South Carolina, apparently made bribery an integral part of the process of transacting legislative business. One South Carolina legislature issued bonds valued at $1,590,000 to redeem bank notes valued at $500,000; it voted a bonus of $1,000 to the speaker when he lost that amount in a bet on a horse race. For a time the legislators of this state enjoyed the services of a free restaurant and bar established for their private use; they billed the state for such "legislative supplies" as hams, ladies' bonnets, perfumes, champagne, and (for one unfortunate member) a coffin. The cost of state printing in South Carolina between 1868 and 1876 was greater than the cost had been from 1789 to 1868. On one occasion, as the legislature was about to adjourn, a Democratic newspaper in Charleston wrote the following epitaph: "In life it has been unlovely, and in death it has not belied its record. As it lived, it has died—an uncouth, malformed and abortive monstrosity, its birth a blunder, its life a crime, and its death a blessing."

Meanwhile, the credit of some of the southern states was impaired as public debts mounted. In Florida the state debt increased from $524,000 in 1868 to $5,621,000 in 1874. In South Carolina a legislative committee reported that between 1868 and 1871 the state debt had increased from $5,403,000 to $15,768,000, but another committee insisted that it had increased to $29,159,000. By 1872 the debts of the eleven states of the former Confederacy had increased by approximately $132,000,000. The burden on taxpayers grew apace. Between 1860 and 1870 South Carolina's tax rate more than doubled, while property values declined by more than fifty per cent. In Tennessee a radical reported that during the first three years after the war taxes had increased sevenfold, though property had declined in value by one third. Throughout the South the tax burden was four times as great in 1870 as it had been in 1860. Such rates, complained many southern landholders, were confiscatory; and, indeed, taxes and other adversities of the postwar years forced some of them to sell all or part of their lands. Sympathy for South Carolina's planter aristocracy caused a northern conservative to ask: "When before did mankind behold the spectacle of a rich, high-spirited, cultivated, self-governed people suddenly cast down, bereft of their possessions, and put under the feet of the slaves they had held in bondage for centuries?"

High taxes, mounting debts, corruption, extravagance, and waste, however, do not constitute the complete record of the radical regimes. Moreover, to stop with a mere description of their misdeeds would be to leave all the crucial questions unanswered—to distort the picture and to view it without perspective. For example, if some of these governments contained an uncommonly large number of inexperienced or incompetent officeholders, if much of their support came from an untutored electorate, there was an obvious reason for this. Howard K. Beale, in a critique of various reconstruction legends, observed that the political rulers of the ante-bellum South "had fastened ignorance or inexperience on millions of whites as well as Negroes and that it was this ignorance and inexperience that caused trouble when Radicals were in power. . . . Wealthy Southerners . . . seldom recognized the need for general education of even the *white* masses."[13] Even in 1865 the men who won control of the Johnson governments showed little disposition to adopt the needed reforms. In South Carolina the Johnsonians did almost nothing to establish a system of public education, and at the time that the radicals came to power only one eighth of the white children of school age were attending school. The Negroes, of course, had been ignored entirely. It was probably no coincidence that the radicals made their poorest record in South Carolina, the state which had done the least for education and whose prewar government had been the least democratic.

As for the corruption of the radical governments, this phenomenon can be understood only when it is related to the times and to conditions throughout the country. One must remember that the administrations of President Grant set the moral tone for American government at all levels, national, state, and local. The best-remembered episodes of the Grant era are its numerous scandals—the Crédit Mobilier and the Whiskey Ring being the most spectacular of them—involving members of Congress as well as men in high administration circles. There were, moreover, singularly corrupt Republican machines in control of various northern states, including Massachusetts,

New York, and Pennsylvania. But corruption was not a phenomenon peculiar to Republicans of the Gilded Age, as the incredible operations of the so-called Tweed Ring in New York City will testify. Indeed, the thefts of public funds by this organization of white Tammany Democrats surpassed the total thefts in all the southern states combined.

Clearly the presence of carpetbaggers, scalawags, and Negroes in the radical governments was not in itself a sufficient explanation for the appearance of corruption. The South was being affected by the same forces that were affecting the rest of the country. No doubt the most important of these forces were, first, the social disorganization that accompanied the Civil War and hit the defeated and demoralized South with particular severity; and, second, the frantic economic expansion of the postwar period, when the American economy was dominated by a group of extraordinarily talented but irresponsible and undisciplined business leaders. These entrepreneurs' rather flexible standards of public morality provided an unfortunate model for the politicians.

Whether southern Democrats would have been able to resist the corrupting forces of the postwar decade had they remained in power is by no means certain. Perhaps the old ruling class would have been somewhat less vulnerable to the temptations of the Gilded Age, but the record of the Johnson governments was spotty at best. In Louisiana the conservative government created by Lincoln and Johnson wasted a great deal of public money. In Mississippi the state treasurer of the Johnson government embezzled $62,000. (This, by the way, far surpassed the record of the only thief in the radical government, who embezzled $7,000.) E. Merton Coulter discovered that during the era of reconstruction some Democratic officeholders "partook of the same financial characteristics as Radicals" and "took advantage of openings" when they found them. He quotes a Georgia editor who claimed that the extravagance and corruption "benefitted about as many Democrats as Republicans"; and he notes that a Democratic administration in Alabama "in lack of honesty differed little from the administrations of the Radicals between whom it was sandwiched."[14]

In the 1870's, when the South's so-called "natural leaders" returned to power, that troubled section did not always find itself governed by politicians distinguished for their selfless devotion to public service. In Mississippi the treasurer of the Democratic regime that overthrew the radicals in 1875 immediately embezzled $316,000, which broke all previous records! Elsewhere in the next decade eight other state treasurers were guilty of defalcations or embezzlements, including one in Louisiana who defrauded the state of more than a million dollars. Georgia was now ruled by a Democratic machine that was both ruthless and corrupt, a machine whose record was so offensive that by the end of the 1880's the white masses—some even willing to accept Negro support—rose in political rebellion against it. Reports about the Mississippi Democratic regime of the late nineteenth century are particularly colorful. One white editor charged that an "infamous ring" of "corrupt office-seekers . . . [had] debauched the ballot boxes . . . incurred useless and extravagant expenditures, raised the taxes, [and] plunged the State into debt." At the Mississippi constitutional convention of 1890, a white Democratic delegate gave the following description of politics in his state during the previous fifteen years: "Sir, it is no secret that there has not been a full vote and a fair count in Mississippi since 1875. . . . In other words we have been stuffing ballot boxes, committing perjury, and here and there in the state carrying the elections by fraud and violence. . . . No man can be in favor of perpetuating the election methods which have prevailed in Mississippi since 1875 who is not a moral idiot." Twelve years later an editor claimed that it would tax "the range and scope of the most fertile and versatile imagination to picture a condition of greater political rotteness" than existed in Mississippi at that time.

In the final analysis the crucial question about the extravagance and peculations of the radical governments is who the chief beneficiaries were. Only a few of the Negro and white radical leaders profited personally. The funds they stole, the money that prodigal legislators used for their own benefit, accounted for only a small fraction of the increased debts of the southern states. Nor did the total sums involved in bribery rise to a very impressive figure. And why was the tar brush applied exclusively to those who accepted the bribes and not to those who offered them? Under these circumstances is it really more blessed to give than to receive? For when the bribe-givers are identified we have located those who profited most from radical misdeeds. These men were the construction contractors, business speculators, and railroad promoters, of their agents, who hoped to persuade legislators to give them contracts, franchises, charters, subsidies, financial grants, or guarantees. They were the men who were also corrupting Congressmen and northern legislatures.

In Virginia much of the history of reconstruction concerns the rivalry of the Baltimore and Ohio Railroad and the Southside line for control of the Virginia and Tennessee Railroad. Both lines fought to control elections and legislators and backed whichever party promised to serve them, until, in 1870, the legislature ended the dispute by approving the consolidation plans of the Southside. Louisiana's reconstruction politics was enlivened by the attempt of a railroad and steamship corporation, headed by Charles Morgan of New York, to prevent the state from subsidizing a rival line between New Orleans and Houston, until Morgan forced the new line to take him in. In Alabama the North and South Railroad and the Alabama and Chattanooga Railroad battled for access to the ore deposits around Birmingham. In the process the competing groups corrupted both Johnson and radical legislatures, and in the latter both Republicans and Democrats.

Most of the debt increases in the southern states resulted not from the thefts and extravagance of radical legislators but from the grants and guarantees they gave to railroad promoters, among whom were always some native white Democrats. In Florida more than sixty per cent of the debt incurred by the radical regime was in the form of railroad guarantee bonds. In North Carolina the radical government, prodded by the carpetbagger Milton S. Littlefield, a skilled lobbyist, issued millions of dollars of railroad bonds. Among those who benefited were many of the state's "best citizens," including George W. Swepson, a local business promoter and Democrat. Most of Alabama's reconstruction debt—$18,000,000 out of $20,500,000—was in the form of state bonds issued to subsidize railroad construction, for which the state obtained liens upon railroad property. When one measure for state aid was before the Alabama legislature, many Democrats were among the lobbyists working for its passage. Yet, complained a radical, the Democrats who expect to profit from the bill "will use the argument that the Republican party had a majority in the Legislature, and will falsely, but hopefully, charge it upon Republicans as a partisan crime against the state."

Indeed, all of the southern states, except Mississippi, used state credit to finance the rebuilding and expansion of their railroads, for private sources of credit were inadequate. This policy had been developed before the war; it was continued under the Johnsonians; and in some cases when the Democrats overthrew the radicals there was no decline in the state's generosity to the railroads. While the radicals controlled the southern legislatures, not only they but many members of the Democratic minority as well voted for railroad bond issues. According to an historian of reconstruction in Louisiana, "Such measures were supported by members of both parties, often introduced by Democrats, in every case supported by a large majority of Democrats in both houses."[15] The subservience of many postwar southern legislatures to the demands of railroad and other business promoters is in some respects less shocking than pathetic. For it expressed a kind of blind faith shared by many Southerners of both parties that railroad building and industrialization would swiftly solve all of their section's problems. No price seemed too high for such a miracle.

In several states, for obviously partisan reasons, the actual increase in the size of the public debt was grossly exaggerated. In Mississippi, for example, there was a durable legend among white Democrats that the radicals had added $20,000,000 to the state debt, when, in fact, they added only $500,000. Mississippi radicals had guarded against extravagance by inserting a clause in the constitution of 1868 prohibiting the pledging of state funds to aid private corporations—a clause which the conservatives, incidentally, had opposed. In Alabama, apart from railroad bonds secured by railroad property, the radicals added only $2,500,000 to the state debt. They did not leave a debt of $30,000,000 as conservatives claimed. In most other states, when loans to the railroads are subtracted, the increases in state debts for which the radicals were responsible appear far less staggering.

As for taxes, one of the positive achievements of many of the radical governments was the adoption of more equitable tax systems which put a heavier burden upon the planters. Before the war the southern state governments had performed few public services and the tax burden on the landed class had been negligible; hence the vehement protests of the landholders were sometimes as much against radical tax policies as against the alleged waste of taxpayers' money. The restoration governments often brought with them a return to the old inequitable fiscal systems. In Mississippi the subsequent claim of the conservatives that they had reduced the tax burden the radicals had placed upon property holders was quite misleading. The conservatives did lower the state property tax, but, as a consequence, they found it necessary to shift various services and administrative burdens from the state to the counties. This led to an increase in the cost of county government, an increase in the rate of county taxes, and a net increase in total taxes, state and county, that Mississippi property holders had to pay.

As a matter of fact, taxes, government expenditures, and public debts were bound to increase in the southern states during the postwar years no matter how controlled them. For there was no way to escape the staggering job of physical reconstruction—the repair of public buildings, bridges, and roads—and costs had started to go up under the Johnson governments before the radicals came to power. So far from the expenditures of the reconstruction era being totally lost in waste and fraud, much of this physical reconstruction was accomplished while the radicals were in office. They expanded the state railroad systems, increased public services, and provided public school systems—in some states for the first time. Since schools and other public services were now provided for Negroes as well as for whites, a considerable increase in the cost of state government could hardly have been avoided. In Florida between 1869 and 1873 the number of children enrolled in the public schools trebled; in South Carolina between 1868 and 1876 the number increased from 30,000 to 123,000. The economies achieved by some of the restoration governments came at the expense of the schools and various state institutions such as hospitals for the insane. The southern propertied classes had always been reluctant to tax themselves to support education or state hospitals, and in many cases the budget-cutting of the conservatives simply strangled them.

Thus radical rule, in spite of its shortcomings, was by no means synonymous with incompetence and corruption; far too many carpetbagger, scalawag, and Negro politicians made creditable records to warrant such a generalization. Moreover, conditions were improving in the final years of reconstruction. In South Carolina the last radical administration, that of the carpetbagger Governor Daniel H. Chamberlain, was dedicated to reform; in Florida "the financial steadiness of the state government increased toward the end of Republican rule."[16] In Mississippi the radicals made a remarkably good record. The first radical governor, James L. Alcorn, a scalawag, was a man of complete integrity; the second, Adelbert Amers, a carpetbagger, was honest, able, and sincerely devoted to protecting the rights of the Negroes. Mississippi radicals, according to Vernon L. Wharton, established a system of public education far better than any the state had known before; reorganized the state judiciary and adopted a new code of laws; renovated public buildings and constructed new ones, including state hospitals at Natchez and Vicksburg; and provided better state asylums for the blind, deaf, and dumb. The radicals, Wharton concludes, gave Mississippi "a government of greatly expanded functions at a cost that was low in comparison with that of almost any other state."[17] No major political scandal occurred in Mississippi during the years of radical rule—indeed, it was the best governed state in the postwar South. Yet white conservatives attacked the radical regime in Mississippi as violently as they did in South Carolina, which suggests that their basic grievance was not corruption but race policy.

Finally, granting all their mistakes, the radical governments were by far the most democratic the South had ever known.

Notes

1. James Bryce: *The American Commonwealth,* 3 vols. (New York, 1888), Vol. II, pp. 476–8.
2. E. Merton Coulter: *William G. Brownlow* (Chapel Hill, 1937), pp. 282–3, 337.
3. "From contemporary usage . . . we derive the following as a nonvaluational definition: the men called carpetbaggers were *white Northerners who went south after the beginning of the Civil War and, sooner or later, became active in politics as Republicans.*" Richard N. Current: "Carpetbaggers Reconsidered," in *A Festschrift for Frederick B. Artz* (Durham, 1964), p. 144.
4. Walter L. Fleming: *Civil War and Reconstruction in Alabama* (New York, 1905), p. 402.
5. In the presidential election of 1872, according to a recent estimate, approximately 150,000 white Southerners voted Republican; they constituted about 20 per cent of the white voters. These scalawags were most numerous in Tennessee, North Carolina, Arkansas, Texas, and Virginia. Allen W. Terlease: "Who Were the Scalawags?" *Journal of Southern History,* XXIX (1963), p. 458.
6. Most of the lower-class whites who became scalawags had been Unionists, but some had supported the Confederacy.
7. South Carolina's first radical legislature contained 87 Negroes and 69 whites. The Negroes, however, had a majority only in the lower house. The upper house contained twice as many whites as Negroes.
8. However, Negro leaders did protest when they thought that white radicals were trying to monopolize the offices.

---

9. The number of Negroes and whites in the various conventions was as follows:

	Negro	*White*		*Negro*	*White*
Alabama	13	90	Mississippi	16	84
Arkansas	8	58	North Carolina	15	118
Florida	18	27	South Carolina	76	48
Georgia	33	137	Virginia	25	80
Louisiana	49	49	Texas	9	81

10. The Democrats accused the Republican delegates of wasting time and of extravagance. The printing bills of some of these conventions were unnecessarily high, but in general these accusations have relatively little evidence to support them.
11. Attempts to accomplish a sweeping disenfranchisement of Confederate sympathizers were defeated either in the conventions or, as in Virginia and Mississippi, by popular vote. The disenfranchisement accomplished by these constitutions seldom went beyond those disqualified for holding office by the Fourteenth Amendment, and all made provision for the eventual restoration of the franchise even to them.
12. Francis B. Simkins and Robert H. Woody: *South Carolina during Reconstruction* (Chapel Hill, 1932), pp. 90–111.
13. Howard K. Beale: "On Rewriting Reconstruction History," *American Historical Review,* XLV (1940), pp. 807–27.
14. Coulter, *The South during Reconstruction,* pp. 152–3.
15. Ella Lonn: *Reconstruction in Louisiana after 1868* (New York, 1918), pp. 36–7.
16. William W. Davis: *The Civil War and Reconstruction in Florida* (New York, 1913), pp. 672–3.
17. Wharton, *The Negro in Mississippi,* pp. 179–80.